ART POLLARD

The Gentleman Racer

Expanded Second Edition

Bob Kehoe

Copyright © 2019 by Bob Kehoe

All rights reserved. No part of this publication may be reproduced, distributed or transmitted in any form or by any means, without prior written permission of the author.

Author: Bob Kehoe
Hillsboro, Oregon and Eloy, Arizona
(bkehoe51@gmail.com)

Book Layout © 2014 BookDesignTemplates.com

Jacket Design by Joe Santana, MKTX, Inc.

Art Pollard/Bob Kehoe – Second (Expanded) Edition (rev. 0)

ISBN 978-10-886791-2-8

Printed in the United States of America.

To the entire Pollard family for putting their faith in me to produce this expanded second edition tribute to Art. And a special thank you to Judy Pollard Dippel for her continued suggestions and proof reading.

And to my wife Karen, who continually supports the time I spend on my book projects.

"Believe you can and you're halfway there."

—THEODORE ROOSEVELT

Photo Credits: Unless otherwise noted, the photos in this book are from the Pollard Family Collection. Thank you to the many others who have shared photos from their collections, including:

Ann Arbor District Library
Bill Throckmorton Collection
Brian Pratt Collection
BSU Archives
Clyde Sullivan Collection
Colorado Motorsports Hall of Fame
Coos Bay – The World
Dick Vermeil Collection
Foster Family Collection
Gary D. Brown Collection
Gapinski Collection
Glenn Binegar
Granatelliturbines.com
Grant King Racers
Idaho Historical Racing Society
Indianapolis Motor Speedway (IMS)

Indianapolis Star
Indycar.com
Jack Corley Collection
John A. Wilson
Kitchel Kollection
Medford Mail-Tribune
Museum of American Speed
Racing Wheels Publication
Ralph Hunt Collection
Speedway Motors
Steve Veltman
Stock Car Racing Magazine
STP Corporation
Vollstedt Family Collection
Vukovich Racing Legacy

CONTENTS

Humble Beginnings in Utah 1
Boyhood Adventures 4
Setting Down Roots in Roseburg 7
The Navy – and Marriage 10
A Growing Family 12
From Boats to Race Cars 15
Oregonians at Indianapolis 21
Moving Up the Ranks 41
Art's Fun-Loving Ways 45
Art Pollard and Dick Vermeil 50
The Road to Indy 56
1965 – Joining the United States Auto Club Championship Car Series 76
First Taste of the Brickyard 80
1967 – The Fred Gerhardt Team 94
A Broken Leg 105
Life Begins at Forty 109
The 52nd Annual Indy 500 120
A Champion with the Kids 134
The 1968 Season Continues 143
Driving for Andy Granatelli 152
Two Championship Car Wins! 160
The Pollard Car Wash Team 173
1970 - The Second Half 180
Life Changes 185
Having Fun Away from The Track 189
1971 - The Jim Gilmore Team 192
1972 - Back with Granatelli 200
A Historian's Perspective 207
Starting the 1973 Season 211
A Sixth Attempt at the '500' 213
May Twelfth, 1973 217
A Race to be Forgotten 223

A Racer Returns Home 226
Racing in Art's Footsteps 229
Remembering Art Pollard 235
Acknowledgements 262
About the Author 263
Index 264

PREFACE

"Why a book about Art Pollard?" you might ask. To answer that, I must first explain a little of my background.

I grew up in Portland, Oregon, nearly in the shadows of the Portland Speedway and the Jantzen Beach Arena. Sadly, the much-beloved ovals of Jantzen Beach and the Speedway are now simply notations in the city archives.

Though no one else in our family was much into cars, I was fascinated with them since a very early age. We lived on busy Vancouver Avenue and one of my favorite forms of self-entertainment was trying to identify not only the make, but also the model of each car that passed by. Without question, doing so was much easier in the 1950s. There was your everyday Ford, Chevrolet, or Plymouth, but on occasion there might be a Hudson or Kaiser. A foreign-built vehicle was extremely rare, and then it was likely a Volkswagen Beetle or Renault Dauphine.

As I grew older, I started sifting through the popular automotive magazines of the day. Most featured articles about racing, and that hooked me. Along with normal sports activities such as sandlot baseball and pick-up basketball, everything else I did seem related to auto racing.

School-yard bicycle races with friends became our own version of the Indianapolis 500 or Daytona 500. We'd strip off those unnecessary fenders and turn the handlebars upside-down. "I'm Fireball Roberts and you're Richard Petty."

There was the weekly bicycle ride to the nearest hobby shop to buy the next installment to my model race car collection. Remember when a good model car kit sold for $2.00 and a bottle of Testors paint was only ten cents?

The biggest thrills came on Sunday afternoons at the Portland Speedway where my favorites were the stock cars, simply because I could better identify with them. My local heroes included drivers like Hershel McGriff, Bill Amick, Dick Bown and Kuzie Kuzmanich. After the day's last event, I would wander out onto the track to find assorted bits and pieces that fell from the cars during the race. Great souvenirs for a twelve-year-old!

As much as I enjoyed the stock cars, the open-wheeled midgets, hardtops and sprint cars were just as fun to follow. It didn't hurt that the daughter of local legend "Wild" Bill Hyde was a classmate in my grade school. Their home, a few blocks away from ours, always seemed to have a sprint car on a trailer parked in their driveway. I was always jealous.

The early days of racing at the Portland Speedway.

(Jack Corley Collection)

The last race at the historic Portland Speedway took place in September 2001. Demolition came in 2003, and the site is now a trucking terminal.

(Author photo)

Of course, the *BIG* race of the year was the Indianapolis 500. In the months leading up to the event, the magazines often had preview articles featuring the new cars being built for that year. Sometimes there were driver profiles for the likes of A.J. Foyt, Rodger Ward, or Parnelli Jones. This was all good, as the local newspapers only seemed to feature auto racing if there was a major crash somewhere.

Come Memorial Day morning, I would anxiously tune the radio dial to the race broadcast, listening intently to the action from start to finish. Sans television coverage this was, and remains, a tremendous way to experience the event. The pictures in your mind, drawn by some of the best racing announcers in the business, allowed a special impression that video coverage cannot provide.

During those early years of the 1960s, my ears would perk up whenever the name Len Sutton would arise. Once Len retired from racing, the same would hold true for Art Pollard.

In later years I had the privilege to befriend men like Len Sutton and Rolla Vollstedt. I went to a high school prom party at the Sutton home, as a classmate was dating one of Len's daughters. Much to the chagrin of my date, I spent most of the time looking at all of Len's racing memorabilia. Years later, Rolla Vollstedt rebuilt the engine in my Mustang Mach 1.

Further endeavors have allowed me to interview many of the greats, such as Parnelli Jones, Cale Yarborough, Ned Jarrett, Donnie Allison and Al Unser Sr., to name a few. I once spent a day driving Phil Hill around Portland to various appearances. Imagine a Formula One World Champion sitting alongside you in the family station wagon! He was a superb conversationalist and I don't believe we ever talked much about racing. He was more interested in discussing the world around us.

But more than all, I regret I never had the opportunity to meet Art Pollard. It was a very sad day when the news of his untimely death came across the airwaves. To this day I've never believed he earned the credit he deserved. Aside from his racing statistics I never knew Art as a person, a dedicated family man, or a friend.

In writing this book I've come to regard him not so much as a racer, but just a great – but humble – human being. I've interviewed many that knew Art personally, and not once did I hear an unpleasant word about him. Everyone spoke of his kindness, his humor, and his way with kids – especially those associated with the Larue D. Carter Memorial Hospital in Indianapolis.

But Art was also a race driver, and a damn good one at that. His competitors described him as being fierce behind the wheel, but at the same time he would race cleanly. If your car happened to be faster than his, he would wave you by. He held great mechanical skills and when it came to setting up a car, he seemed to know exactly what needed to be done. He had an innate feel for the machine.

Art spent many years in the lower rungs of the racing ladder, achieving great success. When he finally got an opportunity in the "big leagues" of Championship Car racing, he was already 40 years old. One could only imagine what his future held if he had been ten-years younger.

I often think about what might have been if Art were alive today. I can imagine chatting with him on the front porch of the home he had intended to build somewhere in the picturesque Willamette Valley. I would mention that I would like to write his biography. But true to Art's nature, he'd probably reply, "Aw shucks, who would want to read about me?"

And that's where this story begins.

(Author's note) – I published the first edition of the Art Pollard biography in 2016 and am pleased to say it was well-received. Since that time, I collected many more photos and stories about Art which I felt should be included in this expanded second edition. My hope is that this version will be enjoyed as much as the first.

Bob Kehoe
Hillsboro, Oregon/Eloy, Arizona
August, 2019

Art Pollard – The Gentleman Racer

FOREWARD

Art Pollard, my dad, was a man who left a life legacy for many reasons—Indy racing being one. Like all championship race drivers, his "dream of dreams" was to win the Indianapolis 500. As a family, we shared his goal. He had raced *something* from the time I was a toddler. Having a dad who raced was all I knew.

I grew up and 20 years passed, and when I was 23 years old, I will never forget Dad's unrestrained excitement on the phone when we talked on his birthday on May 5th, 1973. It was a memorable conversation in more ways than one – it was to be our last.

Judy Pollard Dippel

For him, the mere prospect of being a strong competitor to sit on the 'Pole' with a car that was smoothly turning record speeds at 192+ mph, filled him with confidence and optimism that *this could be the year* he would achieve his life's dream. Everything was lining up perfectly – he was confident, and it doesn't get better than that for a racecar driver – to have a fast car – and one that keeps running until the checkered!

Like so many drivers, mechanical problems are like a plague to the winner's circle, and Dad had his share. Yet, with a smile on his face, more often than not he would say, "That's racing!"

Without pause, the next race was already on his mind – he was rarely visibly down or discouraged, but always looking forward to the next possibility on the track – and in life.

Unfortunately, we know the reality of winning at the famed Brickyard is one dream my dad didn't get to see play out. His fatal accident ended the dream, but nothing can take away the races he won and the people he influenced, due to the remarkable kind of person that he was day-in and day-out.

It is most fitting, in 1973, that Dad's good friend, Johnny Rutherford, took to the track, and electrified the crowd into a frenzy. His third lap of 199.071 mph was just 0.21 seconds shy of the elusive 200 mph barrier. His four-lap average of 198.413 mph secured the pole position. He didn't win that year, but he is one of a select group to have won Indy three times in his career.

Race drivers know that winning is everything! But I dare to say, that as important as it was – a driving force in Dad's life – the people he met along the way agree that he was a winner in more ways than one. He had a rare combination of positive personality traits that influenced young and old alike. He was called "the driver's driver" by many, due to his ability to increase camaraderie and good will among the drivers, pulling these driving celebrities together as a group to do good deeds off the track. Additionally, Dad was in his element when giving the after-dinner speech – once again enjoying the opportunity to share his life, talk racing, and connect with people.

I cannot express in words how meaningful this book is to me, and to the Pollard family. Reading over the chapters before final copy, a relative who was especially close to Dad, emotionally expressed, "Reading the pages of this book makes me feel as if Art's with us again – at least for a short while – and that feels so good."

I am, and the family is, extremely grateful to Bob Kehoe for dedicating two years of his life to this book. You, the reader, will see the results as you turn the pages. He gathered together years of racing stories and pored over newspaper articles to glean interesting tidbits. He discovered websites and Facebook pages, where he found Dad to still be a popular point of discussion. *People who never knew him still care!* For the family, that's a priceless gift.

I'm grateful that Bob was adamant about the accuracy of racing stats, and sought out photos, some of which I had never seen. He found video interviews online – short – but at least I got to hear my dad's voice again! I think he knows how much that means to me. Bob set aside his personal time to discover as much as he could – willing to go anywhere and talk to anyone. Phone calls and travel to interview family, friends and fans – the not so famous and the famous.

Bob shared with me that it was surreal when his wife, Karen, answered the phone one day. "Al Unser is on the phone. He's returning your call." That happened several times for them, returned calls from various drivers who considered Dad not only a fellow competitor, but a friend.

It's important for me to note that Dad valued and respected people equally, for who they were to him – not just those who were his close racing buddies with household names. Thank you to the lifetime friends and family who share their stories in this book. They are part of our family's life history, and reveal the caring, creative, entertaining sides of Dad. Also, I want to publicly thank Dad's former wife, Pat Pollard Arslanian for her contributions to this book, and her husband Dave Arslanian.

Dad was a bright spot in many people's lives. I've known few people in my lifetime, who have a natural way of making every day, ordinary situations interesting and fun – but Dad's good humor and fun-loving spirit prevailed in his life – and I was one lucky girl to grow up with him as my dad, one with patience and unconditional love. I will always miss him, but I don't take for granted that I received more love from him in 23 years than some daughters receive in a lifetime.

Having his story told in this book for posterity is something that our family will cherish for generations to come: and for the other readers, it shows a good slice of his life, the whole person, not only *what he did*, but the *type of person* he was. I know there was a real man behind the racing suit, and he was an exceptionally good one! I'm excited for readers to get to know him more – and for people who did know him, to spend a little time with him again, due to the writing of this book.

Speaking for myself, and for my late brother, Mike Pollard – "Thank you, Bob Kehoe!"

Judy Pollard Dippel
Eugene, Oregon

August 2019 – Judy Pollard Dippel and Mario Andretti at the World of Speed Museum. Art Pollard and Mario both drove for Andy Granatelli in 1969, but in different capacities. As Andretti explained, "The teammate situation was such that we were really two separate teams. I sold our team to Granatelli and retained Jim McGee and Clint Brawner as crew chiefs, but we were two separate operations."

ONE

Humble Beginnings in Utah

Dragon, Utah, is a mere ghost town in Uintah County, not far from the western Colorado border. Today, from a birds-eye view, the desolate site is not much more than a wilderness intersected by a few dirt roads.

But long ago the area was the location of a significant Gilsonite deposit, and commercial mining began there in 1888. Resembling shiny black obsidian, Gilsonite was first marketed by Samuel H. Gilson as a lacquer, electrical insulator, and waterproofing compound. This unique mineral is now used in more than 160 products.

Because the vein formed the shape of a dragon, the operation was known as the Black Dragon Mine. Thus, the surrounding canyon and town adopted its name.

It was in Dragonthat, on May 5th, 1927, Bobbie Pollard gave birth to Artle Lee (Art) Pollard Jr. The little boy joined a sister, Christene, born three years earlier.

Like so many others, the Pollard family story began during a time in this country when many a young man labored long hours to house, clothe, and feed his growing brood. Artle Lee Pollard Sr. was part of that generation.

"Our dad was from Texas and my Mom came from Oklahoma," said Bob Pollard, Art's younger brother who was born in 1930. "How my parents got together I don't know. Those were really hard times in Texas and Oklahoma during the 1920s, with a limited number of job opportunities."

Bobbie Pollard told her granddaughter, Judy Pollard Dippel, how strict her own mother was. She and Art Sr. married in their mid-teens, not uncommon in those years.

Judy recalls: "My Grandma told me it was serious business the day she married my granddad. Her mother, my great-grandmother (Zenie Jaynes) rode in the back seat of the buggy with them when they drove to get married. Apparently, she wasn't about to let them be alone together until they were married. My Grandma often chuckled about that over the years. Those were the days!"

Searching for a better means to support his family, Art Sr. relocated to Dragon, Utah. "I'm guessing our dad heard about job opportunities in Dragon and went there for that reason," surmises Bob.

Art's parents – Artle Lee Sr. and Bobbie Pollard.

Art Sr. was part of a large family that included four sisters and three brothers. The son of the eldest boy Noah, Harvel Pollard was one of Art Jr.'s cousins: "Dad was a Texas farmer that decided in late 1928 to sell everything they had and move to Wasco, California. I was the youngest of the children in our family. Unfortunately, Dad passed away at the age of thirty, when I was just eight months old. Following that, Uncle Art (Sr.) and Uncle Owen spent a lot of time looking after us and they were very attentive."

Art Sr. continued his quest for even better career opportunities outside of Dragon. He eventually packed up his family and joined his brothers in Wasco, where Bob Pollard was born. Roughly 1,000 miles from Dragon, Wasco is a city in California's San Joaquin Valley, lying twenty-four miles northwest of Bakersfield. As Harvel described:

"Our neighborhood was very poor. Uncles Art Sr. and Owen would come over on Sunday and give haircuts to all the kids in the neighborhood. As I look back, I think a lot of Art Jr.'s feeling towards people – and his concern for youngsters in the years ahead – came from his dad. It's amazing how kids take on their parent's characteristics."

One of Harvel's lasting recollections of growing up in Wasco was that the town had some paved roads, but those in the Pollard neighborhood remained dirt. "It didn't make much difference since not many had a car, including us."

Art Jr. and Harvel's brother Alfred (nicknamed "Sonny") were about the same age. Once the families had cars, one of their pastimes was to get Art Sr.'s car and gather up all the neighborhood kids that were old enough to push the car. Harvel remembers: "Art Jr. was always the driver and Sonny would sit up front with him. I couldn't have been more than five or six-years-old. I distinctly remember Art saying 'faster, faster!' We would push that car around and around the block and when we'd wear out, they'd get another group of kids."

Bob Pollard describes his father, Art Sr.: "Dad was a jack-of-all-trades, but was given the opportunity to work for a natural gas company as an installation and maintenance technician. That became his main occupation for the future."

Following Wasco, Art Sr. made a few more household moves to nearby Delano, and then to Shafter, California, to continue his employment with the gas company.

TWO

Boyhood Adventures

As youngsters, Art Jr. and little brother Bob Pollard shared a Huckleberry Finn lifestyle. "Art and I got along well," recalls Bob. "He rarely teased or picked on me just because I was younger and smaller. We camped out overnight a couple of times. Once was in the backyard of our house, and another time in the woods along a river near our home. We always used a tent so, at least, were not exposed to the elements or tiny creatures."

Christene, Bob and Art Jr. with their mother, Bobbie.

"Art took me to the movies several times in the 1930s, but I only remember the films that impressed me, such as *Frankenstein*, *Wolfman*, and the serials they ran between the double-features. In the beginning, I was young enough that I didn't have to pay. If I did have to buy a ticket, it was only a dime."

From Shafter, the Pollard family again picked up roots and settled for a time in Bakersfield, California.

"We lived near some cotton fields, and I remember picking cotton and putting it in a long sack that I dragged behind me along the ground," says Bob. "I believe my sister Christene and Art were also involved since we were being paid by the pound to pick cotton."

Not unlike Henry Ford, a young Art Jr. took a keen interest in all things mechanical, as Bob remembers:

"Art frequently repaired my bicycle. When the brakes quit working, he'd put gasoline through the rear wheel hub oil hole, which would make the brakes work for a while. This was necessary every few days. I guess Art wasn't concerned about the fact that the oil hole meant that *OIL* should only be used, not *GASOLINE!* I don't recall how long I was able to continue using that bike, but that was just one early example of Art's mechanical ingenuity.

Because of the many job opportunities due to the World War II effort, Art Sr. moved the family to Los Angeles around 1942. Bob has a few memories of his big brother from that era.

"I had a paper delivery route, and one day two older kids took my papers away from me," Bob recalls. "Of course this upset me and I told Art. With me following, he went looking for them. We weren't successful, and I don't know what Art would have done if we had found them."

While living in Los Angeles, the Pollard family car was a 1940 Chevrolet. "Art was going somewhere, and I was just along for the ride," said Bob. "We were sitting at a stop light, and a guy beside us indicated he wanted to drag race when the light turned green. Naturally, being a teenager, Art accepted the challenge."

"We took off as fast as we could and were staying fairly even with the other guy when a police car showed up behind us and turned on his lights. Art decided to separate himself from the other car and turned off onto a side street to the right. The police car continued following the other guy's car. After we had returned home, a police car pulled up in front of the house. The officer knocked on the front door and asked who was driving our car an hour earlier. Apparently, he had taken down the license plate number. I don't remember if Art received a ticket or not."

As Art grew older, he naturally took an interest in some of the most important things in a teenaged boy's life – girls and hairstyles. Bob remembers, "Art met his first wife, Claudine, in Los Angeles and they started dating. In that era, Hispanic street gangs were referred to as 'Pachucos' and the duck-tail haircut was popular. Art, always pretty stylish, tried to duplicate that look and I suppose he was he was somewhat successful."

[The origin of the term 'Pachuco' is uncertain, but one theory connects it to the city of El Paso, Texas, which was sometimes referred to as 'Chuco Town' or 'El Chuco.' People migrating to El Paso would say, in Spanish, that they were going "pa' El Chuco." These migrants became known as "Pachucos"].

When the Pollards moved to Roseburg, Oregon in 1944, Art's high school buddies called him "Pachuco" because they had heard about that popular culture in and around Los Angeles. Since Art was a very outgoing person, he accepted the nickname merely as a friendly gesture.

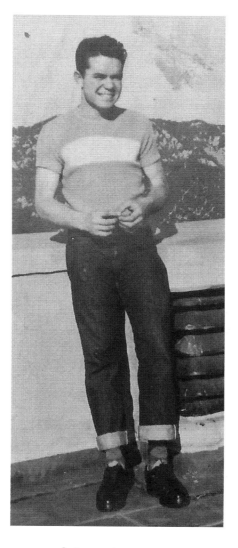

Art as a teenager.

THREE

Setting Down Roots in Roseburg

"We moved from Los Angeles to Roseburg, Oregon when our dad got into the propane gas business," says Bob Pollard. "I was fourteen and Art was seventeen and in his junior year of high school. I think the move was harder on me than Art, as he never complained. I was not as outgoing as he was."

Soon after, some of the other members of the extended Pollard family also traveled northward, including cousin Harvel. "Uncle Art Sr. and Uncle Owen were farm-type people and liked the open spaces, so they moved around quite a bit and eventually came to Oregon," says Harvel. "I was in the seventh grade when Uncle Owen decided to bring me up to a little place called Melrose, just outside of Roseburg. He lived in an old church that had been converted into a house. It had a graveyard out back and we had cows to milk. Nearby was another house and vacant land. Uncle Art, Aunt Bobbie, Art Jr., Christine, and Bob lived there."

Art enrolled at Roseburg High School in his junior year and, due to his outgoing personality, he was quick to make friends. Three closest to him were Jack Rodgers, Don Caskey, and Lee Holmes. Jack and Don were in the same class with Art, while Lee was a year behind.

"When the Pollard family moved in next door to us," Don recalls, "I could see their car and a younger guy, so I went over and introduced myself to Art's dad. He told me about Art, what grade he was in and everything – and I said I'd like to meet him."

Jack added, "I think when Don and I became acquainted with Art, they had just moved up here. Art was overhauling the carburetor on his folks' Chevy, and he had it all worked over."

"The pipes that he had were loud!" laughed Lee.

"All of those things kind of became popular after he moved here," Jack said. "During high school, Art went to classes for half a day and worked the other half at Hanson Motors – the Chevrolet dealer in Roseburg."

Art Pollard, Jr.

**Forever Friends – Lee Holmes, Jack Rodgers and Don Caskey.
Don passed away in 2018.**

(Roseburg High School and author photos)

A natural athlete, Art played football and basketball during his junior and senior years at Roseburg High. In football, he played both offense and defense – either as a running back, defensive back, or tight-end.

Bob Pollard recalls one incident while watching his brother at a game: "Art was playing at the defensive back position. The fellow carrying the ball for the opposing team ran towards Art. As he was in the process of tackling the guy Art ended up with the ball and ran it back for a touchdown. He just took the ball out of the other guy's hands while they were both still in an upright position!"

"When I was still living in Melrose," Harvel adds, "Bob and I went into Roseburg to watch Art play basketball. He was a senior and was a pretty good size for that time. I tell you, Art was a great athlete!"

"I think the only thing Art did was play ball," said Jack. "We were a pretty mediocre team because we were a small school. Art was a left tackle, so he handled the ball. Everybody played both ways, but most of us were pretty inexperienced. Art had a strong arm and could throw the football farther than anyone else."

Always the competitor, Art became involved in boat racing and water skiing and excelled at both. He had a small ten-foot hydroplane with an outboard engine that he would race on the North Umpqua River. He would soon turn to racing micro-midgets at the fairgrounds in Roseburg.

FOUR

The Navy – and Marriage

Soon after high school graduation in 1945 Art enlisted in the Navy. He was stationed in San Diego, but since the war had come to an end he was discharged in 1946. While living in Southern California, Art rekindled his earlier relationship with Claudine B. Smith. She would frequently take the bus from Los Angeles to San Diego, and the pair would meet in Balboa Park to spend the day together. It wasn't long before Art and Claudine were married in Los Angeles in April 1946.

Claudine and Art.

"Art Sr. told me that Art Jr. was lovesick," Don Caskey recalls. "He had left his lady in Los Angeles, so he hooked up with her again when we went into the Navy. Since he was one month older than me, Art was marching out of boot camp as I was coming in."

Don Caskey, Jack Rodgers, and Lee Holmes were into cars just as much as Art was. "I had a '33 Chevy roadster and Art told me I'd better get pipes on it," said Don. "He was going to Los Angeles over the holidays to see his girlfriend, Claudine, so I gave him money to buy me some 'Smitty' mufflers. Well, he came back but there were no mufflers. Art used the money to buy Claudine a ring! Later, I finally got the mufflers, and all was good."

Don added, "When I got out of boot camp I went over to Coronado, California, and who should I run into but Art. I think we bull-shitted all night long. That's when he was learning to run the landing craft. When he went to Long Beach, he ran a twin-engine Liberty boat. It had throttles set up with the handles on them, and he was running it with his feet. They saw him doing that – and he caught hell."

"He went into the Navy for about a year, but when he came back home, he was married to the gal he had gone with down in Los Angeles," recalls Jack. "We all stayed in the Roseburg area, but Art came back married to Claudine."

Not unlike similar occupations, the life of a professional racing driver can cause a great strain on marriages and personal relationships. The rigors of a season-long race schedule, combined with test sessions and sponsorship obligations, demand one to be on the road and away from home for days and weeks at a time. Unfortunately, this also affected the Pollard family in the years ahead.

After 24 years of marriage, Art and Claudine divorced in 1970. For much of that time, Claudine had been very supportive of Art's racing aspirations. Along with their two children, Mike and Judy, Claudine traveled with Art to most of his racing events throughout the Pacific Northwest.

Claudine remained in Medford for many years, but never remarried. She retired from Boise Cascade Corporation in 1992 and was quite involved with many volunteer activities. She moved to Eugene in 2010 to be nearer to daughter Judy's family. Claudine passed away at age 87, in March of 2015, from age-related causes. Besides daughter, Judy, she is survived by five grandchildren, eleven great-grandchildren, and one great-great-grand-daughter.

Claudine Pollard.

FIVE

A Growing Family

Art and Claudine established their first home together in Roseburg after their marriage in 1946. Art began taking auto repair classes and found work at a local car dealership. This allowed him to gain hands-on experience while learning the mechanics' trade. Of course, this went hand-in-hand with Art and his buddies souping-up their personal cars and motorcycles.

"When Art could finally afford a car of his own, he purchased a 1940 Oldsmobile sedan," said Bob Pollard. "First chance he had, he painted it a medium blue. This came after filling in all the areas where he had removed all the exterior trim. He also installed fender skirts and dual exhaust pipes with 'Smitty' mufflers."

Bob and Art Pollard in Roseburg.

Bob remembers that in 1948, Art purchased a brand-new Chevy coupe and quickly customized it in much the same style as the Oldsmobile: "He installed dual exhausts, again with 'Smitty' mufflers, but this time he added a bypass valve to route the exhaust through a normal muffler to avoid being picked up for too much noise. He let me borrow his car every now and then to drive to school, pipes and all."

"Some guy had a BSA motorcycle," said Don Caskey. "One Saturday, Art came by the house with it. I hopped on the back and we went out on Diamond Lake Boulevard. I got off and Art roared up the road, pulling wheelies and all that crap. It came to my turn and I did the same thing. I came back and we took off, Art driving. We just about got back to town and we're following a car, so we had to slow it down. Just then, the rear tire blew out and we had to push it the rest of the way. Yep, we had to fix the tire."

Claudine, Art, Mike and Judy.

Particularly in small towns, hot rods always came under the scrutiny of the local police. Roseburg was no exception. Don noted, "We became known when we had loud pipes."

"That upset the State Police," Lee Holmes chuckled.

"It was all Art's fault," Don noted. "Hell, Art went to Eugene one time and I think he got a ticket in every town he passed through. He did have mufflers, but they 'talked' to you when he got on it. He split the manifold on a six-cylinder Chevrolet. His dad let him do what he wanted with the car. He was easy-going like Art."

"Art was always a real friendly guy," said Jack Rodgers. "I only saw him mad once in my life. He and I went to a movie or something like that, and someone swiped his hubcaps. We looked all over town for them but never found them, but he was really upset. You know, I don't think I ever heard Art swear." "And he didn't even drink," Don added.

Meanwhile, Art and Claudine's young family began to blossom in Roseburg. Son Michael was born in 1947 and daughter Judy arrived in 1950.

SIX

From Boats to Race Cars

In the early fifties, a favorite weekend pastime in Roseburg was water sports. Always the competitor, Art became involved in boat racing and water skiing and excelled at both. He had a small ten-foot hydroplane with an outboard engine that he would race on the North Umpqua River and elsewhere.

"During that period, one of the few times while I was home on vacation, Art tried to teach me to water ski, but that didn't work," chuckled Bob Pollard. Lee Holmes recalls, "We used to race small hydroplanes. We ran our own boats over on Tenmile Lake, and Art won races over there. You had to sit down on your knees to drive the boat."

"Art really enjoyed watching the Unlimited Hydroplane races on Lake Washington, near Seattle," said Bob Pollard "That was back in the days when the boats were powered by V-12 aircraft engines manufactured by Allison, or Rolls Royce's Merlin engine. The Merlin was the most reliable and produced more horsepower. I was living in Seattle from 1953 through 1957. Art, Claudine, their kids, and friends would drive up and we would go to the races together."

Don Caskey added, "We went up to Seattle for the Seafair hydroplane races and were standing near the pits. Art said, 'I'll see you in a little bit'. Pretty soon he was down in the pits talking to those guys. How he got down there I don't know."

For Art, the move from hydroplanes to racing cars was a natural progression. He was hooked on speed – not a daredevil type, but he rapidly developed driving skills with each new type of racing. "Like me," Bob recalls, "he was always working on cars, but he had a lot more experience. In the 1950s, Art got involved with racing micro-midgets, and I thought that was kind of neat that he was racing. He then moved up to hardtops and sprint cars."

Don recalls, "The first time he raced cars was with Bob Book and Ollie Fosback. It must've been in the early fifties. Roseburg had a dirt track, and that's where his oval track racing began."

"In the wintertime, he drove micro-midgets inside one of the livestock buildings at the Douglas County Fairgrounds," Lee recalls. "He had an Indian motorcycle engine and he could win with that."

Bob Book and Art with their Micro-Midget. They won their fair share of race trophies.

These early articles in the Roseburg newspaper described the beginnings of the popular micro-midgets:

Micro Car Races to Start Saturday

Twenty-four cars, all but several built in Roseburg, will inaugurate micro-midget racing at the County Fairgrounds Pavilion Saturday night with a full program of racing events.

About 700 spectators can be seated for the opening event of a season which is expected to end here April 18 in what is currently the state's only winter-time operating car track.

Blacktopping on the track and other improvements to the pavilion were completed Wednesday for the run of the little cars which number about 20 in the Roseburg area and about six visiting autos here from Crescent City for the inaugural. The field, however, is limited to only 24 cars.

Sponsored by the Pacific Racing Association, summer-time promoters of the Roseburg Speedway hardtop events, the proposal for indoor racing was met with enthusiastic response by fans last fall. Several hardtop drivers and other car enthusiasts set on the project of building their own autos.

The engines, mostly Cushmans, are limited to 18 cubic inches while minimum weight of the entire machine is 260 pounds. Other specifications for size and safety must be met.

Cars will burn alcohol and methanol fuel and an adequate ventilating system installed in the pavilion recently will remove all unpleasant odors.

A total of 10 races will be run Saturday night beginning with time trials at 7:30. Races on the program are two trophy dashes, four heat races, two main events, and two additional races pitting winners of heat dashes against each other.

Six cars will compete in each heat race and 12 in each of the two main events.

Reports indicate that a steam-driven micro, being built by Mark Nichols of Roseburg, starter at the track, will be ready to race in future events. It is a 22-horsepower machine built on 12-1/4 inches.

Art celebrating another micro-midget victory with his young daughter Judy at the Roseburg Fairgrounds.

January 24, 1955 – Another turn away crowd lined the County Fairgrounds Pavilion to witness the second event-packed micro-midget racing program Saturday night.

The crowd witnessed resetting of the track record for the 1/15th-mile oval in the time trials and saw Art Pollard in midget number 42 walk away with the biggest share of the winner's loot.

Pollard started the evening by winning the A-trophy dash and then picked up firsts in the fourth heat race and final heat race. The latter event matches the first and second finishing cars from each of the proceeding four heat races.

Pollard Ups Racing Spot; Graves Tops

March 11, 1955 – By scoring 44 points, high for last Saturday's races, Art Pollard moved from fifth to third place in the micro-midget racing point standings this week.

Pollard, Eaton Make Top Micro Showings

March 14, 1955 – Two of the season's leading car drivers, Jay Eaton and Art Pollard, virtually took over the track with top money finishes in Saturday night's micro-midget racing program at the County Fairgrounds.

Art Pollard collected two firsts and two seconds on the 10-event show, including the A-Main title, to share top honors with second-place Jay Eaton who took three firsts and one second.

Pollard Captures Trophy for Top Score in March

April 1, 1955 – A total of 150 points scored in March earned for Art Pollard last month's high point honors at the micro-midget races and the George Ginder Trophy which will be presented at Saturday night's races.

Pollard, consistently in the first and second place money, edged out high-flying Jay Eaton, who leads the season's standings by a four-point count for the month.

After gaining experience and numerous racing wins with the micro-midgets, Art's emerging racing career moved up a notch to racing the larger and more powerful modified stock hardtops. Continuing his partnership with Book and Fosback, the team began campaigning a modified '33 Chevy hardtop powered by a six-cylinder GMC engine. Their first season at the Roseburg Speedway was a learning year, but by the end of the second year in 1956, Art earned a Pacific Racing Association track championship.

Art grabbing the checkers once again.

Celebrating victory lane with Claudine, Mike and Judy.

The following season, a successful Roseburg business owner named Ken Glass (*Ken's 1-Hour Martinizing*) replaced Fosback on the ownership team, and from that point on there was no looking back.

An article, written by Steve Veltman for the March 2005 issue of *Vintage Oval Racing Magazine*, described what took place. Herewith are some excerpts from that report:

Their hardtop was a crude little racer but behind the wheel, Pollard's ability shined. The team managed to capture the title knowing that if they wanted to win bigger races against tougher competition, they would need more race car.

Visits to other venues, including the Portland Speedway, had familiarized the team with Rolla Vollstedt. There was a lightweight Super Modified chassis for sale that Vollstedt had constructed for his friend Ernie Koch. Originally the car had been powered by a DeSoto Hemi-head engine, but Pollard and Company were Chevy guys. They bought the car and lengthened it. They installed their modified Corvette engine, christened the car the 'Ken's Martinizing Special' and went racing. The combination proved (nearly) unbeatable.

Over the next four years, Pollard dominated Super Modified racing on the West Coast. He won in Edmonton, Canada and in Fresno, California. In between, the teamed stormed Monroe, Spokane, Tacoma, Portland, Eugene, Coos Bay, Ashland, Anderson (CA), Sacramento and San Jose. They traveled east to Boise and Salt Lake City. Glass couldn't always go on the long hauls but continued to lend financial support. In one incredible season, Pollard won 22 features in 28 starts! It was an incredible run but like all Cinderella stories, it had to come to an end.

It may not be pretty, but it's fast!

(Clyde Sullivan Collection)

SEVEN

Oregonians at Indianapolis

Historically, the racing community has always been a close-knit bunch, particularly in the amateur ranks during the 1950s. Traveling together from race to race, drivers, mechanics, their wives, and children often bonded for life. Once the dust settled on another race weekend, this unique fraternity shared their everyday lives, just as you or I would.

As Art Pollard continued to develop his racing skills, he also established lasting relationships with other drivers, car owners, and crew members. Art's outgoing personality naturally beckoned people to wanted to "hang out" with him. Fellow Oregonians earned the opportunity to compete in the Indianapolis 500 are Rolla Vollstedt, Len Sutton, Bob Christie and George Amick. Additionally, Pat Vidan served as the Chief Starter at Indianapolis for seventeen years.

Portlander **Rolla Vollstedt** is a racing legend – not only in the Pacific Northwest, but throughout the United States. It all started for Rolla back in 1947 when, as a car owner, he began with a track roadster at the Portland Speedway. The car was built by George 'Pop' Koch and was powered by a 12-cylinder Lincoln Zephyr engine. The purchase price was $500.

In his autobiography *The Rolla Vollstedt Story* (co-authored by Ralph Zbarsky), Rolla said: "I got my interest in racing before WW II when I worked in a speed shop in Portland for Frank Costanzo. I worked there from 1939 to 1942, until I got drafted into the Army. He was my mentor, and eventually became a stockholder in Vollstedt Enterprises. He helped me a great deal, and even more came back to work with us for a few years at the Speedway in Indianapolis."

For the record, Rolla was an infantry soldier – a "Grunt" – as he describes himself, in the European theater during World War II. He was wounded twice in combat, earning a Purple Heart with an Oak Leaf Cluster.

Frankie McGowan was Rolla's first driver, but that came to a quick end. Vollstedt explained it this way: "When I arrived at the Portland Speedway, I learned that Frankie McGowan had quit driving for me, so I was at the racetrack without a driver. The team that hired McGowan had fired Len Sutton, and when I came through the pit gate there was Len looking for job. I hired Len on the spot."

Rolla Vollstedt with one of his first race cars.

(Vollstedt Family Collection)

That quick partnership turned out to be a match made in heaven. Over the next nine years, the Vollstedt/Sutton combination – first in track roadsters and then sprint cars – wore out the competition up and down the West Coast.

In his own autobiography, *My Road to Indy*, Len Sutton described those first years: "While most of our racing took place in Oregon, we found that traveling north to Seattle every other week gave us more exposure, plus an added income. We raced on the Aurora quarter-mile paved track in northern Seattle. Rolla claims we took home between three and four hundred dollars every week we went up there. Washington cars and drivers were very competitive and beating them was not a slam dunk."

Above all, Rolla was an innovator. His first race car was a 1925 Ford T-bodied roadster powered by a Mercury Flathead V8. In 1952, enlisting the assistance of Sutton and Pop Koch, he built a sprint car powered by a powerful GMC engine. Despite much of the competition using the venerable Offenhauser motor, Vollstedt and Sutton won the Northwest Sprint Car Championship in 1953, 1954 and 1955.

Vollstedt is known for building the first rear-engine, Offenhauser-powered Indy car that he and his friends completed in late 1963. After a year of testing, Len Sutton qualified eighth for the 1964 running of the '500'. To that extent, Vollstedt helped start the rear-engine revolution in oval track racing.

A young Len Sutton at speed in Rolla Vollstedt's roadster.

(Sutton Family Collection)

Another achievement that Rolla best known for is bringing driver Janet Guthrie to the Indianapolis in 1977. Janet was the first woman to qualify and compete in both the Indy 500 and Daytona 500.

Janet Guthrie and Rolla Vollstedt.

(Vollstedt Family Collection)

Art Pollard and Rolla Vollstedt were close friends, and Rolla certainly recognized Art's driving skills. This association would eventually lead to Art's first experience at the

Brickyard. As Art's longtime friend Don Caskey noted, "Vollstedt was the one who got Art into the big time. He knew Art was good."

Rolla's sons Kurt and Bruce both inherited their father's involvement in racing. Kurt was a racing mechanic, and Bruce (pictured above) became a successful NASCAR driver. Rolla jokingly referred to the stock cars as "taxicabs".

(Author photo)

Bruce and Rolla Vollstedt with Al Unser, Sr.

(Vollstedt Family Collection)

Rolla Vollstedt passed away in 2017 at the age of 99. For his final years he resided in an assisted living facility in a Portland suburb. His room was filled with racing memorabilia from the past, and he still thrived on watching televised races.

"All my memories of Art Pollard are good ones," Rolla recalled near the end.

Born in 1925, **Len Sutton** was a lifelong resident of Portland, Oregon. After serving in the Navy during World War II, Len returned home and – like many other veterans – began dabbling in racing. He was an exceptional talent almost from the start and, teaming up with Rolla Vollstedt, Sutton won several Oregon Racing Association championships during the 1950s.

In 1954, Len hooked up with Ranald Ferguson of Bickelton, Washington to run in that year's Carrera Panamericana road race in Mexico. Ferguson owned the 1953 Lincoln which finished third in the 1953 Mexican road race, driven by Jack McGrath. On a dark and unfamiliar stretch of road, Len and Ranald suffered a major crash.

In his biography, Len described the incident: "On a straight stretch and coming over an undulation, my headlights caught maybe 10 or 15 head of cattle. In trying to miss them, I got too far onto the left shoulder of the highway and lost it in the gravel. We ended up in a ravine (right side up) with the headlights still burning. A while later some Mexicans found us, helped us out of the car and dragged us up to the highway. We appeared conscious and not bloody, but I had a broken vertebrae and Ranald had several cracked ribs." The result was that Len was in a body cast for four months.

Len Sutton was one of the most versatile and successful drivers to ever come out of the Pacific Northwest. He raced in the AAA and United States Auto Club Championship Car series from 1955 to 1965, achieving 43 top-ten finishes and three victories in 76 starts.

The great Len Sutton.

(Author photo)

He raced in seven Indianapolis 500s, beginning in 1958. His best finish at the Speedway came in 1962 when he finished second behind teammate Rodger Ward. Sutton also competed in a number of stock car races, including the 1963 Daytona 500.

Indy 1962 – Len Sutton finished second to teammate Rodger Ward.

(IMS photo)

Len retired from racing in 1965 following a USAC race at Langhorne, Pennsylvania. He explained that decision: "We had a real, real bad accident. Mel Kenyon got severely burned, I got out of the race car that day and said to myself, 'I think my family's too important. I've got to hang it up.'"

For a number of years following retirement, Len served as the 'guest driver' during the radio broadcasts of the Indianapolis 500 as a member of the Indianapolis Motor Speedway Radio Network. His accolades include induction into the West Coast Stock Car Hall of Fame in 2005, the Oregon Sports Hall of Fame, and the National Midget Auto Racing Hall of Fame in 2009. In December of 2006, Len passed away due to complications of cancer. He was 81 years old.

1964 – Len Sutton drove Vollstedt's revolutionary rear-engine Offy.

(Sutton Family Collection)

1965 (left to right) – Len Sutton, Tony Hulman, Grant King, Rolla Vollstedt and Art Pollard.

(Vollstedt Family Collection)

Bob Christie was born in 1924 and lived in Grants Pass. Like many others from his era, Christie earned his racing credentials on the fairgrounds circuit around the Pacific Northwest. Christie carried the nickname "Caveman." He got that from a 20-foot tall Caveman statue wearing only a loincloth and wielding a club that was located near downtown Grants Pass.

Bob Christie in 1960.

His first attempt at Indianapolis came in 1954, with his own car, but he was unable to qualify. His first opportunity to race in the '500' came in 1956 when he started in the 25th position and finished the race in 13th place in the car that Jack McGrath at raced at Indy in 1955.

Christie then went on to compete in the race for the next seven consecutive years, with mixed results. His best finish came in 1960 when he came home in the tenth position. That was the only year he completed all 200 laps.

In all, Christie raced in the USAC Championship Car Series from 1956 to 1963, with 15 career starts. In 1956, he also began racing in the USAC stock car circuit where one of his best performances was a third-place finish behind Jim Rathmann and Rodger Ward in a USAC stock car race at the then-new Daytona International Raceway in 1959.

Christie loved Indianapolis, even after he retired. He would spend much of the month of May at the track. He was said to be an excellent speaker and would escort special guests through Indy's garage area. Bob Christie died on June 1, 2009, in Grants Pass. He was 85 years old.

Bob Christie's last race at Indy was in 1963.

(Ralph Hunt Collection)

George "Little George" Amick was also born in 1924 in Vernonia. After serving in World War II, he began racing in the jalopy circuit. Amick would drive just about anything on wheels. He won the 1946 Pacific Coast Stock Car Championship before moving to California and switching to USAC's National midget cars. There, Amick finished top ten in points each season, winning 16 feature races. In all, he totaled 38 wins, including the 1957 Turkey Night Grand Prix at the Gardena Stadium in California.

George Amick. Photo at right was taken at the Saugus, California Speedway, where he was driving the Sellers Graham Offenhauser Midget.

(Jack Corley Collection)

Amick graduated to Indy cars, winning three times in 43 starts. He did not qualify for the Indianapolis 500 in 1957. The next year Amick was behind the wheel of a Quinn Epperly-designed roadster owned by Norm Demler and built by chief mechanic George Salih. He started the event from the 25th position and drove an outstanding race to finish second behind winner Jimmy Bryan.

Following the race, in a phone interview with John White, a sportswriter with the *Portland Journal* newspaper, Amick described his Indy adventure: "Ever since I was six years old, I've wanted to drive race cars. I used to listen every year to the Indianapolis races, and when I started getting goose pimples on top of goose pimples, I knew I wanted to drive there myself someday. It was [the 1958 Indy 500] just wonderful."

On April 4th, 1959, USAC staged a Championship Car race at the new, high-speed tri-oval track at Daytona Beach, Florida. The 'Daytona 100' would be the first and only Champ Car event staged at that facility.

George Amick drove the Demler Special to a second-place finish at Indianapolis in 1958, earning the Rookie of the Year Award.

(IMS Photo)

Sadly, the race would take the life of "Little George". Noted motorsports journalist Robin Miller penned this review of the contest which appeared in *Motorsport Magazine* in 2009. The following are excerpts from that article:

That Was No Place for Indycar

Indycars at Daytona. That suggestion today would bring a volley of laughter from drivers, mechanics, owners and race officials. The speeds would easily top 250 mph and it would be borderline insanity running wheel to wheel for two-and-a-half miles on the 31-degree banking. But, back in 1959, safety seldom entered the thought process because there was so little of it.

A professional race driver in the United States Auto Club was long on bravado and short on life expectancy. Danger was simply part of the job description. So when Bill France opened his answer to the Indianapolis Motor Speedway down in Florida, it only seemed natural that the Boys of Indy would be part of the show.

The Daytona experiment was short and savage for Indycars. Marshall Teague and George Amick lost their lives and Indycar never came back. "I always liked the high banks of Salem and Winchester in a sprint car; heck, that's where George Bignotti saw me win an IMCA race and hired me to drive for him," said A.J. Foyt, who finished eighth in his Dean Van Lines Special at Daytona. "But Daytona was scary. It was like sitting on the wing of an airplane.

[Oregon driver] Bob Christie, who wound up third in the Federal Engineering Special, enjoyed the experience but admitted the speeds were ridiculous for a roadster with eight-inch-wide tires. "You really didn't drive it," he said. "You just aimed at it."

During the initial Indycar test session at Daytona in February '59, speeds rocketed past 170 mph and the track claimed its first victim. Marshall Teague, a two-time stock car champion with no previous Indycar experience, had practiced at over 171 mph in the radical Sumar Streamliner that featured an enclosed cockpit and fenders over the wheels. The postmortem in a local paper read: "Going into a turn the car appeared to list, the nose went downhill and dug itself into the ground. The car then hurtled into the air. The cockpit tore loose from the chassis and travelled airborne for 150 feet with Teague in it. Sections of the car came off in the air and were strewn in many directions. There was no indication of mechanical failure and the general consensus was that Teague had just lost it."

Qualifying was a sight to behold as Amick threw down an incredible lap of 176.887 mph and Tony Bettenhausen, who had run 177 mph in the Novi in Italy the year before, had practiced a tick under 180 mph. Pat Flaherty, the 1956 Indy winner, found the pace hard to comprehend: "It's hard to realize your enormous speed, and it's exhausting." Dick Rathmann, elder brother of Jim, who had taken Teague's place for the Sumar team, stuck his conventional roadster in the show at 173.210 mph and said: "There's nothing I'd rather be doing than driving here."

Despite his eye-opening speed, Amick didn't discount the challenge ahead. "Perhaps it takes more experience to drive at Indy, but this course is tough because you don't get a chance to relax anywhere. Then, in what turned out to be an eerily prophetic comment, he added: "If you lose it here, your rump is a grape."

"Little George" Amick, prior to his death at Daytona in 1959.

The 40-lap race turned out to be a preview of the 1959 and 1960 Indianapolis 500s as Jim Rathmann and Rodger Ward staged some of the closest and best racing ever seen before or since. Rathmann led the first six laps before Ward took command, only to yield back on lap 11 to the man he would beat to the checkered flag that May by 23 seconds.

"Ward and I had a helluva duel in the early part of the race before I took the lead for good," said Rathmann, who would come back to conquer Ward at Indy in 1960. "I never got too far ahead of him but I had the best car and it was flying."

Other than Dempsey Wilson's spin into the infield on lap 28, the race was fast and safe as the cars took the white flag. But, as Rathmann headed for the checker, Amick's ghastly accident was unfolding exiting Turn 2.

"George and I had a good battle for third and we must have exchanged places every lap for almost half the race," said Bob Christie. "But on that last lap I said to myself, 'George, I'm going to take you in there real hard this time.' But he didn't make it. Either the wind caught him or he turned the car too sharply."

The newspaper account said Amick's Bowes Seal Fast Special knifed into the guardrail, shearing off both front wheels as it sailed upside down for approximately 900 feet before landing in the infield. The front end was severed from the car and the 34-year-old had no chance.

Christie took third and Amick, who had finished second in his first Indy 500 the previous May, was credited with fourth. Rathmann's winning speed for the 100 miles was an incredible 170.261mph. "It took just over a half hour to run 100 miles and that was pretty much unheard of," says Rathmann, who collected $6400 for his win. "The speeds didn't bother me, I loved fast race tracks. I liked Monza and I liked Daytona, although I think I was in the minority."

The clean-up took forever and it was determined that the second race (a non-points affair) would be shortened from 100 to 50 miles (20 laps), as only 14 drivers lined up. Tony Bettenhausen opted not to run and turned over his Racing Associates mount to Wilson, while George Bignotti parked Foyt. The cars of Eddie Sachs and Len Sutton couldn't be fixed from earlier problems.

Rathmann paced the first lap before Ward took the point, but his day ended in Turn 4 on lap four. "Rodger was leading and I was in third, and I saw some moisture on the track as we approached Turn 2," says Christie. "He lost it and I thought he was going to spin down into the infield so I went high, but he was headed right for the fence and I clipped his tail. That started him spinning down the track and I zigged back and forth almost the length of the straightaway before I finally got my car straightened out. But by hitting him, I saved Ward's life, I know I did."

With Ward gone, Jim Rathmann managed to hold off brother Dick and Christie, but the USAC fraternity was just relieved to get out of Florida without any more fatalities. "It was terrible," says Foyt, who tamed deadly tracks such as Langhorne with relative ease. "We didn't have the proper tires and those cars weren't built to run at a track like that with those speeds. It was like racing a roadster in the snow and you stayed puckered all day. Like I said, it scared the hell out of me."

Even in the macho world of USAC racing circa 1959, the risks were too big. A return for the July 4 race was cancelled. "I don't feel like there's a car that can be built that will be safe at these speeds," said Ward, who would win twice at Indy. "The driver only has a certain few opportunities to escape serious trouble."

NASCAR issued a statement that said the deaths of the two drivers could not be blamed on its track. Then Nat Purcell, executive director of NASCAR, said what everyone had figured out: "The track is engineered far ahead of the automotive industry. Car designers and engineers have a lot to learn about wind resistance."

Another NASCAR release said: "A close examination of driving and aerodynamic conditions existing between 160 and 200mph should be made before Speedway (Indy) cars are sent into competition at Daytona again."

Of course, Indycars never returned to the beach, at least not to race on those daunting banks. Watson said Ward had already hinted he'd never be back and that seemed to be the general mindset of the bravest men of that era. "I enjoyed running stock cars at Daytona," says Foyt, who won NASCAR's crown jewel in '72. "But that was no place for an Indycar."

At the time of his death, George Amick was 34 years old and living in Rhinelander, Wisconsin. In 2009, he was inducted into the National Midget Auto Racing Hall of Fame.

Though ***Pat Vidan*** did not drive a race car at Indianapolis, the Portland native became one of the track's most iconic figures of the 1960s and 1970s and one of the sport's finest ambassadors. Pat became an assistant starter at Indianapolis in 1958, and in 1962 he was named the Chief Starter for the most prestigious race in the world. He served in that capacity for 17 years until his retirement in 1979.

Born in 1914, Pat became fascinated with early auto racing in the Portland area and, in 1946, became the chief flagman at the Portland Speedway and the nearby Portland Meadows track.

He believed it was his responsibility to entertain the spectators during breaks in the racing action. An athletic man, old-timers remember Vidan performing back-flips down the center of the track while the race cars sped by on either side of him.

Pat was known to get on the back of a Multnomah County sheriff officer's motorcycle and perform stunts, including standing atop the rider's shoulders. Also a talented artist and sign painter, Vidan would draw caricatures of people in the grandstands while commenting over the loud speaker. His personal repertoire included that as a skilled ice skater and snow skier, a gymnast and a designer and builder of boats. All told, Pat was a jack of all trades.

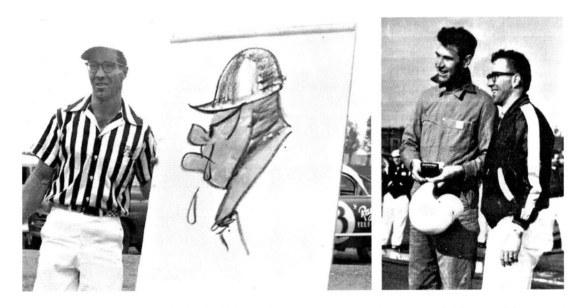

Pat Vidan's many talents included his artistic capabilities. On the right he is with racer Len Sutton in the early days at Portland Speedway.

(Ralph Hunt Collection)

At the Portland Speedway in the 1960s, Art Pollard accepts another racing trophy from the race queen and flagman Pat Vidan.

Vidan's flair at the racetrack became known across the country, and he was invited to flag the Tangerine Bowl race in Florida. Tony Hulman, the owner of the Indianapolis Motor Speedway, happened to be there and subsequently invited Pat into the world of Championship Car racing in Indiana.

On that occasion, the *Oregon Journal* newspaper provided this article on March 16, 1958:

Portland's Pat Vidan Named to Indianapolis Post

Pat Vidan, Portland's jumping Jack of auto racing starter, has never seen the 500-mile Memorial classic at Indianapolis. He will this year. Vidan has been named assistant starter at the world series of racing. He's the first person from the Pacific Northwest ever so honored.

"I figured if I ever got back to Indianapolis," he laughed, "I'd have to pay my way in. It's a wild dream as far as I'm concerned. I still can't believe it."

For 12 years the colorful Vidan, whose regular job is at McCuddy's Marine, has thrilled racing fans with his acrobatics while handling the flags at tracks throughout the Northwest. He's worked in Portland, Salem, Spokane, Seattle, Yakima and Tacoma races in a race-crazy state. And that led to his big break. "I understand Tony Hulman, who owns the Indianapolis Speedway, saw me in action in Miami", said Vidan. "Where did you get that starter?" asked an amazed Hulman. He found out. And Vidan was on his way to the big time.

"I guess they'd never seen anything like it in Florida," said Vidan, discussing his work that led to the Indianapolis assignment. "I'd have the cars come at me single-file, and then divide," he said. "As they divided, I'd run towards the cars and do a round off a sort of quick flip, and then a series of back flips."

It was Vidan's reputation, as one of the nation's most acrobatic starters, that led him to the top. And he comes by his acrobatics naturally. For an all-around athlete, he's hard to beat. He's been – among other things – a star ice skater (hockey fans will recall his exhibitions between periods), a three-meter diving champion, a motorcycle stunt rider, a top swimmer, a gymnast, a skier, a designer and a builder of boats.

"Everything but baseball," he said. "I just couldn't get interested in the game." To stay in the top physical condition required in his hazardous job, Vidan still works out three times a week in weightlifting and muscle-building sessions.

Although cars roar by him just inches from his body, Vidan never has been injured on a track. "I guess they were really shook up in Florida when I jumped over a midget which was coming at me. But I've done that before. It's only a matter of jumping three feet.

What's the most important requisite for his job? "Not getting excited," he said. "A track in no place to get shook up. You're the only means of communication between (the drivers) and what's going on at that track," he explained. "Those fellows depend on you."

Pat will leave Portland about May 1st to prepare for the Indianapolis race on Memorial Day.

Pat Vidan – Chief Starter at Indianapolis for 17 years.

(IMS photo)

During his years at Indianapolis, Vidan was always dressed in his customary white dinner jacket, tie and black pants while distinctively displaying the flag – green, yellow, blue, red or checkered as dictated during the race. Until safety issues dictated otherwise, he worked from the actual track surface, dropping to one knee with an elaborate flag-waving routine as a competitor crossed the finish line at the end of the race.

The athletic Oregonian resided for many years in the town of Speedway, Indiana. There, he operated a health studio that was frequented by numerous drivers. Much in demand as a public speaker, his act included a racing-related "lightning cartoon" segment that entertained both children and adults.

Pat Vidan's early days of flagging took place at Portland Meadows and the Portland Speedway.

(Ralph Hunt Collection)

(IMS photos)

In 1983, at the age of 69, Pat Vidan passed away and chose his final resting place to be in Indianapolis. In 2012, he was posthumously inducted into the Auto Racing Hall of Fame.

EIGHT

Moving Up the Ranks

In the book, *Early Modifieds,* Art's early sponsor Ken Glass said in an interview with author, Gerald Hodges:

"I met Art down at Bob and Ollie's station. He had been racing their micro-midget and now they were fiddling around with a 1933 Chevy that had been cut down. It looked pretty crude at the time, but I'd seen Pollard race, and I knew that by the time they got it on the track, it would be hard to beat."

That '33 Chevrolet was competitive at tracks throughout Oregon, including the Portland Speedway, where most of the premier cars and drivers ran. According to Lee Holmes, "Those guys up there had sexy coils and all kinds of carburetors. They'd just eat Art up on the straight-aways but come to the turns he would just drive around them. They couldn't figure that out. Art would tell 'em they don't need all that power."

In 1958, Art continued his winning ways by replacing the Chevrolet with a Corvette engine-powered 1934 Willys 77 coupe for the modified hardtop class. It was at Portland that the team had witnessed first-hand the potential of having a more powerful and advanced race car.

(Clyde Sullivan Collection)

On August 29, 1959 the *Salem Statesman* reviewed one race evening:

Pollard Sets Track Record
Roseburg Driver Also Captures 50-Lap Main Event at Salem Oval

Art Pollard, Roseburg's top modified hardtop driver, set a new track record at the Salem Speedway in Saturday's races. Pollard circled the track with a fast time of 16.11 seconds to break the record set earlier this season by Dean Wilcox of Eugene. Wilcox's record was 16.13 seconds on the quarter-mile asphalt track.

In the 50-lap main event Pollard continued to add points to his total by finishing ahead of the other drivers. Pollard crossed the finish line with Dick Pace, a Portland driver, close behind. Pace threatened to overtake Pollard right up to the checkered flag, but Pollard managed to nose him out at the end.

Following close behind Pollard and Pace were Jim Roberts and "Sparky" Yarbrough, both of Eugene. Less than a car length separated the third and fourth-place finishers.

Jack Timmings of Portland won the A Trophy Dash and Chuck Hammond of Eugene took the trophy in the B Trophy Dash. The heat races were won by Gordy Wilson, Portland; Kurt Harris, Roberts and

Bobby Etchison, Eugene. Etchison won the final heat and drove the fast heat race of the evening's action.

Pollard continues to hold a slim lead in the race for the top driver in the Northwest. The Roseburg speedster will travel to Eugene to compete in the races scheduled for Labor Day. A special 100-lap Mid-Oregon Championship race will highlight the Labor Day event on the three-eighths-mile asphalt track in Eugene. Competing in this race will be the top drivers from all over the Northwest.

**Lined up for a heat race at the Portland Speedway (left to right):
Art Pollard, Bill Hyde and Dick Pace.**

(Ralph Hunt Collection)

Art's hometown newspaper, the *Roseburg News-Review*, did a nice job in keeping up with his racing activities, like this piece that appeared on November 25th, 1960:

Art Pollard Will Compete in Sacramento Race Event

Art Pollard will enter the second annual modified stock car 100-mile race at the Capital Speedway in West Sacramento, Calif., driving the 'Martinizing Cleaning Special' Sunday.

Pollard won the Northwest modified racing crown for the second straight year driving the car with the big number one on its side and will now try to add to his driving laurels.

Qualifying and practice runs will be held Saturday at Sacramento and the starting positions will be decided from the finishes in the time trials. Approximately 150 to 200 cars are expected to be circling the half-mile clay track in the qualifying races. In the championship race, 50 cars will go to the starting line and the winner will take home $1,000 in silver dollars.

Pollard won over half the races he started in the Northwest during the past season and finished third or better in every race he completed. He came into his own midway through the season to set four track records for qualifying speeds. Pollard now holds records at the Jantzen Beach Speedway, the Salem Speedway, the Eugene track and the Ashland Speedway.

The chassis of the much modified 1934 Willys driven by Pollard is set up strictly for track use. Magnesium wheels, spot brakes, a quick-change rearend, open axle and knock-off lugs are some of the special equipment on the car. The machine is powered by a full-race Corvette V8 engine.

Another win, this time at the Jantzen Beach Arena in Portland.

The combination of a great car, driver, and crew surged forward with tremendous success. "I was always on his crew and traveled around with Art," says Art's high school friend Don Caskey. "Art was a finesse racer and knew how to set up a car. He just had the feel of it right off the bat."

NINE

Art's Fun-Loving Ways

With Art as both the family man and the maturing racer, there are always several stories and anecdotes from those who knew him well. These memories convey his lifestyle both on and off the track.

Bob Pollard and his wife Diane remember their wedding day in 1950. "Art and my brother, Jack Rodgers, went to high school together," said Diane. "Art was the best man at our wedding and always called me his favorite sister-in-law. That was fine, but I was his *only* sister-in-law!"

Diane and Bob Pollard.

(Author photo)

To which Bob added, "I asked Art if we could leave our car in his garage on our wedding day, so the guys couldn't decorate it and tie tin cans to the bumper. We had bumpers in those days! I suppose I should have known better, because when we went to get our car it was completely decorated and had tin cans hanging from the bumper. I was in the Air Force at the time and we were on our way back to Denver, where I was stationed. We traveled many miles down the highway towards Grants Pass, with friends following and everyone blowing their horns!"

After playing football for one season at Bakersfield College, Art's cousin Harvel Pollard joined the Air Force due to the Korean War. Following his enlistment, Harvel returned to California, reentered college, and married his high school sweetheart, Mary Lou. His next reunion with Art was when Harvel was playing football for San Jose State College in 1957. His team was playing against the University of Oregon in Eugene.

"I was a running back and during warm-ups I was fielding punts," Harvel recalls. "I heard this guy yell, 'Harvel, Harvel'. I look over and there's Art, and he's coming across the field. He said, 'I just wanted to let you know I was here. I'll see you after the game.'"

I asked Art how he knew I was playing," says Harvel. "Art said he was watching a Pacific Eight Conference highlight reel and I was featured a couple of times. I thought it was nice of him to drive three hours to Eugene to watch me play."

Mary Lou and Harvel Pollard with their children Laurie, Mark and Brad.

(Courtesy Harvel Pollard)

Always close since they were young kids, Harvel and Art were more like brothers. Following the game, the two cousins had a nice visit. Harvel introduced his good friend, Dick Vermeil, to Art. Years later Vermeil would become the head football coach at UCLA, and subsequently go on to coach the Philadelphia Eagles, St. Louis Rams, and Kansas City Chiefs of the National Football League.

"In the spring of the next year I got a call at my home in Bakersfield one night and it was Art," Harvel says. "He and his family were driving back from San Jose, and he said he had a timing gear go out. Dick Vermeil and I drove up and towed Art and his family all the way back to our house that night. I think he had an early '50s Chevy."

Knowing the extent of the repair, Art said he'd have to take the car to a garage the next day. Dick mentioned that he didn't have to do that. Art questioned 'Why not?' It turned out that Dick had a mechanical background that he gained under the tutelage of his father Louie, who made a living with his own auto repair shop. It didn't hurt that Louie Vermeil just happened to be a well-known builder of sprint car and midget racers in California.

"So, Dick, Art and I put the car in Dick's garage and Dick climbed underneath to change out the timing gear," Harvel recalls. "Art asked Dick, 'How in the world did you know how to do that?' Dick explained that his dad had taught him. Art was really impressed, and that was the start of a lasting relationship between Art and Dick."

Art Pollard was an all-around talented mechanic, as his brother Bob recalls. "When Art was at home, if he wasn't doing anything else or getting together with friends, he would be working on his race car," said Bob. "Though he didn't always have help from others, he was constantly coming up with new modifications." Bob remembers that lacking a proper power outlet in the garage, Art would run a line from an electric welder back to the house and plug it into the range receptacle in the kitchen.

Bob described one time he was with Art as he was towing his racer to an event in Sacramento. "In his earlier racing days Art may or may not have a pit crew." Bob was living in the area and went with Art to help at the track. "I did a few things, but I was pretty useless when it came to things he needed to be done," said Bob. "Most of the time he did all his own work."

Art was a mechanic by trade and was periodically sent to school in Portland by his employer. That may have played into Art's innovative ways with a race car, along with his creative "Let's just try it." personality.

Bob remembered another story regarding his big brother's mechanical aptitude. "Art used to haul his race car on a trailer, and during one of his trips to California a spindle on the left side of the trailer broke off. The wheel and tire took off down the highway, and a Greyhound bus just happened to be coming towards him in the opposite lane. The trailer wheel hit the front left side of the bus and did some damage.

Later, this minor damage became a major issue, because Greyhound wanted payment for the time the bus was out of service while being repaired. I don't know what the total cost was in the end, but Art's insurance company paid the bill as far as I know. Fortunately, no one was injured. Anyhow, he had to leave the trailer and race car parked alongside the highway. Since he was close to Sacramento, where we were living at the time, Art and Claudine stayed with us while he repaired the trailer."

"Art used to repair and modify his race cars, as necessary, to help him win races," Bob noted. "A lot of the modifications were experimental in nature, while others were exactly what he wanted in order to improve the performance of his race car."

A talented mechanic, Art was always a "hands-on" type of guy with his race cars.

(Ralph Hunt Collection)

Art working on his race car in the garage at Indy.

Art was involved in every aspect of a car's performance. Here he's talking things over with acclaimed IndyCar Chief Mechanic George Bignotti.

TEN

Art Pollard and Dick Vermeil

Legendary football head coach Dick Vermeil's friendship with Art Pollard began when Art's cousin, Harvel, and Vermeil were football teammates at San Jose State College.

"I met Art one weekend," Dick recalls. "Harvel and I were both seniors in college at the time. Art blew a timing gear in an old Chevrolet. With his mechanical experience, Art thought he would have to take the engine out and pull it apart. We [Harvel and Dick] went out and towed him in. We had a little one-car garage behind our house and put his car there."

"I had learned from my dad, Louie, how to change a timing chain in a Chevrolet without taking the engine apart," said Dick. "I pulled the radiator out, took the timing gear cover off and all that stuff. It was a process that I actually don't remember now how I did it. That was a long time ago."

Coach Dick Vermeil with one of his father's restored sprint cars.

(Dick Vermeil Collection)

Dick continued, "I had my tools and just pulled them out and did it like I did when I was working in my dad's garage. We sort of bonded at that time, and Art appreciated it. He didn't have a lot of money and was working his way up [in racing]. I was just tickled to death to do it because I grew up wanting to be an Indianapolis race car driver. Looking back, it was a big thrill for me to help Art with his car. He was someone who became a friend and successful Indy driver. My dad, Louie, was big into sprint cars."

Jean Louis "Louie" Vermeil was born in 1906 in San Francisco to Albert and Clotilde Vermeil. The family soon moved to San Mateo, California, where Louie attended school. After a visit to the San Carlos board track in the early 1920s, Louie quickly took a keen interest in automobile racing. He witnessed racing legends such as Ralph DePalma, Peter DePaolo, Tommy Milton and Jimmy Murphy circle the track at triple-digit speeds. Louie was so smitten with the experience that he quit school to pursue a career as an auto mechanic.

At the age of 20, Louie moved to Calistoga where his grandfather lived in the former home of writer Robert Louis Stevenson. Twelve years later Louie married his sweetheart, Alice Wilson. Continuing to build on his rising career as a mechanic and, along with his racing interests, Louie opened a small auto repair shop.

The legendary Louie Vermeil.

(Dick Vermeil Collection)

Louie's first year as a race car owner came in 1938, in the first races held at his hometown track—Calistoga Speedway at the Napa County Fairgrounds in Northern California. Jack Pacheteau was his driver. People recall that the track was a "dust bowl" and just twelve race cars were presented.

In the years following, Louie's race cars competed throughout California. In 1950, Louie earned the American Racing Association (ARA) car owner's championship with Mike Riley driving the "Black Beauty" special. In 1955, Louie took on the position of an ARA official. In 1960, he helped pick up the pieces of the then-defunct ARA and became one of the founding fathers of the Northern Auto Racing Club (NARC). In those days, his duties ranged from being a referee to business manager, and most positions in-between.

(Clyde Sullivan Collection)

Louie served as president of NARC from 1965 to 1985, spending countless hours and, in some cases, money from his own pocket to ensure the long-term success of the series. He once said, "The people are the greatest. I wouldn't trade a moment of the time I have spent in this sport."

Louie and Alice, married for over 50 years, were known for their hospitality and generosity at their 115-year-old home in Calistoga. Behind the home was Louie's Owl Garage, which came by its name when he operated a 24-hour towing service. The shop was open all the time for racers to work on their cars while Alice provided plenty of food and fine Napa Valley wines for the hungry crews.

The Owl Garage also housed Louie's collection of unrestored midgets and sprint cars. Racing machines included those that had been driven by veterans such as Jack Pacheteau, Hal Cole, "Tex" Peterson, Rajo Jack, Mike Riley, Clay Walsh, Don Branson, Bob Veith and Jim Hurtubise.

Alice Vermeil preceded her husband in death. Louie lost his long fight with cancer in 1987. He was named Motorsportsman of the Year in 1982 and was inducted into the National Sprint Car Hall of Fame in 1995. Other honorees that year were veteran drivers Pat O'Connor, Bob Sweikert, Pete DePaolo, and Johnny Rutherford.

Since 1937, the half-mile dirt oval that is Calistoga Speedway has beckoned the most famous and talented competitors. They are the ones that have propelled auto racing into a major spectator sport. Many of the drivers that have raced at Calistoga went on to become legends of the Indianapolis 500. The track is located at the northern end of the Napa Valley in the picturesque town of Calistoga, where the roar of racing engines still draws big crowds today.

Beginning in 2008, each Labor Day weekend, Calistoga Speedway hosts the Louie Vermeil Classic to honor this racing pioneer's memory. The event draws many of today's up-and-coming racers.

Louie and Alice Vermeil raised four children: Laura, Dick, Stan, and Al. Stan followed in his father's footsteps as both a driver and car owner. He supported and worked with Louie to establish Calistoga Speedway as the premier sprint car venue it is known for today.

Dick graduated in 1959 from San Jose State University, where he was a quarterback. Following college, he served as an assistant football coach at San Jose's Del Mar High School for one season, and then took on the head coach role at nearby Hillsdale High for three seasons. He went on to serve as an assistant coach at San Mateo College, and as the head coach at Napa Junior College. While at Napa, Dick's younger brother Al played for him. In the 1965-66 season, Dick coached the freshman football team at Stanford University.

Dick was hired as the National Football League's first-ever special teams coach by the Los Angeles Rams in 1969. He retained that position until 1974 when he was named as head coach of the UCLA Bruins. In 1975, he led the Bruins to their first Conference Championship in ten years, plus a win in the Rose Bowl.

Dick rose to an even bigger football arena when he became an NFL head coach, beginning with the Philadelphia Eagles in 1976. There, he was named the NFL's Coach of the Year in 1980 while leading the Eagles into Super Bowl XV.

After retiring from the game following the 1982 season, Dick spent the next 15 years as a sports announcer for the CBS and ABC television networks but returned to football in 1997 as the head coach of the St. Louis Rams. In 1999 St. Louis earned their first Super Bowl victory by defeating the Tennessee Titans. With this accomplishment, Dick was named NFL Coach of the Year for a second time. Despite another retirement following that Super Bowl, Dick took the helm of the Kansas City Chiefs from 2001 to 2005.

Dick and his wife, Carol, have three children and twelve grandchildren. Staying true to his roots in Napa Valley, Dick partnered with *On The Edge Winery* and produced his own *'Garage Cabernet'* wine, named in honor of his father Louie. Dick's life is best summed up in an August 2013 interview with *The Weekly Calistogan* newspaper: "Growing up in Calistoga, there were three things my family was passionate about – sprint cars, wine and football. I am lucky enough to have been involved with all three."

According to Dick, the Owl Garage was 25 yards behind the family home and was Louie's full-time life. Considering his passion for racing, Louie surprisingly attended just one Indy 500, in 1946. "That's the only vacation he ever took in his life," Dick recalls. My dad is extremely well-respected in Northern California. I run into people from the east coast that knew Dad."

"My dad's driver drove a midget during the week and a sprint car on the weekend," Dick explained. "As a kid, I would travel with Dad's driver to the midget races, and then to the sprint car races wherever they were on the weekend. In the old days, they wouldn't let kids in the pits. Dad became the president of the association, and then he was pit steward. He wouldn't allow anyone to break the rules, let alone me! It was good for me in the end because I would've started driving and never gone into football."

Dick remembers, "I saw all those guys driving midgets with the old BCRA (Bay Cities Racing Association). Drivers like Billy Vukovich, Johnny Parsons, Bob Sweikert and Mike McGreevy. got going, and he came through Calistoga. In fact, I can remember Dad giving him money to get home. Another was Rajo Jack, one of the only African-American race drivers ever. He was a good friend of Dad's, and I got to know him at Calistoga. I think he was driving a big old Ranger."

"I went all the way up to Portland [Oregon] one time," Dick said. "I towed a sprint car up there with my Dad's friend, Jack Flaherty. We got up there and blew a head gasket in qualifying. It was a Studebaker V8. We drove all day and night to get up there from California."

(Dick Vermeil Collection)

Regarding the track at Calistoga, Dick observes, "There are probably no better non-winged sprint car races in the country. There aren't many half-mile dirt tracks like this left anymore, with long straights and narrow turns. They run in under 19-seconds and really fly!"

Though he spent several decades fully devoted to his role with professional football, Dick Vermeil never forgot his family's deep-seated roots in racing. "As a fan, I stayed involved," he says. "I would watch my brother race his midget."

That close involvement with racing was bolstered when Dick worked as a football analyst for both the CBS (1983 - 1987) and ABC (1988 - 1996) sports networks. "During my CBS career, because they knew my interest in racing, I used to work the IROC (International Race of Champions) Series," he said. "It was a lot of fun and a great thrill for me. I got to know Chris Economaki [the *'Dean of Motorsports'* and founder of *National Speed Sport News*]. He was a big-time wine guy and a friend of my dad. So when I got involved with the IROC series, I always brought Chris Napa Valley wines that he couldn't get on the east coast. He loved that."

Dick has attended the Indianapolis 500 several times, once as a guest of his friend, Roger Penske. "I did a feature on the differences between a football player and a race driver," he explained. "I remember one of the key lines was, when you go off-sides [in racing], it's more than just a five-yard penalty."

Dick is the proud owner of two beautifully restored vintage racers that once belonged to his father. The Number 7 car was originally built by Al Bignotti in 1926. It was purchased by Grant Douglas of San Francisco and raced by Buck Whitmer and Gene Figone. After World War II, Louie Vermeil acquired the car and put Jack Pacheteau behind the wheel. This combination earned the American Racing Association Championship in 1950. In 2006, Dick and D.L. George began a three-year effort to restore old Number 7 back to its original condition. "I've taken it out to California three times to run it in the Louie Vermeil Classic," said Dick.

Dick restored the historic #2 sprint car that is part of his collection.

(Dick Vermeil Collection)

In 2011, Dick began work on a second restoration project on the Number 2 car, which some say was one of the best cars of its time. Built in 1936 by Urb Stair and Wally Schock of Los Angeles, the car's driving duties were shared by Schock and Tex Peterson. Peterson took ownership of the car in 1939, and it was successfully driven by notable drivers such as Spider Webb, Bud Rose, Sam Hanks and Jimmy Miller. The car was retired in 1958 and purchased by Louie Vermeil in 1980.

"These are my Ferraris," Dick told the *Weekly Calistogan*. "When I grew up in Calistoga I wanted to be a sprint car driver. My brother and I would spend most of our childhood nights working on Dad's race cars."

"I follow NASCAR and the Indy Cars," Dick said. "I follow Tony Stewart because I like the way he came up. I met A.J. Foyt a number of times. In fact, when I was doing the IROC series, everybody was afraid of him. They would send me over to do the pit interviews because Foyt knew of my dad through racing, and me through football. He would give me the interview. A.J. and Mario Andretti have to be the two finest drivers, right?"

ELEVEN

The Road to Indy

In late 1960 or so, Art, Dude Rose and Ken Glass made a down payment of $400 for a Rolla Vollstedt-built, DeSoto-powered car that was built for driver Ernie Koch. The balance of $1,300 was financed through a bank loan. Because of its light weight, the three owners were convinced it had the potential to be a winner. Others felt it was crazy that they were spending so much on a race car.

Art Pollard shows off his new sprint car to (left to right) Ken Glass, Don Caskey and Bob Green. Glass, well known to racing fans while living in Coos Bay for some time, is a part owner of the modified sportsman.

(The World, Coos Bay)

After performing several modifications, which included replacing the DeSoto engine with their own Corvette V8, it was time for some serious racing with the 'Ken's Martinizing Special.' An article and photo that appeared on March 31st, 1961 in the *Roseburg News-Review* described this new car:

Art Pollard Set to Drive New Machine

A new look will be seen on the racetracks of Oregon this summer with sprint cars and Modified Sportsmans to take over the scene from the modified hardtops.

An example of this type of machine, and the first of its kind in the Roseburg area, is the new 'Ken's Martinizing Special' to be driven by Art Pollard.

The car is an open type sprint car built specially to run on tracks from one-quarter to one mile in length, either dirt or asphalt. Utilizing special equipment, the car is capable of circling the tracks at a high rate of speed.

The 'Special' is powered by a modified Chevy Corvette V8 engine and has aircraft spot brakes. Special equipment on the chassis includes a Halibrand open rear axle with a quick-change rear end, magnesium wheels with knock-off hubs and Nordum sprint car steering. The body was hand built from aluminum and fiberglass by Bob Green and Dude Rose.

Competing as a sprint car, the machine will be in action about six times a year, while by adding a top the car will run as a Modified Sportsman in about 18 races. The Modified Sportsman is a new class of cars growing out of the old modified hardtop classification.

'Ken's Martinizing Special' is owned by Pollard, Rose and Ken Glass. The flashy auto is sponsored by Ken's Dry Cleaning of Roseburg and Eugene, with the work being done on the car at the local Union Garage.

Pollard, the 1960 champion modified hardtop driver in the Northwest, will be behind the wheel as the car takes to the track. The pit crew will be composed of Don Caskey, Bob Green, Rose, Jim Byrd and Glass.

Local fans will have a chance to see Roseburg's newest entry in the auto racing field at the first annual Autorama sponsored by the Umpqua Regional Timing Association April 7-9 at the Douglas County Fairgrounds.

The 'Ken's Martinizing Special' at the Portland Speedway. The track did double-duty as a drive-in movie theater.

(Ralph Hunt Collection)

The 1961 racing season proved to be a huge success for Art and his small team. The year began on a positive note, as described in this article in the *Roseburg News Review* on April 10th, 1961:

Pollard Breaks Eugene Record

Art Pollard opened the 1961 racing season with a brilliant display of his skill on the Eugene track, setting a new record as he sped around the oval for the first time in the Modified Sportsman Class Sunday. Pollard had the fast lap time of the day as he whizzed around in 20.32 seconds to break the mark of 20.44 which was set last year.

In addition to setting the new mark, Pollard won the 'A' Trophy Dash, the fourth heat race and the A-Main Event. Roseburg drivers dominated the field as Bob Cummins joined Pollard in the winner's circle taking the top awards in the 'B' Trophy Dash and the B-Main Event.

Winning the first heat at the Eugene Speedway was Eldon Linder of Portland, while Lyle Knox came in second. Chuck Hammond of Florence and Floyd Summers of Eugene placed first and second in the second heat, beating out Cummins who finished third.

The *Roseburg News-Review* typically kept local fans informed of the team's progress, such as this feature that appeared on May 12th, 1961:

Pollard to Race on Eugene Oval

Racing fans are in for plenty of excitement Sunday when the Modified Sportsman take over the Eugene Speedway at 1:30 p.m. with three local drivers appearing.

Art Pollard, driving the 'Ken's Martinizing Special' will lead the contingent of local drivers headed for Eugene. Pollard won the driving crown for two consecutive years in the Northwest Modified Hardtop loop, and now has switched to the Sportsmen and the sprint car races.

Holding track records from all over the northwest, Pollard has been Roseburg's top entrant in auto racing. The Special is sponsored by Ken's Dry Cleaning of Roseburg and Eugene and is owned by Pollard, Ken Glass and Dude Rose.

The sleek machine is capable of running in both Modified Sportsman and sprint competition as it sports a removable top. The Special was completed earlier this year as the new Sportsmen class of racing has taken the spotlight throughout the Northwest.

Bob Cummins will also be competing for the top honors at Eugene. Cummins is also an old hand at auto racing as he competed in the modified hardtop circle before switching over to the Sportsmen.

Art continued to display his talents at Eugene just a few weeks later, as described in another *Roseburg News Review* feature dated May 31st, 1961:

Pollard Wins Eugene Race

Art Pollard continued his winning ways Tuesday with a victory in the 100-lap R.J. Bugbee Memorial Race at the Eugene Speedway, while Roseburg rookie Bud Van Osten finished fifth.

Van Osten, competing in his first race of the season, and his first in several years, exhibited top driving form as he stayed close on the heels of the leaders in the 100-lap main event. Van Osten was piloting a machine sponsored by Byrd's Flying A Service of Roseburg.

Pollard edged out Jerry Fanger of Medford in the main event. Fanger, competing in his second season, led for the first 23 laps, before Pollard took the lead and held it until the waving of the checkered flag. Pollard was pushed all the way in the main event.

In addition to winning the 100-lap main event, Pollard set a new track record with the fastest lap time of the day. Pollard's new mark is 20.13, bettering the old record of 20.32.

Following Pollard and Fanger in the main event were Al Gilman of Portland, Bobby Etchison of Eugene and Van Osten. For the win Pollard was presented a rotating trophy by the family of R.J. Bugbee, who was the founder of the Racing Association in Eugene.

Also, in 1961, at one of his favorite events, Art won the Western States Race of Champions at the Kearney Bowl in Fresno, California. The two-day event began on Friday when Art qualified on the pole and set a new track record. That evening, he won the 'A' Dash and the Fast Heat races, plus all three of the 25-lap Main events. On Saturday, Art's charge continued by again setting another track record, followed by additional wins in the 'A' Dash and Fast Heat events. He then won two out of the three 25-lap Mains, finishing second in the third race.

At the end of the weekend, Art was crowned Champion and was awarded a nine-foot trophy, after recording 1,150 points out of a possible 1,200! Too large to keep in his home, Art asked Ken Glass to house this tall trophy. For decades after, it remained in the Ken's Martinizing dry cleaning business in Roseburg, Oregon.

Team partners with the Western States Championship trophy.

The Ken's Martinizing Special team traveled to Edmonton, Alberta, for the 1961 Edmonton Gold Cup race. At the time, the event was billed as the most prestigious auto race in Canada. Again, Art and his car were the class of the field. Twenty-four cars started the

200-lap event on the quarter-mile asphalt oval. Art started from the pole and led the entire distance for the victory.

(Ralph Hunt Collection)

As crew member Don Caskey remembers, "We went up to Edmonton in 1961 for the Gold Cup, and Art won that hands down. The engine was a Chevy 283 cubic-inch bored out a little, with a single Pontiac carburetor. We worked it over pretty good. Art qualified quickest, naturally. And hell, he took those guys into the first corner so fast that those hot rods were clear up agin' the wall. Art just disappeared! It wasn't long before he had a lap on them, and I'd get out there and signal him to 'COOL - IT!'"

The next year, Art repeated his winning ways by grabbing Edmonton's Gold Cup a second time. With these back-to-back wins, Art joined several other Edmonton winners that would go on to make their mark in racing, such as Billy Foster, Jim Malloy, Tom Sneva and Eldon Rasmussen. Art was quickly becoming a household name in racing. During the 1961 season, he won an amazing 22 of 28 feature events. It was an incredible run!

The local press described Art's second win at Edmonton in this article:

EDMONTON, Alberta – Veteran American race driver Art Pollard won Western Canada's ninth annual 200-lap Gold Cup Race for the second straight year on August 10th, 1962.

Timing in at 14.20 to win the pole position, Pollard was never really pressed after the 29th lap when Bill Crow of Boise, Idaho, left the race with a blown block. Pollard's car, powered by a 1962 Corvette modified motor, streaked home a full lap ahead of Dean Wilcox of Eugene, Oregon. Norm Ellefson of Edmonton was third, the same position he held in the 1961 classic.

The handsome Pollard, who calls Roseburg, Oregon, home, was born in Dragon, Utah, 35 years ago and only became seriously interested in racing seven years ago. Since then he has won many trophies in the Pacific Northwest, including the Copper Cup at Salt Lake City in 1961. He is the first man to win the rich Gold Cup Race twice, although previous Americans have won this coveted trophy – Cecil Hunt, Spokane, in 1957; Ernie Koch, Portland, in 1958; and Larry McDonald of Seattle in 1959.

At the Portland Speedway.

(Ralph Hunt Collection)

The late 'Tiger' Matan of Edmonton was the first winner back in 1954 and the following year ace driver Gavin Breckenridge of Edmonton took the honors. Then followed well-known Edmontonian Ray Peets in 1956. Norm Ellefson in his Chrysler-powered Crosstown Special was the last Canadian winner in 1960.

As a result of a 48-hour delay due to rainstorms, only 18 of the 24 qualifying cars entered the big race and there were ten finishers – thus all ten shared in the prize money. Behind Pollard, Wilcox and Ellefson were: (4th) Frank Taylor, Edmonton; (5th) Eric Van Camp, Fort Saskatchewan, Alberta; (6th) Larry Squires, Great Falls; (7th) Eldon Rasmussen, Calgary.

Wilcox might have made it a great race, but an early pileup cost him a lap and he could never quite make it back on Pollard, although he passed Ellefson twice to regain second position. The same mixup on the corner put Calgary's most fierce competitor, Frank Janett, out of the classic for the ninth straight year. He has never finished a Gold Cup Race although he has entered them all.

George Robertson of Lewiston, Idaho, who has probably won more position money than any other American driver on this quarter-mile track, dropped out early in the race with differential trouble.

[Author's note]: In the first edition of this book, I included a photo of Art accepting the Edmonton Gold Cup trophy from the race queen but was unaware of her name. Months later, I received an email from a lady in California – Darolyn (Cooke) Greenhut – informing me she was the gal in the photo.

Darolyn and her husband Mike are racing enthusiasts and had read the book. Unfortunately, she told me, she no longer had the photo in her possession and Mike would very much like a copy. Was it possible that I could forward a copy to them? I gladly sent them an enlarged print.

Every year, Darolyn and Mike drive their RV to Canada for an extended stay, naturally with a stop-over in Oregon for a few days. Twice now, I've had the pleasure of meeting them in person and, for this extended version of Art's biography, I asked Darolyn if she would share her personal memory as a race queen, which I now thank her for:

Art and Queen Darolyn Cooke in Edmonton.

"I was working for a two-man, two-girl office – Seymour E. Bushe & Sons and insurance agent Archie Dunlop. A gentleman came into the office one day looking for Marilyn, Mr. Bushe's secretary, to enter the contest. She had been a runner-up for Miss Edmonton.

She said her boyfriend wouldn't let her enter any more contests, but how about Darolyn? I said, 'Don't be silly', and Marilyn said, 'Oh come on, it'll be fun!' I got talked into it.

My next memory is the first time the contestants were to ride in convertibles around the track, in swimsuits, before a race. As I had auburn-colored hair, the woman in charge of us assigned me to a silver Mercedes. When it was time to get into the cars, one of the other contestants was sitting in the Mercedes and wouldn't get out. The only other car was a red Mercedes and I got into it. The woman said, 'No, not with your hair.'

Just then, a young fellow in a black Cadillac convertible drove in. He was asked if he would like to chauffeur a Miss Gold Cup contestant around the track. He said 'Sure' and became my driver. The Cadillac was the one Queen Elizabeth used when she was in Canada (1952?) and had the insignia on the doors.

As we travelled around the track, we came to the end where a bunch of guys were sitting and they yelled, 'Hey, here comes the Queen!' Of course, I blew them a kiss.

At the banquet, my chauffeur and his girlfriend were seated with my parents. When it was announced that I was the winner of that year's Gold Cup contest, I was floored and never in a million years thought I might win. I hadn't even prepared a response, and the rest was just a blur. I saw my driver standing in the crowd whooping – it was quite a night!

When photos were being taken, Art Pollard was standing beside me and we congratulated one another on our wins. He was a very sweet, delightful man. I was saddened when I heard of his fatal accident. Years later, a girlfriend and I made a car trip from Vancouver, Canada to San Diego. On the way, we attempted to contact his widow in Medford. However, she was out of town according to some people in the restaurant we stopped at. I was sorry not to have met her."

Darolyn and Mike Greenhut in 2019.

(Author photo)

Another huge weekend for Art and his crew during the 1961 season took place in mid-August at Salt Lake City. The event was the prestigious annual Copper Cup Race. Hi McDonald, a sportswriter for the *Deseret News*, summed up all the action in his report of August 19th:

Pollard Leading Copper Cup Race

It looked like money in the bank Saturday for Art Pollard of Roseburg, Ore., as the Copper Cup stock car invitational moved into the final night at the Salt Lake Fairgrounds.

The booming Pollard, winner of Canada's Gold Cup only last week, jumped into a substantial point lead Friday night as a host of out-of-state and local drivers opened a fender-grinding bid for the $1,000 first prize.

Pollard racked up 74 points in a night of sterling performances which saw him:

- Set a new track record of 14.67 seconds – substantially below Mel Andrus' best mark set only a week ago.
- Win the trophy dash, gunning through a hole left by Andrus on the last lap.
- Win the 40-lap A-Main after hasty repairs on a bent axle received when he was bumped into the fence during the fast-car heat race.

Another out-of-stater, Eldon Rasmussen of Edmonton, Alberta, Canada, stood second in the Copper Cup battle with 58 points. Eldon put up a stirring battle with Pollard in the A-Main but was forced to settle for second. He captured first-place honors in the fifth heat.

Right behind Rasmussen was Salt Lake City's Dick Card with 57 points. Sam Sauer, Denver, stood fourth in the unofficial point standings with 42.

Friday night's opener was a bump-and-grind affair with the driver's nerves sharpened by that dangling $1,000 first prize with $600 for second and $400 for third.

It was a night which saw the out-of-staters dominate most of the races. In addition to Pollard and Rasmussen, Boise's Bill Crow showed plenty of skill in winning the fast-car heat race, and George Robertson of Lewiston, Idaho, took the third heat and won the B-Main hands down.

The locals ran into a bevy of troubles. Andrus, running solidly in third place in the A-Main, spun out and dropped way back in the pack. The new-found Andrus horsepower gave him an even break with the field up to that point.

Fred Sorenson lost a wheel in the A-Main and was forced out. And Dick Card found himself boxed in much of the race and unable to move up.

In a follow-up report, Hi McDonald filed this report that appeared in the *Deseret News* on August 21st, 1961:

Near-Perfect Pollard Captures Copper Cup

A bump into the fence which put Roseburg, Ore.'s Art Pollard out of a heat race appeared Monday to be the only thing that kept him from scoring a complete sweep of the two-night Copper Cup Invitational stock car extravaganza.

Except for that one incident, the incomparable Pollard swept everything in sight as he racked up 170 points out of a possible 200 in the Salt Lake Fairgrounds feature. It gave him $1,000 first-place money to add to the $4,000 he won the week previous in Canada's Gold Cup.

Pollard won every race he entered in Saturday night's finale. The fence incident, coming in Friday night's opener, might have cost him the first-place money except for some quick work by pit crewmen who straightened an axle and had Pollard back on the track in time for the A-Main.

The speedy Pollard, running a 1956 Corvette engine, was the only driver on the track with enough power to pass on the outside. And that was his key to victory as he set a new one-lap record for the second night in a row Saturday night, a 14:53-second tour of the quarter-mile oval.

Speed must have been infectious. Salt Lake City's Mel Andrus broke the Salt Lake Racing Assn.'s track record with a 14:80 clocking. His record will stand as the official mark, while Pollard's time will remain only as the Copper Cup record since his car does not meet local specifications.

Eldon Rasmussen of Edmonton, Alberta, Canada placed second in the final standings with 133 points for the $600 second-place money. Andrus and Dick Card tied for third and split the $400 money with 117 points.

It was another zany night as Card dropped his drive shaft and limped out of the trophy dash. Gary Hill of Blackfoot, Idaho, led all the way in the second heat race and lost in the last quarter lap with mechanical troubles. Bad-luck Fred Sorensen, leading the fast-car heat, was bumped by Pollard and put out of the race when he blew up his transmission. And Andrus spun out in the A-Main, taking the flagmen, flag bag and all. Some speedy footwork saved the flagmen, but the flags suffered for the extra wear.

The team continued to dominate Super Modified racing in the western United States during 1962. The tracks they competed at included Portland, Salem, Tacoma, Monroe and Spokane, Washington; Boise, Idaho; Salt Lake City, Utah; Sacramento, San Jose and Fresno, California; and Victoria, British Columbia, and Edmonton, Alberta, Canada.

During this time, Art and Victoria's up-and-coming racer – Billy Foster – became both close competitors and friends. This race report appeared in the *Times-Colonist* newspaper on September 5, 1962:

Billy Foster Captures 'Daffodil Cup' for Cars

Victoria's Billy Foster, competing against 25 of the top drivers in the Pacific Northwest, won the 150-lap Daffodil Cup modified sportsman car race Monday before 7,898 fans at Western Speedway.

Ahead early, Foster lost the lead on the 57th lap, and stayed behind Portland's Art Pollard for the next 50 laps. Pollard continued the chase, but hit an oil slick while trying to pass on the 130th lap, and Foster built up a lead of almost a lap before he recovered. At that, Pollard was only three car lengths behind at the finish. Bob Gregg of Portland placed third.

This article appeared in the *Racing Wheels* publication dated September 15th, 1962:

Pollard Wins Big at Evergreen '100'

MONROE, WASHINGTON – The "Medford Menace", Art Pollard took home the lion's share of the $5,000 guaranteed purse Sunday at the big Evergreen Motor Speedway 100 lapper. Art won $100 for fast time of the day with a time of 24.86 seconds; $490 lap money for leading the race for 98 laps, plus $1,500 for winning the race. In addition he won two of Buck's racing tires; one for leading the most laps and one for winning the event; and also a set of Monroe shock absorbers for leading the 50th lap.

Billy Foster drove a tremendous race in the straight-up, three abreast Indy type start. Billy arrived late and was unable to time in, so started at the back of the 38-car field. He quickly moved up eleven positions by the end of the first lap, a total of 21 positions by the end of the second lap, by the tenth lap was running fourth, and was second the 14th circuit. This was as far as he could go. Having engine difficulties all the way, he chased Pollard throughout the remainder of the race a half lap behind.

A real duel for first spot developed early in the race between Pollard and Don Walker. When traffic built up Don was able to slip by to lead the event for two laps. Walker was forced out with bearing troubles. Al Smith of Victoria was never in contention for first spot. He must have developed engine trouble as he putted around the track for some time.

At left is Pollard waving the checkered, to the right is second-place finisher Billy Foster, and in the middle is the trophy presentation by Miss Evergreen Speedway, Sharon Blackburn. It was reported to be the first time Art was awarded a trophy by a bathing suit-clad lovely, and he was momentarily speechless.

(Racing Wheels Photos)

We also located this article that appeared in the *Racing Wheels* publication dated March 17, 1963.

Pollard Maintains Winning Ways

Art Pollard of Roseburg, in Ken's Martinizing Special, showed he is the man to beat in '63, not only in the Modified Sportsman, but in the Indianapolis type Sprint cars. It took him only four laps to charge from tenth position into the lead he held unchallenged in the 25-lap Main event Sunday on the ½-mile paved oval at the Portland Speedway. He also took the third heat.

The real show maker this chilly 37-degree day though was Bob Gregg. Bob was stuck in heavy traffic for five laps but gained steadily on Pollard when he got clear. Gregg warmed fans in the fourth heat when he and Pollard waged a wheel-to-wheel duel, with Bob winning by inches, taking Pollard on the outside.

Promoters Paul and Ron Ail, of Valley Sports, Inc., made a fine gesture by presenting Bob and Mrs. Gregg with beautiful watches, commemorating Bob's 25th anniversary in auto racing. The old pro still has those good reflexes.

Two hard luck boys were Howard Osborn of Portland, who won the Dash and set fast time, and Billy Foster from Victoria, B.C. Howard noticed he had an oil leak and scratched his car to avoid making the track slick for the others. Foster, a 26-year-old topnotch driver, burned two rods in his car while practicing Saturday afternoon.

Bill Crow, the 'Kissin Crow from Idaho', was unable to drive Sunday because an old arm injury flared up, so offered young Foster his '121 Club Special'. This car blew a radiator.

Billy can be seen again next Sunday, March 24, back at the Speedway along with Northwest champion Art Pollard, when a top field of Modified Sportsman begin their racing season.

The Martinizing Special was eventually sold, ending the partnership between Art and Ken Glass, though they remained good friends during the years ahead. Art continued to race whenever possible for other car owners, such as Bob Cochran of Eugene and Levy Jones from Puyallup, Washington.

1963 – The Canadian American Modified Racing Association

In January of 1963, representatives from eight cities in the Pacific Northwest, Utah, and western Canada met in Spokane, Washington for the purpose of organizing a regional super-modified racing series. The coalition became known as the Canadian American Modified Racing Association, or CAMRA. The first president was Bill Crow of Boise, Idaho.

The original eight tracks were in Salt Lake City; Meridian, Idaho; Seattle and Spokane; Nanaimo, Victoria, and Vancouver, British Columbia; and Edmonton, Alberta. The series became a long-term success story and would help further the professional careers for a number of Northwest drivers.

1963 - At left is Idaho's Bill Crow and Art. To the right is Art, Bill Crow and Victoria's Billy Foster.

CAMRA's first race was held on May 17th, 1963 in Nanaimo. The 100-lap feature event was won by Bill Crow. The following night in Victoria, Crow repeated as the victor. At the end of the first season, Victoria's Billy Foster became CAMRA's first Champion, followed by Bill Crow and Lewiston, Idaho's George Robertson.

Denver's Jim Malloy earned back-to-back Championships for the 1964-65 seasons. Second and third in the standings for 1964 were Foster and Bob Gregg of Portland. Art finished in seventh place overall. In 1965, behind Malloy in the season standings, were Eldon Rasmussen of Edmonton and Bob Gregg.

Veteran driver and team owner, Dick Simon, was among Art's close friends and competitors over the years. Dick offered an example of the two racing each other in the 1960s at the Salt Lake City Fairgrounds:

"I felt more comfortable running wheel-to-wheel with Art than anyone in history. He beat me every time by about six inches, but we had standing ovations from the crowd. We put on a show all around the racetrack. I'd be on the inside and Art would be on the outside. Then he'd be on the inside and I'd be on the outside.

The way they did qualifications in Salt Lake was that the fastest cars started in the rear, so we would have to work our way up through the field. On a quarter-mile fast track, to get through the field in a hurry and survive all that is one thing. But the next thing is to find that right next to you is Art Pollard!"

Veteran racer Dick Simon with car owner Rolla Vollstedt and Janet Guthrie.

(Ann Arbor District Library)

Hi McDonald, a sportswriter for *The Deseret News* in Salt Lake City described one such night:

"If Art Pollard NEVER comes back to race in Utah, it'll be too soon for the Salt Lake circuit stock car drivers. But like Marley's ghost, Pollard's image may be around for some time to haunt the local hub-to-hub club. He plans to materialize next for the Copper Cup Invitational in August, the event he won as convincingly last year as he captured the Intermountain Championship Saturday night.

In Saturday night's grind, he ran up 180 points and captured the A-Main for the second night in a row to further his cause. But it was neck-and-neck all the way with Boise's Bill Crow, last year's Intermountain titlist, coming within an eyelash of taking the cumulative title.

Pollard, heavily favored to add the Intermountain title to his Copper Cup crown he won last year, was no disappointment either in horsepower ability or driving savvy. He left no room for doubt as he boomed to an early lead and just kept on rolling to widen his margin of victory."

Jim Malloy was the CAMRA Champion in 1964 and 1965.

(Photo courtesy of the Idaho Historical Racing Society)

On September 12, 1964, *Racing Wheels* provided a review of a CAMRA-sanctioned event at the Portland Speedway:

PORTLAND, ORE. – Jim Malloy started things rolling at Sunday's CAMRA race at the Portland Speedway by setting a new all-time track record of 22.15, knocking .35 off the old record on the ½-mile paved oval.

The association changed the running of the "200" by having two 100-lap mains. The first 100 was run straight-up with the fastest cars in front. Fast-time Malloy held the lead for 23 laps until Ray Walker of Medford, driving Billy Foster's #27 car, took over on the 24th lap.

The 55th lap proved disastrous for Eldon Linder and Jim Roberts. Going into turn #3, a rock punched a hole in Linder's radiator, causing him to spin. He hit the guardrail on flipped on his side but was unhurt. Jim Roberts, who was running fourth and really charging as usual, hit the water, lost control and clipped the guardrail. This gave him a boost for his altitude record. After flipping several times, he came to a stop upside-down.

Roberts regained consciousness this morning (Monday, Sept. 14) and is being held for observation. He suffered a fractured shoulder and concussion. Jim Malloy accidentally hit the kill-button and coasted into the pits, thinking a wire had broken. He found his trouble and went back out without stopping.

Jim Malloy (#5) and Art Pollard (#1) charge full-bore into a turn during a championship race at the Portland Speedway.

The 63rd lap saw Ray Walker pit with a broken axle, Pollard leading the race at this point. Malloy took the lead from Art on the 87th lap. Pollard was forced to slow down due to a flat left rear tire but continued to a second-place finish.

The field was started in reverse of their finish for the second 100-lap event. Art Pollard took the lead on the fourth lap with Malloy on his tail for 40 laps before starting to drop back a little each lap. Bob Gregg took over McTaggart's car, but had trouble with a gas leak. He was in and out of the pits during the race.

Since points were given to each car, Malloy won the race by turning in a faster qualifying time than Pollard. If points were not given, there would have been a tie for first place since Malloy and Pollard each had a first and a second.

CAMRA's final year came in 1984 when Jan Sneva won his second straight title, with his brother Blaine in the runner-up spot. CAMRA then merged with the Washington Racing Association, which became the short-lived USAC-Washington series. During its long run, CAMRA served as a memorable chapter in the history of super-modified racing.

Its list of Champions includes Norm Ellefson, Jim Roberts, Tom, Jerry, and Blaine Sneva, Don Selley, George Robertson, , Bob Cochran, Marc Edson and Marty White.

These days were just a lull in the action, however, for Art Pollard's shot at the big time was just around the corner.

Art with his son, Mike, at the Portland Speedway.

(Ralph Hunt Collection)

At the Portland Speedway with Art Sugai's famous 'Pink Lady'.

(Ralph Hunt Collection)

Portland Speedway – 1964.

(Ralph Hunt Collection)

Another trophy to add to Art's growing collection.

(Ralph Hunt Collection)

Art in the pits at a race in Meridian, Idaho.

Presenting Art with the Earl Mossman trophy at the Portland Speedway are Jeanie Morgan and Bunny Geiger.

(Racing Wheels Photo)

Art at another race at the Portland Speedway.

(Ralph Hunt Collection)

TWELVE

1965 – Joining the United States Auto Club Championship Car Series

Of course, Art's primary obligation was tending to the well-being of his family in Roseburg. In 1965 he was offered the service manager's position at the Fairway Oldsmobile dealership in Medford, Oregon, about 97 miles south of Roseburg.

Art moved his family to Medford, Oregon when he became the service manager at the Fairway Oldsmobile dealership.

(Medford Mail-Tribune)

Art, Claudine, Mike and Judy (now teenagers) made the move south to their new home on Johnson Street. Racing on a regular basis had to take a back seat for Art – team members now lived farther apart, the competition was making strides, and it was more difficult for Art to find the money and time to stay ahead in racing.

"Art, like most of the sprint car drivers, usually operated on a very low budget," Bob Pollard explained. "Buying a race car and maintaining it was a difficult task. Even though Art won a high percentage of the races he entered, a minimal amount of prize money was awarded. Art had a sponsor, which helped, but paying someone to help him in the pits was not always possible. The only large thing awarded after winning a race was the trophy, and Art had a room full of them."

Despite keeping busy with everyday life, Art was able to continue his climb up the professional racing ladder.

1965 – Art's first USAC ride was in the Vollstedt/Offy, piloted in 1964 by Len Sutton.

(Medford Mail-Tribune)

His first experience racing in the United States Auto Club (USAC) Championship Car series came in the late summer of 1965. Courtesy of Rolla Vollstedt, Art's debut took place on August 22nd, 1965, at the Milwaukee Mile in West Allis, Wisconsin. The event was the Tony Bettenhausen 200.

Milwaukee's historic one-mile oval is the oldest operating motor speedway in the world, hosting at least one race every year since 1903 (excepting the World War II years). Long a dirt track, it was paved with asphalt in 1954. A multitude of famed drivers have competed and won there.

Vollstedt provided the car, which was a Vollstedt/Offy previously driven Len Sutton. Len was now behind the wheel of the new Vollstedt/Ford that was built to compete in 1965. Art's car was now owned by Jim Robbins and was sponsored by Autotron Electronics. Also entered in the race was Rolla's own Vollstedt/Ford, sponsored by Bryant Heating & Cooling, and driven by the up-and-coming Billy Foster.

In his autobiography, Rolla Vollstedt explained how he prepared Art for the race: "We were staying at a place owned by a race car driver named Frank Burany, called the Sleepy Hollow Motel, in Milwaukee. He had cottages and so forth around a circular driveway. To get Art used to driving a rear-engined car, we had him sit in the car – in neutral – while we started it. We started the car, Art putting the clutch down and engaging the gear. We practiced that several times going around Burany's driveway."

Art faced a field of drivers that read like a "who's-who" of the sport. Guys like A.J. Foyt, Bobby and Al Unser, Johnny Rutherford, and Mario Andretti were all there. It must have been something for Art to be a name on that entry list!

Art qualified in 25th position but experienced a spin and completed only 77 laps. He finished 22nd out of a field of 26 cars, earning just $186.00 from the total purse. Billy Foster started the race 15th but fell victim to mechanical problems on just the seventh lap. Race winner Gordon Johncock (Gerhardt/Offy) drove to the win and earned $11,870.

Trenton, New Jersey. Art dueling with eventual race winner A.J. Foyt. In a fine performance, Art drove the Vollstedt/Offy to a fifth-place finish.

(Vollstedt Family Collection)

In just his second race in the 'Big Leagues,' things went extremely well for Art. The date was September 26th, 1965 and the event was the Trenton 200 in New Jersey. Again driving the Vollstedt/Offy for Jim Robbins, Art qualified 13th and crossed the finish line in the fifth position behind race winner A.J. Foyt. Joe Leonard finished in second place, followed by

Jim McElreath and Roger McCluskey. Art's portion of the purse was $1,480. "Decent money in those days," as Art's daughter, Judy, recalls.

In October, the series switched back to the front-engine sprint cars on the one-mile dirt track at the California State Fairgrounds in Sacramento. Art was entered to drive Don Collins' Hemi V8-powered Kurtis. Unfortunately, the engine lost oil pressure and did not qualify for the race, which was won by Don Branson in a Watson/Offy.

The final race of the 1965 USAC season took place on November 21st at Phoenix International Raceway. The Bobby Ball Memorial would be a 200-lapper on the paved one-mile track. Art qualified the Jim Robbins' car 15th on the grid, but a crash on lap 70 resulted in a 19th place finish. The win went to Foyt, driving the Sheraton/Thomson Lotus/Ford.

The 1965 season championship was awarded to Mario Andretti, followed in order by Foyt, McElreath, Branson, and Johncock. Despite participating in just three events, Art was ranked 30th in a list of 57 drivers who had competed at one time or another during the season.

At the Sacramento Fairgrounds.

Throughout his career, Art was always a hit with the fans.

THIRTEEN

First Taste of the Brickyard

Every race driver's dream is a victory in the Indianapolis 500. Early in 1966, Art was offered an opportunity he couldn't refuse – a chance to qualify for his first Indianapolis 500. One can only imagine how he felt, to finally compete in the pinnacle of racing at 39 years of age.

Art's daughter, Judy, says it felt as if that was the way life was supposed to be for her family – a natural progression. Because her dad had raced *something* from the time she was a toddler, she didn't give the next step a lot of thought; racing felt comfortable when she was a teenager. Plus, he had almost always won most races he entered, so she had confidence he would continue to do great.

"I suppose Dad and Mom must have had serious discussions," says Judy. "I don't really know, but my brother and I just took the racing in stride. There were never any controversial conversations in our house over Dad choosing to go big-time racing—only the money factor. I do remember my parents talking with us about the fact that we might have to tighten our belts until regular income, or bigger money, could be earned racing. After all, my brother and I were teenagers. We were pretty oblivious, except if we'd have had to give up movie or gas money or something. After all, those types of *essential* teenage necessities did have our attention!"

Thus, Art signed a contract with car owner, Dick Compton, of Oregon. Compton had obtained a rear-engine, Offenhauser-powered racer which was built in 1964 by Rolla Vollstedt and driven by Billy Foster in his rookie year at Indy in 1965. He had qualified the car in the sixth position with a speed of 158.416 mph, but a faltering water manifold ended his day on lap 85 of the race. Foster was credited with a 17th place finish.

"You don't just decide one day that you are going to race at Indy," Art explained to a *Medford Mail Tribune* writer in February of 1966: "You have to work your way up in racing circles. That goes for both the cars and the drivers."

From the *Medford Mail Tribune* on February 13th, 1966, by Staff Writer Jim Ochs:

Art Pollard to Drive at Indianapolis in Effort to Qualify for 500-Mile Race

On May 1, approximately 60 of the nation's top race drivers will congregate at Indianapolis, Ind., to begin preparations for one of the biggest of all races – the Indianapolis 500 on May 30. Among those drivers will be Art Pollard, service manager at Fairway Oldsmobile in Medford.

Pollard recently signed a contract with Dick Compton, Portland, to drive Compton's car, a rear-engine Offenhauser which was built in Portland in 1964 by Rolla Vollstedt. The car is a 255 cubic-inch, four-cylinder model which develops approximately 430 horsepower.

Compton, however, is planning several modifications before the big race in May. Plans call for installation of a new supercharged Offenhauser motor which will be capable of developing 600 horsepower with only 180 cubic-inches. The present displacement of the motor is the Indianapolis maximum. Also, the weight of the car – 1,425 pounds – will be cut down before the race.

A few days later, this follow-up article appeared in the *Roseburg News-Review*:

Ex-Roseburg Driver to Try for Big One

Art Pollard, former Roseburg race driver, will be one of the nation's top drivers to congregate at Indianapolis in an effort to qualify for the Indianapolis 500.

Pollard started his racing career in the Roseburg area in 1955 as a hardtop driver at the Roseburg Speedway. "It was just a weekend hobby in those days," said Pollard. "But after you have a little success you just keep going."

Pollard graduated from the hardtops to the modified super sportsmen, driving Ken's Martinizing Special to victories in featured races throughout the Northwest, winning the Northwest championship title in the super sportsmen for three straight seasons.

He then stepped up to the sprint cars in 1960. Last year he moved into the Indianapolis-type car, competing in two races at Milwaukee, Wis., one at Phoenix, Ariz., and placed fifth in the 200-mile event at Trenton, N.J.

Pollard will be classified as a "rookie" driver in the Indianapolis race, and must pass a rigid driver's test under the supervision of a board of more experienced drivers before being allowed to compete.

Pollard now resides in Medford where he is a service manager for the Oldsmobile agency. If he qualifies for the May 30 classic, he will be only the third Oregon driver to do so. Previously Bob Christie of Grants Pass and Len Sutton of Portland have competed carrying the Oregon banner.

The first order of business for Art, as it was for all first-time drivers at Indy, was to pass the mandatory rookie test. Back then the test consisted of ten laps each at 135, 140, and 145 mph.

Like an incoming freshman class in high school or college, a new group of Indianapolis rookies was the rule for the experienced Brickyard drivers, such as Johnny Rutherford, who said:

"I had been in USAC since late 1962, so I was kind of established as still a rookie, so to speak, when Art came in. Others, like Jim Rathmann and Rodger Ward, were established. I was just getting my footing after making my first race in 1963, so I knew the lay of the land."

"Every year it seemed we had new groups from different parts of the country, such as the east coast, led by Bobby Marshman. Then we had the ones from the Pacific Northwest. Jack Turner, Shorty Templeton, Billy Foster, and all those guys from out there led the way. Art Pollard was just another guy from the Northwest. Len Sutton was ahead of me by a few years, and Len was a dear friend. They were all friendly and nice."

"All of the guys that came from those areas were the cream of the crop, and they showed well at Indy," Johnny went on to say. "It's a giant learning curve, and you have to have a background somewhere."

On May 2nd, behind the wheel of the #66 Autotron Electrics Special, Art became the first driver to pass his rookie test under the scrutinizing eyes of two-time Indy champion Rodger Ward. "I really know now why they call us rookies," Art explained to a reporter: "Until you have driven at Indianapolis, you definitely are one."

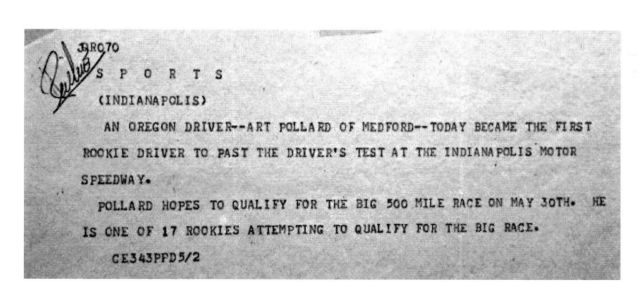

In another interview, Art observed: "I feel I was a little slow getting established here, but once I got over my jitters I started settling down. Driving here is quite a thrill. This place is so big, but I had no trouble getting adjusted. In fact, I was surprised it came as easy as it did.

I'm sure I'll be thrilled even more when I get going real well, but driving the Speedway is going to be a real challenge."

On May 3rd, *The Oregonian* newspaper reported on Art's early progress via this *Associated Press* article:

Pollard Zips in Indy Test

INDIANAPOLIS (AP) – The first weekend of practice at the Indianapolis Motor Speedway this season got off to a cold start with a rain-dampened opener Saturday and chilly weather Sunday.

Chief Steward Harlan Fengler imposed a 150 miles-an-hour limit for the first few days until some of the dirt is blown off the track.

Chuck Hulse returned for practice at the track for the first time in two years. He ran his Wynn's Offenhauser at 149.8 mph for Sunday's fastest time.

Two rookies passed the first two sections of their driver's test and are expected to complete the tests Monday. They are Art Pollard of Roseburg, Ore., and Jackie Stewart, both eyeing their first Indianapolis 500 in the 50th running this Memorial Day.

This additional UPI report appeared on May 4, 1966 in the Medford *Mail Tribune*:

Year Makes Difference for Pollard

What a difference a year makes. Art Pollard couldn't get a ride for last year's 500-mile speedway auto race, but he was determined to make the big show. A year later, he's shooting for one of the 33 starting positions in the world's richest gasoline derby. He has already passed one exam at the famed 2.5-mile oval, earning the distinction of becoming the first "500" rookie to pass his driver's test.

His next test comes May 14, the opening day of the time trials and Pollard is confident he'll qualify on the first day. "I feel I was a little slow getting established here," said the 38-year-old Oregonian, "but once I got over my jitters I started settling down."

Art removing his rookie stripes – an age-old tradition at Indianapolis.

A critical jury of drivers and USAC officials found nothing wrong with his driving ability during 100 miles of cruising around the speedway at speeds up to 145 miles per hour.

The exam over, the ripped the three stripes – signifying rookie drivers' tests – off his rear-engine machine and now Pollard is on his own. With the 150-mph speed ceiling lifted, he hopes to work up to the 160-mph bracket by next week.

Pollard has been in racing since 1955, mostly competing in super-modified sprint cars on the West Coast. Compared with the quarter and half-mile tracks he is used to, the speedway is huge. "Driving here is quite a thrill," he said. "This place is so big, but I had no trouble getting adjusted. In fact, I was surprised it came as easy as it did. I'm sure I'll be thrilled even more when I get going real good, but driving the speedway is going to be a real challenge."

Art Pollard removes the rookie stripes from his car after becoming the first to pass his test at the Speedway. Watching the happy occasion is Pollard's chief mechanic, Keith Randol.

(Indianapolis Star Photo)

Pollard is driving the same car which Canada's Billy Foster qualified for last year's race at a speed of nearly 158.5 mph – good enough for a second-row spot. It was the fastest Offenhauser-powered machine and Pollard is confident it will be still faster this time, although his crew made few changes. "Basically, it's the same machine as last year," said Pollard. "We only made some refinements."

Pollard, a mechanic by trade, will spend the next few days practicing at gradually increased speeds until he can reach a 160-mph average. Then, he figured, he'll be ready to qualify.

"So far we haven't had any problems," said Keith Randol, 41, Portland, Ore., Pollard's chief mechanic. "We felt we were ready when we got here because this is a good car. "We won't be the fastest outfit on the track, but we'll be up there. We just want to make the show."

Some of the old-timers are already eyeing him as one of the newcomers to watch and that's all right with Pollard, who figures after 10 years in the "minors" he's ready for racing's big time.

Close friends and competitors from the Pacific Northwest – Art Pollard and Billy Foster. Billy hailed from Victoria, British Columbia.

When it came to qualify for the race, Art posted a four-lap average of 157.985 mph. On the final day of qualifications, however, he was "bumped" from the field by Ronnie Duman. Art's time was 35th fastest, but two positions shy of making the 33-car field.

This disappointing news was given to all of Art's local fans and supporters in Medford's *Mail Tribune* newspaper:

Art Pollard Eliminated from Lineup of Indianapolis Race

Sunday was a sad day at the Art Pollard home on Johnson Street here as Pollard was eliminated from the lineup of drivers who will compete in Monday's 50th annual Indianapolis 500.

Mrs. Pollard told the Mail Tribune yesterday that "time simply ran out" as Pollard attempted to try out another car which became available. However, he thought it "not very smart" to take a car which he wasn't thoroughly familiar with, Mrs. Pollard explained. As it stands now, two drivers would have to drop from the roster of 33 starters before Pollard could participate.

Qualifications for the $700,000 classic were completed late Sunday with two drivers gaining berths by "bumping" slower cars, including Pollard's. The lucky ones were rookie Larry Dickson, Marietta, Ohio, and Ronnie Duman, Dearborn, Mich. Dickson's qualifying speed was 159.144 mph, fast enough to bump Dick Atkins, a rookie from Hayward, Calif. Dickson is among seven rookies in the lineup. Pollard, at 157.985 mph, was eliminated by Duman who set a 158.646 mph pace.

Mario Andretti, Nazareth, Pa., who won the post position with a record-breaking qualifying speed of 165.699 mph has been a "tremendous friend" to Pollard, Mrs. Pollard said. She pointed out that participating in the pre-race events has "opened many doors" for the Medford driver who may enter the Milwaukee, Wis., race June 5.

The Pollard family is still undecided about leaving for Indianapolis now that the local man has been eliminated. Many Medford residents, who in previous years have shown little interest in the 500-mile event, have been following the activities at Indianapolis this year because of Pollard's participation. Among his local fans is a group of small children in the Johnson Street area. They may be seen in the neighborhood wearing small replicas of the uniforms worn by the Indianapolis pit crews. They were sent to them by Pollard.

1966 Indianapolis 500 Champion Graham Hill.

(Indycar.com)

Art and Graham Hill having a chat at Indy in 1970.

Indy 1966 – Unsure of the occasion for this photo, but driver Bobby Grim is on the far left. Art, in the Firestone cap, is standing at the rear of Grim's car.

(Photo courtesy of the Kitchel Kollection)

The 1964 Vollstedt/Offy now resides in the World of Speed Museum in Oregon. In three years of competition, it was driven by Len Sutton, Billy Foster and Art Pollard.

One week later, at the Milwaukee Mile, Art quickly turned his luck around. At the Rex Mays Classic on June 5th, Art qualified a Gerhardt/Offy seventh on the grid.

The car's owner was listed simply as 'GCR', which was an acronym for a trio of notable men: astronauts Gus Grissom and Gordon Cooper, plus racing legend Jim Rathmann (winner of the 1960 Indy 500). The 'Astronauts Car' made its debut the month before at Indy but was crashed in practice by both Lee Roy Yarbrough and Greg Weld, and did not make the race. Now teamed with GCR, Art would pilot the car for the remainder of the 1966 season.

In the race at Milwaukee, Art drove well and brought the car home in the fourth position behind winner Mario Andretti, with Roger McCluskey and Joe Leonard finishing in the second and third slots, respectively. For their effort, Art's team took home $2,697 of the overall purse.

On June 12th, the series was at the Langhorne Speedway, another one-mile paved oval in Langhorne, Pennsylvania. Art qualified 17th for the 100-lap race but suffered a spin on the 26th lap. He couldn't return to the action and finished last in the 22-car field.

About this same time, a legal development faced Art regarding the recent Indy 500. Two weeks after the race, Art was arrested on an affidavit signed by Richard (Dick) Compton, owner of the car that Art attempted to qualify at Indianapolis. Pollard was charged with taking a drill press, two magnesium racing wheels, a race car starter, an air compressor, and small tools. In a newspaper article, Art explained that the case evolved out of a civil suit he had filed against Compton: "I merely took the equipment as security for back wages Compton owed me."

A judge ultimately ruled there was no criminal intent on Art's part, and the case was dismissed. Pollard was also cleared of any wrongdoing by the United States Auto Club.

Daughter Judy remembers: "I was happily driving alone in the car in Medford – a typical day in the life of a teen – and a news report comes on the radio that 'Art Pollard has been arrested.' Crazy! I was upset because of what people who didn't know him might think, but I knew my dad, and I knew there had to be more to the story. I then realized that it didn't take long for his celebrity to matter to the media."

"Fortunately, the whole thing was settled right away, and the full truth was known. As I remember, the local radio reported the truth of the situation and the positive outcome, too. I can't help but laugh and say, though I was a typically self-centered, sensitive teen, I wasn't traumatized over it."

The season's next racing challenge with the GCR team came on June 26th at the 1.5-mile paved track at Atlanta International Raceway in Hampton, Georgia. Their effort was previewed in this article dated June 19, 1966 in the Medford *Mail-Tribune*:

Pollard Will Race Grissom-Cooper Car

Art Pollard, Medford race driver, will leave Indianapolis this week for Atlanta, Georgia, where he will drive the car owned by Astronauts Gordon Cooper and Virgil I. Grissom and 1960 Indy winner Jim

Rathmann. The 300-mile championship race will be held Sunday, June 26. Practice driving at the track will start June 22, Mrs. Pollard said, with qualifying to be held June 23 and 24.

Pollard appeared in Speedway, Ind., magistrate's court Thursday to answer to a charge by Richard Compton, Portland, that he took tools and racing equipment worth nearly $3,000. Pollard, who was freed on $20 bond after the complaint was filed, told his wife here that trial on the charge has been set for the last week in July. However, in the proceedings, Compton did reduce the valuation of the equipment he charges Pollard with taking to $1,000.

The complaint arises from a disagreement between the two men while they were in Indianapolis prior to the Indy 500-mile Memorial Day race. Pollard drove Compton's car and qualified for the race but was later eliminated by a faster qualifier.

Prior to leaving for Atlanta, Pollard will assist in preparing the Grissom-Cooper car for the June 26 race. The car is a rear-engine Offenhauser.

The GCR Team. Art drove for partners Jim Rathmann (1960 Indy winner) and Astronauts Gus Grissom and Gordon Cooper.

After qualifying fifth for the 300-mile race, Art and the team were optimistic. However, bad luck struck again after a fire took place during a pit stop on the 64th lap. No one was injured, but the Gerhardt/Offy was retired, credited with 22nd place in the 30-car field.

The next stop on the 1966 USAC schedule was in late July when the series took to the road course at Indianapolis Raceway Park in Clermont, Indiana. Aside from a one-weekend stint racing a Corvette at Pacific Raceways in Kent, Washington, Art had very limited experience on a road course. Seven drivers failed to qualify for the race, including Art. The win went to Mario Andretti, followed by Al Unser, Sr. and Jim McElreath.

Still on a learning curve, terrible luck continued for the GCR team on August 7th, upon a return to the Langhorne 150. Art started the race in 15th position, but a broken suspension took him out on just the 20th lap. The only driver he finished ahead of was Lloyd Ruby, who completed only nine laps due to a broken radius rod.

Billy Foster.

(Foster Family Collection)

Art didn't compete in the next USAC race on the one-mile dirt track at the Illinois State Fairgrounds, but the following event was back at the Milwaukee Mile. For the Tony Bettenhausen 200, Art was optimistic after the team's good showing at the same track in June. He qualified the Pure Firebird-sponsored Offy sixth on the grid. He completed 194 laps of the 200-lap race, recording a seventh-place finish and earned $1,601 for the effort. Andretti continued his winning ways, with superb cars that complimented his driving skills.

Another Pacific Northwest standout, and close friend of Art's, was also in this race. British Columbia's Billy Foster qualified ninth and finished fifth in a Vollstedt/Ford. To everyone's sadness, Foster's life was cut short when he was killed while practicing for a NASCAR race at Riverside, California in January 1967. Billy was just 29 years old.

The multi-talented driver and good friend of Art's – Victoria's Billy Foster. Sadly, his life was cut short in a racing accident at age 29.

(Foster Family Collection)

In early October of 1966, the series crossed the Pacific Ocean for an exhibition (non-points) race at the Fuji International Speedway in Shizuoka, Japan. Art's wife Claudine accompanied Art, as did other driver's wives and girlfriends. It must have been a logistical nightmare to transport the cars and equipment across that wide ocean.

It was truly an international field of drivers entered for the race, from the regulars of the USAC circuit to Formula One stars Jackie Stewart, Graham Hill, and Jimmy Clark. In all, 32 drivers made qualifying attempts. Ten failed to make the race, including Pollard, Andretti, Dallenbach, Johncock, and Al Unser. Jackie Stewart won the 80-lap event from the pole, driving a Lola/Ford for owner John Mecom. Bobby Unser finished second in an Eagle/Ford.

The next-to-last race of the 1966 season took place on the one-mile dirt oval in Sacramento. Art qualified the #31 Don Collins-built Vollstedt/Offy in 14th and finished ninth in the Golden State 100. California driver Dick Atkins, driving for J.C. Agajanian, drove a Watson/Offy to the win.

The season ended following the Bobby Ball Memorial on November 20th at Phoenix. Back in the GCR Gerhardt/Offy, Art started the race from the 12th position, but an engine meltdown on the 16th lap ended his day. It was also the end of his association with GCR.

The final season standings for the USAC Champ Cars show that Mario Andretti was crowned the 1966 champion, winning eight of 15 races. Behind Andretti, in order, were Jim McElreath, Gordon Johncock, Joe Leonard, and Al Unser, Sr.

In his first championship season, and despite competing in just seven races, Art finished 26th overall in driver standings (out of 57 total drivers), with $5,876 in total earnings. By comparison, Andretti earned $94,856 for the year.

"Art was good, calculated, and able to get whatever there was out of his car," said Johnny Rutherford. "That was from his abilities of running the cars in the Northwest, and the types of cars he was racing. If you run half-mile dirt or paved tracks you tend to get pretty sharp, plus being able to get the car nailed, set-up wise. Art was obviously very good. Whatever [type of car] he got in he eventually got the most out of and became noticed."

FOURTEEN

1967 – The Fred Gerhardt Team

Now with one partial Championship Car season under his belt, Art began 1967 with new vigor and optimism with an experienced team that was promising from the start.

The Fred Gerhardt team putting the finishing touches on Pollard's car. At left is chief mechanic Phil Casey, Don Gerhardt is in the center and Fred Gerhardt is on the right. Lower left is mechanic Red Stainton.

He signed with Fresno, California-based Fred Gerhardt, who had become a noted car builder. Working out of his Commercial Truck Body factory, and with the expertise of chief mechanic Phil Casey, Gerhardt cars were very competitive. The past two seasons, drivers such as Jim Hurtubise, Ronnie Duman, Gordon Johncock, Mel Kenyon, and Mickey Rupp had driven Gerhardt's designs. In the 1966 Indy 500, Johncock and Kenyon finished fourth and fifth, respectively, in Gerhardt-built cars.

Fred was quite the innovator. A multifaceted talent, he also invented and manufactured the engine starters used by the Champ Cars, as well as designing the hydraulic lift-gate that is still used on today's race car haulers.

Gerhardt's primary sponsor for 1967 was Thermo King, a major manufacturer of automotive air conditioning systems. Fred would field two turbocharged Offys for the season: #15 for Mel Kenyon and #16 for Art Pollard. Mel's brother Don Kenyon would serve as his crew chief while Phil Casey would handle Art's car as crew chief and head mechanic.

Mel Kenyon

Mel Kenyon grew up in Illinois and began his racing career in 1954 with a 1937 modified Chevy stock car. In 1958, Mel began an illustrious career racing midget cars. He won hundreds of races around the country, leading to his first USAC National Midget Championship in 1964. His records earned Mel the title, 'King of the Midgets'.

Kenyon failed to qualify for his first Indianapolis 500 in 1965. Just a few weeks later, while racing at Langhorne Speedway in Pennsylvania, his engine blew and sent hot oil all over the car, his driving suit, and the track. His car hit the wall and he was knocked unconscious. Jim Hurtubise and Ralph Liguori also slid on the oiled-down track surface and ran straight into Kenyon's fuel tank. Suffering severe burns, Mel went through multiple operations and lost nearly all the fingers on his left hand.

1967 – Fred Gerhardt's team drivers Mel Kenyon and Art Pollard.

Determined to return to racing, during the lengthy healing time Mel, his brother Don and their father Everett designed a special glove. It featured a rubber grommet sewn into the palm, which then hooked onto a peg on the steering wheel. This enabled Mel to grab the wheel with his right hand and steer with the palm of his left. In doing so Mel gained the admiration of his fellow drivers, including Art, who considered Mel a friend he held in high esteem.

Mel and Art at a dirt track.

Phil Casey served as a chief mechanic for 35 years and was a nine-time winner in the United States Auto Club National Championship competition.

Heading up Fred Gerhardt's team from 1965 through 1972, Phil had a major hand in the construction of numerous cigar-shaped and wedge-shaped versions of the much sought-after

On the left, Art is with his 1967 Chief Mechanic Phil Casey at Indianapolis. At right is Phil Casey in recent years. He was inducted into the Auto Racing Hall of Fame in 2015.

(Pollard Family Collection and Fresno Bee newspaper)

Gerhardt chassis. His nine championship-level wins were earned for Gerhardt's team with Gary Bettenhausen (two), Vel's Parnelli Jones Racing with Al Unser, Sr. (two) and Interscope Racing with Danny Ongais (five). In 1983 Casey was the winning chief mechanic when John Paul, Jr. edged Rick Mears for the win on the final lap of the Michigan 500.

Other key assignments came with Roberto Guerrero in 1985 and 1986, and A.J. Foyt in 1990. When Janet Guthrie made history as the first female to qualify for the Indianapolis 500 in 1977, Phil was her crew chief.

He took on the role of technical director for the newly formed Indy Racing League in 1996 and is credited in taking part of the development of the SAFER (Steel and Foam Energy Reduction) Barrier.

Phil Casey recalled the beginning of that year with Pollard: "Art was 39-years-old when we got him. He'd driven a car for Rolla Vollstedt for a few races, and we knew Vollstedt. Rolla talked about how good a driver Art was, and Fred Gerhardt and I had seen him race at Fresno. Jim Hurtubise had left us that year, so we ended up getting Art as our driver. Art was a real nice guy. We did some things for Thermo King at a car show at the Cow Palace in San Francisco. I went there with Art when he started with us and got to know him better."

The 1967 Champ Car season made its debut on April 9th at Phoenix for the Jimmy Bryan Memorial. The Thermo King team came ready to go, with Art qualifying his #16 in the fourth position while Mel would start the #15 19th. As the 150-mile race came to a close, both cars finished in the top ten: Art in seventh and Mel in tenth. Lloyd Ruby took the win in a Mongoose/Offy, followed by Roger McCluskey in an Eagle/Ford. Fred Gerhardt's team appeared off to a good start.

In late April, the series traveled to New Jersey for the Trenton 150. Art started a career-best third behind pole winner Andretti and second fastest Jim McElreath, while Mel Kenyon started tenth. At the race finish, there were only eight cars running. Mel finished a respectable fifth, and Art finished eighth. Andretti took the checkered flag in the Dean Van Lines Brawner/Ford.

Now it was time to gear up for the biggest race of the season at the Brickyard. In 1967, the race for the pole position was set for May 13th. In the preceding practice days, Mario Andretti had been setting the pace and was labeled the favorite for the fastest in qualifying. On May 12th, Andretti had turned the quickest practice lap in Indy history at over 168 mph.

Five Indianapolis rookies were on hand including Art, who was the eldest of the group, having just turned 40 on May 5th. The other rookies were New Zealand's Dennis Hulme (age 30), Austrian Jochen Rindt (25), Wally Dallenbach (30) and Lee Roy Yarbrough (28).

In an interview for the *Indianapolis Star* newspaper in early May, Art described what he had to achieve in trying to match the speeds being posted by veterans like Andretti, Foyt, McCluskey and Leonard:

The Art of Looking Lively Pollard's Now

Art Pollard celebrated his 40th birthday today, but his big present was yesterday at the Indianapolis Motor Speedway.

Pollard, who jokes about being a rather old 500-Mile Race rookie driver, passed his refresher test with flying colors, then turned around and put his name down on the list of drivers to keep an eye on.

The Medford, Ore., native, whose son Mike is a sophomore at Southern Oregon College and daughter Judy is a junior in high school, recorded a perfect 10 straight laps at 145 miles per hour in his refresher yesterday. He passed the required 100-mile rookie test last year but failed to make the starting field.

Minutes after completing yesterday's test, he followed up premature present No. 1 with a four-lap session of pouring it on, registering a 161.6 mph lap around the 2.5-mile track. And that puts him right up there with a host of pre-qualification favorites. "But don't worry," smiled Art. "I'll go even faster tomorrow. I want to go as fast as those guys did today."

That would put the 12-year racing veteran in pretty fancy company – with Mario Andretti, who yesterday matched his official one-lap record of 166.328 mph; A.J. Foyt, 165.5; Roger McCluskey, 165.1, and Joe Leonard, 163.0.

"There's only one thing to do to catch those guys, too," said Pollard, "and that's just go into the corners a little deeper and get on the gas a little quicker. It's not my car holding me back. It's set up just the way I want it. So that's all they're doing different."

His car, the No. 33 Thermo King Special, he feels, is one of the reasons for his early success. The rear-engine racer is powered by one of the new turbo-charged Offenhauser engines. "The turbo is definitely here to stay," said Art. "It's going to really give those Fords a bad time."

While Andretti's speeds were a focus of attention, an even bigger story leading up to the '500' was Andy Granatelli's revolutionary turbine-powered STP machine, piloted by 1963 Indy champion Parnelli Jones. There were lots of grumblings and raised eyebrows in the garages regarding what was being called the "Whooshmobile," due to the whispering sound it made at speed. It was quite a phenomenon to hear because everyone was used to the loud notes of traditional Offenhauser or Ford racing engines.

In his autobiography, *They Call Me MISTER 500*, Andy Granatelli offered this explanation: "Of course, the moving force among the Old Guard was fear – fear that this car of tomorrow would wipe them out. Take their jobs, their accessory prize money, their own hard-won reputations for greatness. So, in Gasoline Alley, the haters were way out front of the lovers."

"It's just a damn ol' airplane," A.J. Foyt told all who would listen. "It ain't no car and it just don't belong here."

One designer, however, was reportedly fascinated by the car's engineering and design. He was Englishman Colin Chapman, the famed owner and constructor of the Lotus Formula One machines. As Granatelli wrote:

"Colin and his crew were fascinated by the machine. That evening some of them swarmed all over the thing with tapes, measuring everything and writing it down. It did my heart good. It also proved to be an academic exercise, since I was later to give all the plans and specifications to Chapman anyway."

Pole Day came, and Andretti turned in a four-lap average of 168.982 mph to pace the field in his Dean Van Lines Hawk/Ford. Joining him for the front row was Dan Gurney's Eagle/Ford and Gordon Johncock's Gerhardt/Ford. Parnelli Jones qualified the turbine car sixth with an average of 166.098 mph.

Andy Granatelli and Parnelli Jones with the STP turbine car, which came so close to winning the 1967 Indianapolis 500.

(STP Corp.)

Art qualified his Gerhardt/Offy in the 13th starting position with a speed of 163.897 mph.

(IMS photo)

Art was the 17th car to make a qualifying attempt and averaged 163.897 mph for his run, which was good enough for the 13th starting position. Art's teammate, Mel Kenyon, was just a tick slower at 163.778 mph and would start in 14th alongside Art. On the third day of qualifications, Bob Veith, driving a third Thermo King Offy for Fred Gerhardt, grabbed the 28th starting spot.

To illustrate just how competitive it was to make the 33-car field at Indy in 1967, there were an additional 28 cars that were either withdrawn or failed to qualify.

This report from *United Press International* dated May 22, 1967 appeared in the *Medford Mail-Tribune*:

Pollard to be in Fifth Row in Indianapolis Race

Art Pollard of Medford, Ore., will be in the fifth row of the 500-mile Indianapolis Memorial Day auto race. Final qualifying was held Sunday. Pollard, driving a turbo Offy, qualified earlier at 163.897 miles per hour at the Indianapolis Speedway.

Five veterans of the grand prix road racing set will add an international flavor to the 51st annual 500-mile Memorial Day auto race, but the strongest U.S. contingent of the postwar era will try to return the championship back home for the first time in three years.

Qualifications for the richest event in racing, with more than $700,000 in prize money at stake, ended on their usually hectic note late Sunday with the 33 starters checking in at a record speed of 164.173 miles per hour, nearly four miles faster than last year's high of 160.251.

Defending "500" champion Graham Hill of London, England, became a last-day qualifier, and even more dramatic was the last-day comeback of Scotland's Jackie Stewart, whose original car was one of 10 "bumped" by faster machines Saturday and Sunday. The 10 eliminations tied the record set in 1954.

Nobody came close to the record clip of pole-sitter Mario Andretti, who averaged nearly 169 mph on the first day of the trials. The only second-weekend qualifier who exceeded 165 mph was veteran Roger McCluskey at 165.563.

Hill, jinxed with engine trouble most of the month, finally qualified a Lotus-Ford backup car at an average of 163.317 for the inside position in the 11th and last row of starters.

Stewart's original car was ousted Saturday and he blew an engine Sunday morning in another backup car. However, last year's "500" rookie of the year was back on the track a few hours later and qualified at 164.099.

Only three other successful qualifying runs were made Sunday – by Jerry Grant, Austria's Jochen Rindt, and Al Miller. The other foreigners in the field are Jim Clark of Scotland, the 1965 winner, and New Zealand's Dennis Hulme, who qualified Saturday at 163.376.

From the *Medford Mail-Tribune*, dated May 25th, 1967:

Pollard to be Seen on Closed Circuit Video at Portland

Auto racing fans who wish to witness the performance of Medford's Art Pollard on the television screen on Memorial Day in the Indianapolis 500-mile race will have to be in Portland.

The racing classic will be shown on closed circuit television, exclusively in Oregon and Southwestern Washington, at Portland's Memorial Coliseum. Doors open at 8 a.m. Pre-race action will be shown starting at 8:30 a.m. The race is to get underway at 9 a.m. Ron Ails of Valley Sports has the Oregon Franchise for the showing. Radio commentary on the 500 will be heard here over station KMED, beginning at 8:30 a.m. and continuing through the race.

Art Pollard's starting berth in his 13th year of racing draws in the inside post on the fifth row for the starting flag. His qualifying speed ranked 15th in the field, but, according to race rules, he kept his 13th spot by qualifying on the first Saturday of the trials. The car Pollard is driving was built by Fred Gerhardt of Commercial Body Sales and Manufacturing Company, Fresno, Calif., and is sponsored by Thermo King Corporation, Minneapolis, Minn. The vehicle has a turbo-charged Offenhauser engine mounted in the rear.

On Tuesday, May 30th, the field took the green flag as starter Pat Vidan waved the field on under threatening skies. Vidan was a native of Portland, Oregon. A colorful character that started flagging local races in 1946, he became known at Indy for his crisp black and white apparel and wild flourishes with the racing flags. Vidan became the Assistant Starter at Indianapolis in 1958. In 1962, he took over the role of Chief Starter at the Brickyard for the next seventeen years. He retired to Portland and passed away in 1983 at age 69. In 2012, Pat Vidan was posthumously inducted into the Auto Racing Hall of Fame.

Andretti led the 1967 field into Turn One, but Parnelli Jones in the all-wheel drive turbine went high and quickly passed four cars. Coming out of Turn Two, the STP machine dove beneath Andretti to take the point down the backstretch, and immediately began building a sizable lead.

After just a few laps, Andretti was forced into the pits with mechanical problems. On the 18th lap, rain began to fall, and the race was halted on the next lap. The rain continued, and five hours later officials were forced to postpone the remainder of the race to the following day.

Jones picked up right where he left off and began dusting the field. Andretti was able to restart, but his day ended on the 58th lap when a wheel came loose. During the second half of the race, Jones was challenged now and then by Foyt, but clearly the turbine remained the car to beat. But then, as has been so well documented, with just four laps to go a $6.00 transmission bearing failed on Jones' car and he quietly rolled to a stop. Foyt inherited the lead.

One last bit of drama occurred when, on the final lap, there was a four-car accident coming out of Turn Four. With his skill as a seasoned driver, Foyt avoided the wreckage and logged his third win at Indy. He was followed across the line by Al Unser, Sr. and Joe Leonard.

Art Pollard running ahead of Bobby Unser at one point during the 1967 Indy 500.

Pollard, the rookie, drove a smart and clean race to finish his first '500' in the eighth position, credited with completing 195 of the 200 laps, and earning $16,928. Teammate Mel Kenyon finished 16th after being involved in a wreck with Cale Yarborough (driving for Rolla Vollstedt) on the 177th lap. Bob Veith, in the third Gerhardt entry, finished in the 11th position.

Phil Casey remembers that: "We were running real good. Art was running real fast, up there with Foyt and McCluskey, and turning laps about as fast as they were. All of the sudden there was a yellow and we made a pit stop. Art leaves [his pit stall] and I'm waiting for him to come back around, but he doesn't come by. Another lap goes by, and still he doesn't come through. I thought, 'I couldn't have missed him', then all of the sudden here he comes."

After the race, Casey asked Art, "Where did you disappear to?" Art replied, "Well, I was going down the back straight and I was trying to catch up with the field, and I kinda' gassed it."

Casey explained that in those days of the turbocharged Offy, when the blower kicked in, the car's probably going from 200 to about 600-horsepower: "It spun the rear tires and Art spun into the infield. It took the safety crew a little while to get him pushed back onto the track and restart. We lost a couple of laps, but he made up one of those. I always figured that Art would've finished in second, or perhaps even winning that race. It's funny now."

(IMS and The Indianapolis Star)

In a post-race interview with the *Indianapolis Star*, Art shared his thoughts about the race:

Art Pollard Feels 'Great' After Race but Regrets 'Goof'

INDIANAPOLIS, Ind. – "I'm not too happy, yet I'm a little happy too," Art Pollard, driver from Medford, Ore., declared today after finish of the 500-mile auto race at Indianapolis Speedway. Pollard, who started in 13th position in the race, finished in eighth spot after once moving up to third.

"I feel great," said Pollard, "but I'd feel better if I hadn't goofed." He spoke of the spinout in the third turn on about the 81st lap which dropped him from third position back to 16th. Pollard reported that he had just refueled and that the rear end operated a "little loose" for this reason. Then, a car ahead of him lost some oil and "I got into it. I just lost it," remarked Pollard, who was battling Bobby Unser at the time of the spin. He was down a lap from the leader at the time.

"Do you hope to be back in the race next year?," Pollard, who was driving his first Indianapolis race, was asked. "You bet," he answered, "I've got to do better next year, that's for sure."

"It was a pretty good race," Pollard reported. "The car ran just beautifully," he said, giving high praise to the members of his pit crew. Pollard drove a turbo-charged Offenhauser-powered car built by Fred Gerhardt, Fresno, Calif., and sponsored by Thermo King Corporation.

Other than for the spinout, "everything was just great," according to the Medford driver. "At least I did finish," he said, "and I'm real happy about that." He was particularly pleased to have finished in the top 10 yet somewhat unhappy that he did not place up around second or third.

Pollard won $16,928 in his first Indianapolis appearance. Pollard remarked that yesterday's rain "upset everything" and that the drivers had to get "pepped up again." Pollard will drive the same car in a 150-mile race at Milwaukee, Wis., on Sunday.

As Art's daughter, Judy said: "I recall that Dad was really happy to finish in the top ten. He considered it a great year, even without a win at Indy. My whole family did. After the awards banquet, we were all Indy insiders, I guess. It was pretty awesome."

And Art described to reporters: "I had a ball. The car ran just beautifully at the end of the race. I sure want to come back here and do a lot more racing. I wish the race would have been longer."

Spoken in the Art Pollard way—with humility, appreciation, and optimism.

FIFTEEN

A Broken Leg

The next item on the Thermo King team's agenda was a Firestone tire test back at Trenton, New Jersey, but a bit of a disaster took place on that Wednesday. As Phil Casey recalls: "One of the guys from Firestone was beating on the right front wheel to tighten it but was doing so in the wrong direction. We changed the wheel. The second time out on the track, the end of the hub broke off and the wheel came off. Art hit the wall, broke his leg, and suffered some burns on his face as well."

The break was below Art's knee and would take some time to heal. After the leg was set properly and put in a cast, Art returned home to Medford to recuperate. It was a relief to his family when he stepped off the plane, even with a broken leg and burns, that he was okay otherwise. Around the same time, Art's son Mike was just out of the hospital after surgery for a shoulder injury. He had suffered a concussion while playing basketball at Southern Oregon College. They looked quite the pair – getting stares from those passing by.

After a few months away from the cockpit, in late October Art returned ready-to-rock at the 1.5-mile oval at Hanford Motor Speedway in California.

In qualifying, he pushed his #16 Gerhardt/Offy to a speed of 154.816 mph. That was fast enough for Art to grab his first Champ Car pole position! He would be joined on the front row by Gordon Johncock, driving the Gilmore Broadcasting Gerhardt/Ford. Mel Kenyon would start the race 13th in his #15 Thermo King Offy.

Pollard Qualifies Gerhardt-Offy at 154 mph to Win Hanford Pole

HANFORD, Calif., Oct. 22 – First man to ever win a pole position on Hanford's brand-new 1.5-mile oval was Art Pollard in the Thermo King Auto Air Conditioning special.

Pollard drove the turbocharged Gerhardt-Offy around the D-shaped oval in 34.88 seconds at a speed of 154.816 mph to comfortably edge out Gordon Johncock, the eventual winner of the USAC 200-mile championship race which followed. Johncock turned a 35.19 for a speed of 154.286 in the Gilmore Broadcasting Gerhardt-Ford.

Once the green flag waved, Art controlled the 26-car field by leading the first 108 laps before the car malfunctioned. "He had a good lead when all of the sudden he comes in and said he was out of fuel," said Phil Casey. "I wondered; how can he be out of fuel? We went to fill it and found the right-side tank was full, but the left side was empty. What happened was that the flapper valve [which controls the fuel flow between the two tanks] had broken, letting all the fuel go to the right side. He would've won that race easy."

Due to that stop, Art gave up the lead to Joe Leonard, who was driving a Mongoose/Ford for Vel Miletich. Gordon Johncock took the top spot on lap 130 and was first when the checkered flag dropped on lap 134 in his Gilmore Broadcasting Gerhardt/Ford. One lap down, Art came home fifth to earn $2,299 and gained 200 driver points. Teammate Mel Kenyon finished tenth.

In early November of 1967, Art came home to Medford prior to the last race of the season at Phoenix. The time off allowed him to bring his race car along to make some personal appearances for his legion of fans in Southern Oregon.

Judy Pollard in her Dad's race car at their Medford home in 1967. Neighborhood kids (and family dog, Hilde) were thrilled! Note the neighbor boy's STP uniform.

The penultimate race of the 1967 Champ Car season took place on November 19th at Phoenix:

Pollard Smashes Record

PHOENIX, Ariz. (UPI) – Mario Andretti and Art Pollard were unofficially credited with breaking the one-mile track record at Phoenix International Raceway during Saturday's practice sessions for the 200-mile Bobby Ball Memorial race here today. Andretti, Nazareth, Pa., toured the tricky triangle in :29.29 for an average speed of 122.86 mph while Pollard, of Medford, Ore., turned in a :29.35 for an average speed of 122.657 mph.

Andretti, the defending champ in the Ball race, drove his Dean Van Lines Special, a rear-engine Ford, while Pollard used his Thermo-King Offenhauser which hit the 155-mile mark three weeks ago in Hanford, Calif. Lloyd Ruby, Wichita Falls, Tex., holds the official mark at 29.43. In Saturday's practice runs, Ruby, in a turbo-charged Offenhauser, toured the track in :29.65.

Mario Andretti went on to pick up another win, followed by Al Unser. It was a rather uneventful day for the Thermo King teammates, with Kenyon finishing ninth and Pollard end up 14th.

In the season-ending race, the Champ Cars made their debut on the road course at the historic Riverside International Raceway in Riverside, California. November 26th turned out not so well for Pollard and Kenyon, as each suffered mechanical woes during the race. Art's car lasted only five laps, sidelined by a bad valve, and finished 30th. On lap 26, Kenyon's turbocharger failed, and he was credited with the 21st position. Dan Gurney collected the win in his Olsonite-sponsored Eagle/Ford. He was followed in order by Bobby Unser, Andretti, Ruby and McCluskey.

Though Mario Andretti recorded eight wins during the season, it was not enough to overtake A.J. Foyt's points total for the driver's championship (Foyt won five races). He had competed in 20 events while Andretti drove in 19. Eighty points separated the two drivers at season's end.

SIXTEEN

Life Begins at Forty

While many of Art's competitors were much younger, 1968 would turn out to be another significant year for the 40-year-old Oregonian. At the beginning of the season, the Thermo King team remained intact and was hopeful to perform much better than they did in 1967.

Art's Offenhauser-powered race was now running as #11, based on his overall finish in the point's standings the year before. As the reigning Champion, A.J. Foyt's car was now designated #1. That's how it was done in those days.

The 1968 USAC Champ Car season got underway in mid-March at Hanford for the California 200, but several race previews were offered by the *Fresno Bee* newspaper leading up to the St. Patrick's Day event:

HANFORD, Calif., Feb. 23, 1968 – Engines are being fine-tuned, welder's arcs flash and spit in the shops, skeletons of steel and aluminum are being wedded – a sure harbinger of spring in the world of auto racing. And if you are in a hurry to hear the roar of 550 horsepower, you might be able to hear it at the Hanford Speedway today where Art Pollard and Bill Vukovich are turning 150 mph laps in tire tests.

The San Joaquin Valley is blossoming, not only for the invasion of Indianapolis but also prepping for the local track campaigns. King of the Indy classic builders, Fresnan Fred Gerhardt and son Don, expect to have three new cars and a grand total of perhaps 20 built over the last three years in Indiana in May, trying to qualify for the 500. The Gerhardts already have delivered one new car, turbo-Offy powered, out of their Commercial Body plant on South Orange Avenue, to Gordon Johncock, the winner of last fall's 200-mile championship race at Hanford.

Pollard will have the twin of Johncock's Gerhardt-Offy for the Memorial Day 500. A 1967 model, the one he drove to No. 8 last year, will be his backup. Mel Kenyon will be in the same Gerhardt-Offy he tooled to 16th last year.

Fresno owner Myron Caves hopes the third time will be a charm for his Gerhardt-Offy after failing to get a spot in the fastest 33 the past two years. Caves has signed veteran Chuck Hulse of Los Angeles (seventh-place finisher last May) to drive for him, confident he has the bugs out of the car.

Vukovich, burning up the midget tracks in recent weeks in the manner of his late, great father, will be ready for Indy in J.C. Agajanian's new Brabham Mongoose (turbocharged Offy) for the Speedway. George Snider, who learned his driving in Fresno but now calls Bakersfield home, is trying to get a ride with the A.J. Watson stable.

Pollard Tops 157 MPH in Hanford Tire Testing

HANFORD, Calif., Feb. 23, 1968 – Those words to the old song – "We're having a heat wave" – can be changed to "We're having a speed wave." That comes about because speeds at the Hanford Speed Bowl are climbing higher and higher as tire testing for the California 200 continues.

Yesterday Joe Leonard of San Jose ripped around the triangular oval at 156 miles an hour. Bill Vukovich of Fresno followed that with a speed slightly higher. Art Pollard, not to be outdone, came up with a track record 157.5 in his run.

Leonard and Pollard will continue tire testing for the March 17th J.C. Agajanian 200-mile race but Vukovich will be on the sidelines for a while. His engine blew, so he will be on the sidelines while it is being repaired.

Art Pollard First Entry in Car Race

HANFORD, Calif., Mar. 6, 1968 – Art Pollard of Medford, Oregon, and Mel Kenyon of Lebanon, Indiana, a pair of entries with a local flavor, are the first entrants for the second annual "California 200" – mile USAC Indianapolis car race at the Hanford Motor Speedway on St. Patrick's Day, Sunday, March 17, at 2:30 p.m.

They signed entry blanks with Racing Director J.C. Agajanian to pilot a pair of rear-engined turbocharged Offenhauser specials entered by Don and Fred Gerhardt of Fresno in the opening U.S. Auto Club championship car event of 1968.

Pollard is no stranger to the mile and a half Hanford track, where he holds the official one-lap track record of 154.816 miles per hour, set during qualifying runs for last fall's inaugural.
He'll pilot a brand new Thermo King Auto Air Conditioning special entered by Don Gerhardt, son of race car builder Fred Gerhardt. He led the Hanford race until a fuel stop late in the race dropped him to a fifth-place finish.

The St. Patrick's Day race is expected to draw the nation's top drivers including three-time Indianapolis 500 winner A.J. Foyt, two-time USAC driving champ Mario Andretti, last year's winner Gordon Johncock, Al and Bobby Unser, Lloyd Ruby, Joe Leonard and Chuck Hulse.

17 Indy Veterans Will Go at Hanford

HANFORD, Calif., Mar. 15, 1968 – Seventeen veterans of Indianapolis 500 driving will headline the field for the California 200-Mile Championship Race at the Hanford Speed Bowl Sunday.

**Resting on his elbow, Art chats with fellow racer George Follmer.
Behind them sits Mario Andretti and Bobby Unser.**

Experienced Indy drivers who have entered are A.J. Foyt, Mario Andretti, Bobby and Al Unser, Gordon Johncock, Roger McCluskey, Joe Leonard, Bud Tingelstad, Art Pollard, Chuck Hulse, Lloyd Ruby, Dempsey Wilson, Wally Dallenbach, Arnie Knepper, George Snider and Johnny Rutherford.

But they will not be sporting the same numbers as they did in last fall's 200. The United States Auto Club recently assigned the prestige numbers (the top ones) to last year's leading drivers. So, the numbers will go like this: No. 1, Foyt; 2. Andretti; 3. Bob Unser; 4. Johncock; 5. Al Unser; 8. Roger McCluskey; 9. Leonard; 10. Tingelstad; 11. Pollard; 14. Hulse.

Ruby qualified for No. 6 but when offered it was announced he would rather retain the No. 25 he had last year. The No. 7 man, Jim McElreath has not filed his entry yet.

Several Indy car rookies are in the field including Fresno's Billy Vukovich, Bruce Walkup, Bob Hurt, Gary Bettenhausen and drag-racer Danny Ongais.

USAC also ruled that drivers must have their names painted on their helmets. But this ruling did not come in time for all the drivers in the California 200.

"But," asked Bob Unser, "how will Rutherford, Tingelstad or Bettenhausen get their names on a helmet?"

Something new has been added: This year Chevrolet will challenge the Ford and Offenhauser monopoly on the racing circuit.

Four cars with Chevrolet engines have been entered and while the Fords and Offys are battling each other, the Chevy cars just could slip in for the victory.

Drivers from all parts of the nation will try for the $20,000 guaranteed purse, against 40 percent of the gate admissions when racing starts at 3:00 p.m. Last fall's race paid a purse of over $58,000 to the drivers.

Speeds of over 150 miles an hour average will be common-place as shown by Art Pollard's official one-lap track record of 154.816 mph set last year. Speeds over 157 mph were turned during practice runs.

Racing director J.C. Agajanian announce that more than 30 cars have been signed to try for the 26 starting positions in Sunday's 200-mile event on the mile and a half super-speedway.

Hanford 1968: Fine-tuning Art's Gerhardt/Offy prior to qualifying.

During qualifications, Art ran second quickest, positioning him beside pole-winner Bobby Unser, who was now driving the Rislone-sponsored Eagle/Offy for car owner Bob Wilke. Art's teammate Mel Kenyon qualified tenth.

HANFORD, Calif., Mar. 17, 1968 – So you will be wearin' the green today? From here, it looks both good and bad. A bit of Irish luck might be needed at the Hanford Speedway today to fend off predicted morning showers, allowing the 200-miler to go on as scheduled and saving a costly postponement. But the folks of the Emerald Isle, we have heard, owe their national colors to r-a-i-n. Whether it is a shamrock, a shirt or a tie of green you wear to observe St. Patrick's anniversary, you could save it until tomorrow. That is the day Fresnans celebrate with the annual Fresno County Golf Championship of Ireland and the follow-up $100-a-twosome dinner at Fort Washington.

Anyhow, keep your distance from the pits if you are Hanford-bound today, and wearing green. American automobile racers, the most superstitious people in all of sports, just do not like the color. Ten years ago, you might have gotten your skull creased with a tire iron if you showed up in the pits wearing a green necktie and munching peanuts.

"I think a lot of these crazy superstitions have disappeared with many of the modern generation of drivers," offered Art Pollard, who may be "disqualified" for such an opinion because he is half Irish himself – he thinks.

"When Jimmy Clark won the Indy 500 in 1965, the younger drivers began to laugh at the old guard. Me? I wouldn't mind driving a green car with a bag of peanuts and a flock of green bills (currency, which is green) in my pockets. I'd even take No. 13 on my car."

Pollard, who will be driving Fresnan Don Gerhardt's No. 11 Offy turbocharged job today in Hanford, and no other driver, either, will have No. 13 on his car. The United States Auto Club, which runs championship car racing, does not allow that number. Superstition, of course, from way back. "If you finish 13th in the USAC standings," explained Pollard, "you get No 14 on your wheels (car) the following year."

Of all the American car racing taboos, the traditional St. Patrick's hue is the black cat, the walking-under-the-ladder and the hair off a blind frog wrapped in one.

Scotsman Clark hammered a nail in the myth when his Lotus-Ford was a green blur on Memorial Day, 1965. After all, Grand Prix sports car champion Clark was doing only what was natural. Green is the "national" color of English racers, just as red is for the Italians, white for the Germans, blue for the French.

"I used to drive for Rolla Vollstedt of Portland," said Medford native Pollard. "With him, it (the color green) got to be a little ridiculous. If there was anything anywhere on the car, printing on a radiator hose, a green smudge, Vollstedt made my mechanics scrub it off with acetone or gas."

Many drivers either wear or tape a St. Christopher's medal on the dashboard of their cars. St. Christopher is the Catholic patron saint of travelers. "Sure," added Pollard, "I know a lot of Protestants who do it." A priest traditionally blesses the 33 starters in the Indianapolis 500.

Peanuts are anathema at the tracks, and not because they take four hours to digest and present the risk of gas pains. "There was this driver – I've forgotten his name – at old Gilmore Stadium (Los Angeles) several years ago," contributed Hanford race promoter J.C. Agajanian. "He had qualified for the trophy dash, was putting on his helmet. He looked into the cockpit of his car, turned white, screamed and jerked off his helmet. Somebody had put some peanut shells, maybe by accident but I doubt it, in the seat of his car. Nobody could get him back into the race program that night." Pollard volunteered that the peanut-ban started years ago when someone put peanuts in five cars entered in this race. There was a big pileup of cars, and all five drivers "peanutted" died.

Just where the hated green superstition originated escapes our research department. Most agree it was the result, in the early days, of a series of mishaps involving those wearing the color. There have been some great Irish drivers in recent years. There was the late Pat Flaherty who not only won the 1956 Indy 500, but defied the jinx by wearing a green shamrock on his helmet. There was Pat O'Connor, who was eighth in the 1957 Indy, and killed in a crash on the same track the next year. Today, we hope to check out Roger McCluskey to see if he really is a good Irishman. With our green necktie out of sight in our pocket, of course.

At the start of the 134-lap race, Art shot into the lead and led the first three laps before being passed by Bobby Unser. Unser traded the lead several times with Roger McCluskey, then lead the race from lap 20 through lap 91. Art picked up the lead for the next eight laps. For reasons unknown today, Art crashed out of the race on lap 120 and wound up 16th. Mel Kenyon finished eighth.

Art led the field in the early stages of the Hanford 200, but crashed on lap 120 and wound up finishing 16th.

(BSU Archives)

The *Fresno Bee* newspaper featured this full race report the following day:

Johncock 'Luck' Holds In '200'

HANFORD, Calif., Mar. 18, 1968 – Because an Englishman had the luck of an Irishman, Gordon Johncock of Hastings, Mich., holds his second consecutive California 200 championship.

His luck came yesterday on St. Patrick's day when, driving with caution as his brakes had not been functioning too well, and with a spinout and a brush with the wall pushing the leaders aside, he was able to move up from third into the lead on the 121st lap and then outrun Al Unser of Albuquerque, N.M.

Going into that 121st lap Bobby Unser, Al's brother, and Art Pollard of Medford, Ore., (driving a Don Gerhardt car) were fighting for the lead. Actually, Pollard and Bobby had battled for the lead most of the race, with Roger McCluskey of Tucson, Ariz., the only other driver ever to get out front.

Bobby Unser had the lead going into that 121st lap, with Pollard right on his tailpipe, pushing hard. Unser went into a partial spin, but kept control, even though he did lose the lead. Pollard fared worse. He went into the wall and that put him out of the race, with Johncock taking over.

Bad and good luck rode with two other drivers; Joe Leonard of San Jose, and Danny Ongais of Wilmington, Calif. Leonard escaped serious injury in a flaming crash on the 52nd lap. The cars came into the No. 3 turn bunched when the racer in front of A.J. Foyt got into trouble. That forced Foyt to brake and go to the inside. When Foyt hit his brakes, Leonard had to hit his also, and his car pulled to the outside and into the wall. The car burst into flames. Leonard, however, managed to get out unscathed. His car hit the wall with such force that it tore out a chunk of concrete.

Ongais also came through a flaming mishap unhurt. In his qualifying run his car scraped the wall in the No. 1 turn, damaging the rear end, causing his engine to catch fire. He drove his racer out of the turn, off the track and up to a fire truck, where the firemen extinguished the flames. The car, though out of the race, was not seriously damaged.

Another lucky fellow, Johnny Rutherford of Fort Worth, Tex., escaped unhurt when the engine on his car blew in front of the stands just before turn No. 1, forcing the car into a spin and along the wall, shearing off a wheel. The yellow flag was out four times for a total of 36 laps – a big boost for the fuel-burning Offenhausers.

After Leonard hit the wall, the yellow flag stayed out for 17 laps, much to the consternation of the fans, who began to boo. The had one bit of excitement – a jackrabbit dashing along the wall in one of the yellow flag laps.

The race started on a record-breaking note: A track mark twice broken. First Pollard broke the one-lap Hanford mark he set last year with a 154.905 miles-an-hour speed while qualifying. Bobby Unser followed that up with a higher speed of 155.700.

That gave Unser the pole post and Pollard the No. 2 spot, but Pollard jumped into the lead at the start of the race. Bobby Unser passed him late in the second lap, setting the stage for a sizzling duel between the two and Mario Andretti, who qualified for the No. 3 berth.

McCluskey got into the act by passing Pollard and Andretti and began pushing Unser. McCluskey caught him in the No. 2 turn on the 16th lap and shot into the lead. Unser kept on McCluskey and managed to move back out in front in the 19th lap. The race then settled down into a three-way dogfight – Unser, McCluskey, Pollard and then Unser, Pollard, McCluskey. (Suspension trouble had forced Andretti out on the 40th lap). On the No. 2 turn of the 91st lap McCluskey shot around both to take the lead, which he held until fuel troubles hit him in the 106th lap and he had to head into the pits for refueling.

Then Unser and Pollard slugged it out for the lead until the 121st, when Johncock went by their little tangle to win. "I like this track," Johncock said after the race, "second to Indy. Last year I had to edge out Bobby Unser to win. This year brother Al pushed me." He also revealed he had not been pushing his car, because early in the race brake trouble developed.

A great photo of Mario Andretti, Al Unser Sr., and Art Pollard at Hanford Motor Speedway.

"I think the heavy load of fuel (about 75 gallons) caused it. I think the brakes were over-heating and that caused a malfunction. As the race went on the load became lighter and those runs under the yellow flag helped cool the brakes. But still they had me worried, right to the end. I could not run with the leaders in the corners."

Johncock drove a turbocharged Offy in this race but will switch to a Ford for Phoenix and Las Vegas races. He remains uncertain about which engine he will use for the big Indy 500 but knows it will not be the car he drove yesterday. "It's too old – four years old. We probably will sell it."

Both Johncock and Al Unser drove smart races. The managed to pull into the leading five about halfway through the race and kept there until that big 121st lap. In fact, they had a hot duel of their own going for fourth place. Al kept right on Johncock's tail most of the time as the battled 'round and 'round the triangular oval. Fresno's Bill Vukovich ran into throttle linkage trouble and had to drop out in the sixth lap. Chuck Hulse, driving Myron Caves' Fresno-based car, went out in the 71st.

Why that long yellow flag run after Leonard's accident? Safety reasons and a situation caused by the crew handling the car. The crew would not move the charred racer as the owner wanted to wait and put it onto a trailer and haul it away. Officials feared that as long as the car was left it would draw a large crowd close to the track. A speeding racer making the turn could accidentally have hit the dirt and spun into the crowd. So, the yellow flag stayed out until promoter J.C. Agajanian telephoned to USAC officials to push the racer back and get the race moving again.

By winning, Johncock corralled almost $12,000 as the winner's share of the purse. The purse paid by promoter J.C. Agajanian from the gate was $35,031. On top of that came $2,590 in lap money and $6,858 in accessory prized for a total of $46,747.

The gross gate was $86,181, paid in by 15,501 fans. Drivers are paid a share of the gross gate (minus tax deductions) on a percentage basis. The winner takes 25 percent; the second-place man 15 percent; third, 8 percent; fourth, 6.5 percent; fifth, 5 percent; and on down to one-half of 1 percent for the 26th and last car.

Sunday's victory gave Johncock a 400-point send-off toward the United States Auto Club individual title. The race paid off at two points a mile.

The 200 is the first of 24 races in the USAC circuit this year – the longest in the history of the tour. The cars will run in Hanford this fall and will wind up the season at Riverside a month later.

Two weeks later, the series made the short hop from Hanford to Las Vegas for the Stardust 150 – the one and only Champ Car race held there. The three-mile, 13-turn road course and drag strip in Spring Valley were built in 1965 by the Stardust Hotel and Casino, with hopes of attracting the rich and famous to the gambling complex. In 1966, the track began hosting the season finale for the Can-Am Series. The hotel was eventually sold in 1969 and the new owners basically abandoned the racing facility. Several years later, the land became a housing community.

With a little time on their hands before heading to Las Vegas, Art and Claudine spent a few days visiting cousin Harvel's family in Bakersfield. Art mentioned to Harvel that he should accompany them to the Las Vegas race and be on his pit crew. Harvel says, "I asked him what the hell am I going to do? Art said that I could put gas in the car. Of course, nowadays, they certainly wouldn't allow that."

Eighteen cars qualified for the 150-lap Stardust race. Dan Gurney was on the pole in his Eagle/Ford. Bobby Unser and Mario Andretti held the second and third positions, respectively. Art would start the race 12th in the Thermo King #11. Gurney dropped out even before the first lap with suspension woes, so Bobby Unser and Andretti dominated, with Unser taking the win. Art drove a careful race and finished eighth, five laps down from the leaders.

Art drove the Gerhardt/Ford to an 8th-place finish at the Stardust 150 after qualifying 12th.

(John A. Wilson photo)

Staying in the southwest part of the country, the series raced at Phoenix on April 7th in the 150-lap Jimmy Bryan Memorial. Bobby Unser started from the pole and led a total of 74 laps in taking the win, followed across the line by Lloyd Ruby. It was a great day for the Gerhardt team: Mel Kenyon started in ninth and finished third, while Pollard started 16th and finished fifth behind Wally Dallenbach.

A few weeks later, 22 cars took the green flag for the Trenton 150 behind pole sitter Andretti in his Brawner/Ford. Kenyon's Gerhardt/Offy, now sponsored by the City of Lebanon, Indiana, was starting 13th while Pollard's Thermo King Gerhardt/Offy started 12th. Once again, Bobby Unser was dominant after grabbing the lead from Andretti on the ninth lap and then cruised to the checkered flag. Kenyon finished tenth, but only completed 84 of the 150 laps due to a universal joint failure. Pollard completed a total of 56 laps after a spin and finished 13th, but no driver points were allotted.

Now it was time for all the Champ Car teams to take a short breather as they geared up for the hectic month of May at the Brickyard.

It wasn't apparent at this time that Trenton would be the last race Art would drive for the Thermo King Team.

SEVENTEEN

The 52ⁿᵈ Annual Indy 500

At the 1967 running of the Indy 500, Andy Granatelli and driver Parnelli Jones grabbed most of the headlines with Granatelli's controversial turbine-powered racer. Jones dominated the race until a mechanical failure sidelined the car just four laps shy of the finish.

To better equalize the competition, in the off-season USAC mandated that for 1968, the turbine's air-intake annulus area be reduced 25 percent, from 23.9 square inches to 15.9 square inches.

Nonetheless, Granatelli collaborated with race car designer Colin Chapman for another attempt at Indy with a new turbine car design. The four-wheel drive Lotus 56-3 featured the latest aeronautical engineering techniques, with power supplied by a 500-horsepower Pratt & Whitney gas turbine located directly behind the cockpit. The wedge shape of the bodywork was penned by designer Maurice Phillippe, and an aluminum monocoque chassis helped keep the car's weight at 1,370 pounds, just 20 pounds over the allowable minimum weight. Some observed that the car was "the most innovative race car ever seen."

(granatelliturbines.com)

In February of 1968, three Indy champions were announced to drive the turbines at Indy: Parnelli Jones, Jimmy Clark, and Graham Hill. Jones was slated to again drive the 1967 turbine, but then elected not to race in the '500' because he felt the car would no longer be competitive.

On April 7th, the racing world was shocked when Clark was killed in a crash on a road course in Hockenheim, Germany. Several weeks later, Granatelli announced Scotsman Jackie Stewart as Clark's replacement. The Granatelli team also hired British driver Mike Spence, who was a road racing veteran in Europe. Spence had experience test driving the new turbine in England for Chapman. As Andy Granatelli described Mike Spence:

Mike Spence

(IMS Photo)

"We took him on a provisional basis, but he didn't stay provisional for very long. He was so good, in fact, that we had trouble holding him down for his rookie driving tests. Chief Steward Fengler warned him about 'unconventional cornering', as he was coming in too low. But he had obvious talent. More, he was pure brilliant."

On a side note, two other unique turbine-powered race cars were entered for the 1968 race by Carroll Shelby of Ford Cobra fame. In early practice runs the cars were under-performing, and Shelby elected to withdraw the entries.

On the practice day of May 7th, Graham Hill turned a lap at 169.045 mph, nearly three miles-per-hour faster than Jones' qualifying time in the turbine in 1967. Late that same day, Spence went out in his car and exceeded Hill's time with a 169.555 mph run. Tragedy then struck when Spence crashed in Turn One. That night, he succumbed to his injuries. Understandably disturbed by the event, Colin Chapman returned to England the following day.

One week later, Granatelli lost the services of Jackie Stewart. He was suffering from a hairline fracture in his wrist and was forced into a cast, making him unavailable as a driver. Now down to just one driver, Graham Hill, but with three cars entered, Granatelli signed Joe Leonard and Art Pollard.

Of course, Art was still driving for Fred Gerhardt prior to Granatelli's offer, but the team was struggling to find speed in the #11 Thermo King entry. The Medford *Mail-Tribune* reported on the team's struggles:

Seeks Higher Speed

Medford auto racer Art Pollard, who planned to make his Indianapolis 500 qualifying run yesterday, if weather and position in the draw allowed it, said Friday he hadn't gotten the Offenhauser-powered Thermo King Special up to the speed, in practice runs, he really wanted. He has driven the car around 166 miles per hour and was aiming for 167 or 168. When we talked to him in early afternoon on Friday, he hadn't been out on the track for a practice run that day because rain was falling.

The Fred Gerhardt-built car is basically the same as the one Pollard drove to eighth place in last year's Indy race – with refinements. It is a little smaller and lighter and hopefully faster. There have been some "minor" problems, Pollard said. The turbocharged engine was changed Thursday.

Pollard figures that 163-164 mph will be the minimum speed that can qualify for the 500. He said that the speed which will take the pole position will depend on the weather. If weather is good, he thinks the speed will be around 172. Three Lotus turbine cars have been over 170. There are only 15 or 16 cars faster than those of last year, Pollard reported. The rest are about the same speed or slower.

Andy Granatelli made Art an offer he couldn't refuse. He was offered a $50,000 signing bonus and Granatelli would buy out Art's contract with Gerhardt. Phil Casey of the Gerhardt team reflected on that decision for Art: "He had the chance to go to Granatelli, and I couldn't blame him for that. We were really good friends and he liked Fred and Don Gerhardt. I talked to Art and he didn't want to leave everybody, but it was the opportunity of his life to win at the Speedway. The turbine was a good car, and they were in a class of their own. Art and I remained good friends after he left."

Granatelli's #40 STP turbine from 1967 had also been configured to meet the 1968 rules, and both Leonard and Pollard turned some practice laps with it. In this article from the *Indianapolis News*, Art described his familiarization run in Granatelli's unique machine:

Ride in Turbine Turns on Pollard

"It's real impressive. It's just like driving a passenger car." That summarizes Art Pollard's feelings toward a turbine-powered race car. And Pollard, who just turned 41 Sunday, impressed more than himself at the Indianapolis Motor Speedway yesterday when he took the now famous No. 40 STP turbine, vacated by Parnelli Jones last week because it was "non-competitive", around at 163.6 miles per hour. "It's amazing," the Medford, Ore., driver said after the shakedown run. "It's really super." And so, the adjectives flowed.

But what makes the turbine so competitive? "It just makes driving here easier," he answered. "Actually, it isn't the turbine, but the four-wheel drive and engineering and chassis. Andy Granatelli (the car owner) and Parnelli have talked about that, but now I know. It's different to drive, too. You have to anticipate the throttle. There's a lag there. It's probably more psychological because of the instant response with a gas engine. You have to get on the turbine much sooner. If you wait too long, you bog down."

Pollard will be shooting for his second 500-mile race come qualifying. He finished eighth last year in his first try. He is scheduled to drive the No. 11 Thermo-King Special, a turbo-charged Offenhauser.

But as he said after becoming only the sixth driver to top the 163-mark in practice, "Whenever I get in that car, I definitely think it's a car that could win. This car could run 162 all day long. And I think that'd win. At least I hope so."

On May 12th though, Leonard lost control and hit the wall in Turn One. The driver was fine, but the car would never race again. This *Associated Press* article told the story:

Granatelli Turbine Out of Indy Race

Andy Granatelli's No. 40 turbine engine car which narrowly missed winning last year's Indianapolis 500 is apparently out of this year's 500-mile classic.

It was badly damaged when it hit the wall on the first run yesterday with San Jose's Joe Leonard at the wheel. Leonard had just turned a lap of 166.4 miles per hour when the accident occurred as he went into the first turn of his fifth lap.

Leonard said he was shaking down the car and lost control on the same turn where British driver Mike Spence was fatally injured in another turbocar Tuesday.

Granatelli said the frame of the car was bent and thrown out of alignment. He doubted there would be enough time to make the extensive repairs required in time for the car to qualify in the time trials the next two weekends.

The No. 40 turbine narrowly missed winning last year's race with Parnelli Jones driving, and it held all but six of the 500-race records.

Earlier Sunday, Art Pollard took the car around the oval in a lap speed of 166.805, the fastest the car has ever run.

The withdrawal of the famous "Guppy" turbine leaves only five of the original nine turbine-powered cars entered in the race this year. Carroll Shelby withdrew his two turbines after the death of Spence in another turbine.

All three of the newest turbines made the field on the first day of qualifications. Colin Chapman had returned to Indianapolis and Parnelli Jones was lending his expertise to the Granatelli team. The second car out on the track was Graham Hill, who posted a four-lap average of 171.208 mph. Bobby Unser, in Dan Gurney's Eagle chassis with turbo-Offy power, set the second fastest average speed of 169.507 mph. It was then Joe Leonard's turn in his STP turbine. He really put his foot into it and topped teammate Hill's speed with an incredible 171.559 mph average. He was on the Pole!

Late in the afternoon, Art pulled onto the track in his #20 turbine. Though he had only six practice time laps to familiarize himself with the car, his average speed of 166.297 was good enough to earn the 11th starting spot in the middle of the fourth row. The front row consisted of Leonard, Hill, and Bobby Unser.

Though he had only six practice laps in the turbine, Art earned the 11th starting slot by posting an average speed of 166.297 mph, which positioned him in the middle of the fourth row.

(IMS Photo)

Indy Pole to Leonard

INDIANAPOLIS (AP) – Lotus turbine cars driven at record speeds by Californian Joe Leonard and Englishman Graham Hill yesterday earned the first two starting positions in the 500-mile race, May 30, at the Indianapolis Motor Speedway.

Joining them on the outside of the front row will be a bitterly disappointed Bobby Unser, who reported the track was slippery with oil when he made his run.

Leonard, a former motorcycle champion, left the record at 171.539 mph with a best lap of 171.953 after the first of four sessions of 10-mile time trials.

Hill had held the record four hours before his teammate ran and took about $10,000 in special prizes away from him. The Lotus team's third car also was qualified by Art Pollard at a relatively modest 166.297 mph.

The day following, May 20, 1968, Medford's *Mail-Tribune* reported the good news about the hometown hero:

Art Pollard Qualifies for Indy 500 in Granatelli Turbine Car

"It was a surprise for everybody," declared auto racer Art Pollard of Medford on Sunday. He referred to his Saturday qualifying run for the Indianapolis Speedway's Memorial Day 500-mile race.

Switching by mutual agreement of car owners, Pollard qualified in one of the three turbine-powered cars entered by Andy Granatelli. "I'm really happy to be in a turbine," said Pollard. "I think it'll better my chances by 400 percent ... it'll definitely make the race easier for me ... my chances of winning have increased.

Art visiting with Ray Firestone at Indy.

Pollard averaged 166.927 in Granatelli's No. 20 car and qualified for the 11th position. It puts him in the middle of the fourth row.

The change to the Granatelli team was made Saturday after the Thermo King Special, with its piston-powered Offenhauser engine could not be gotten up to the speed desired. Granatelli, who had pressured Pollard during the week, talked to Fred Gerhardt, builder of the car. Gerhardt agreed and Thermo King was in agreement.

This was with an hour to go before the slated 6 p.m. closing of the track for the day. Pollard, driving this particular turbine car for the first time, took it for 10 practice laps and the decision was made to qualify. He had gone one lap when the 6 p.m. gun sounded but he was allowed to continue the other three of the 10-mile qualifying run.

Pollard was instructed not to try a run with No. 20 but to "just get it into the program." Owner Granatelli did not want to risk a crash. But, Pollard declared, "The car will be real competitive on race day." He'll drive practice runs to become accustomed to the car and become more competitive. His fastest lap Saturday was 166.574 mph.

Pollard will hold his fourth-row position against possible faster qualifiers unless bumped from the race. But he has little fear of that. In his 11th spot it would take 23 faster qualifying times. And, Pollard reported that most of the cars left to try to qualify are slower than the 16 which gained spots during the weekend.

While Pollard was in the No. 20 for the first time, he had driven the turbine machine in which Parnelli Jones raced at Indy last year. The Pratt and Whitney-powered Lotus turbines were built by Englishman Colin Chapman. The car burns a kerosene mixture fuel.

The engine drives all four wheels and that, according to Pollard, is the secret of the good handling of the cars. The car "goes right where you point it," he explained. In contrast to autos with just rear-wheel drive, they have a tendency for rear wheels to drift. The turbine, said Pollard, "is the ultimate in race car design."

Mentioning the Thermo King car, Pollard brought out that it was a new car and "not all sorted out." He drove a Thermo King-sponsored machine built by Gerhardt to eighth place last year. Pollard had high praise for Gerhardt, saying, "He's a great guy."

Indy 1968 – Andy Granatelli appears to be talking race strategy with his drivers Joe Leonard and Art Pollard.

A historic note for the 1968 Indy 500 field was that this would be the final time a front-engine car would appear in the lineup. Jim Hurtubise qualified a Mallard/Offy in the 30th spot, but his race would come to an early end on lap nine with a burned piston.

The Mallard/Offy in 1968. Jim Hurtubise was the last driver to qualify and race a front-engine in the Indianapolis 500.

(IMS Photo)

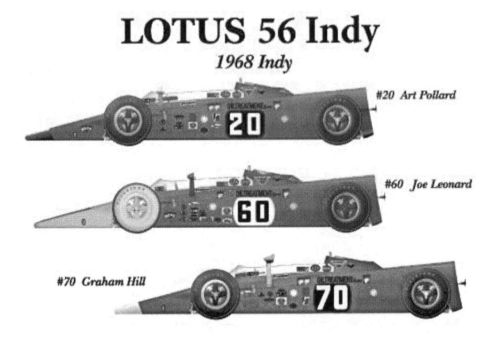

Granatelli's lineup for the Indy 500 for 1968.

As the Ford Torino pace car left the track and the green flag waved, Joe Leonard, in the #60 turbine, immediately took the lead ahead of Bobby Unser and Roger McCluskey. On lap eight, a charging Unser passed Leonard and held the top spot until lap 56. After a series of pit stops, Lloyd Ruby led for a bit until Unser retook the lead on lap 90.

The second caution of the race occurred on lap 110 when Graham Hill's turbine suddenly lost a wheel, sending him into the Turn Two wall. Hill was unharmed, but not there would be only two STP turbines left in the running.

After the green flag restarted this hotly contested battle, Leonard regained the lead on lap 113 for the next seven laps, until Unser moved back in front. When Unser pitted on lap 166, he was overtaken by Ruby and Leonard. The popular Ruby, who always seemed to be the victim of bad luck at the Brickyard, led the next nine laps until he was forced into the pits with a faulty ignition coil.

Up to this point, Art Pollard had been driving a calculated race by staying out of trouble and saving his car for a strong finish. When Ruby pitted, Leonard again took the lead ahead of Bobby Unser and a closing Dan Gurney. Things were looking promising for both turbine cars, but then Carl Williams crashed on the backstretch – bringing out an extended caution to clear the track.

The green flag again waved over the field on the 191st lap, but just past the main grandstand Leonard's car suddenly lost power and rolled to a quiet stop. Almost at the same instant, Pollard's turbine slowed to a crawl. Both cars came to a rest with the same problem, which was a snapped fuel pump driveshaft.

This photo shows Billy Vukovich Jr. (#98) dicing with Art Pollard (#20) at Indianapolis in 1968. Driving J.C. Agajanian's Shrike/Offy, Vukovich recorded a 7th-place finish.

(Vukovich Racing Legacy)

Granatelli's long quest for an Indy victory was again dashed within sight of the checkered flag. "I sat down heavily on the pit wall and looked at the track for a long, long time," Andy said. "It had happened again."

In the end, Bobby Unser picked up the well-deserved win with nearly a full lap lead for the first of his three Indy victories. Dan Gurney placed second while Art's former teammate Mel Kenyon brought his Gerhardt/Offy home in third after starting 17th. Leonard and Pollard were credited with 12th and 13th place, respectively.

Bobby Unser's winning Eagle/Offy, entered by Dan Gurney.

(IMS photo)

These post-race reports on the STP team appeared in the *Indianapolis Star* newspaper:

Hill Hits Wall; Joe Leonard, Art Pollard Cars 'Just Die'

"One thing should come of all this ... at least I don't think they'll have the guts now to ban the turbine." With that, Andy Granatelli rose from behind his desk, took off his coat, sat down again, shook a dozen sympathetic hands, watched the reporters walk from the garage, and then took out a handkerchief – and dabbed at his eyes.

His three bright red wedge-nosed STP babies had failed. Graham Hill kissed the wall midway through the 500-Mile Race and the machines of Joe Leonard and Art Pollard just plain died. "We don 't know what happened," he had said a minute earlier. Later it was learned the turbines were on the wrong kind of formula – an unleaded white gasoline. "It's not important what happened. Whatever happened was meant to happen. Anyone will tell you, no one comes here with a brand-new car and wins the race ... especially Andy Granatelli."

There was some quiet cussing among the STP crew yesterday, and some brooding, and there were a few tears. But this time there was no funeral, no wake, not like last year when Parnelli Jones and the No. 40 went out on the 197th lap. Last year newsmen battled for position with the crowd outside a set of bolted doors for 25 minutes while the STP team composed itself.

The doors were open yesterday. Inside, owner, driver and crew were numb. It was almost as if they knew that, in the end, the wine would again turn to vinegar for Andy Granatelli ... as it always has at the Indianapolis Motor Speedway. Leonard, outwardly calm, keeping an iron grip on his poise, stood in the middle of the very, very quiet three-stall garage and said softly: "It was as if I had turned off the key. It just stopped, just like that. No warning at all. It just went clunk."

The No. 60 STP Lotus-turbine went clunk on the 192nd lap, with Leonard in command and less than eight minutes away from a date in Victory Lane. "Of course, I thought we had it," Joe said. "I thought we had a victory for Andy Granatelli. I feel bad enough ... think of how he must feel right now." And he gestured toward Andy, pale and perspiring, sitting 10 feet away.

Everyone had expected Granatelli's three turbines to run away from the field – everyone, that is, except Andy, drivers and crew. Qualifying laps at 171 miles an hour is nice and all that, but they don't win races, and they can be misleading. "If I get my nose in the breeze, I can run some fast laps," Leonard was saying, "but in traffic it's a different story. Yes, we were definitely underpowered. We've said it all along. Maybe someone will finally believe it. I had instructions from Colin Chapman (designer-builder) and Andy not to pass anyone in the short chutes. But I had to do my passing there. I couldn't pass anyone anywhere else."

"When we're in traffic, the turbine sucks up the exhaust fumes from the other cars. The engine heat goes shooting up maybe 500 degrees, and our power falls right off. It's just like a jet taking off on a hot summer day ... it uses a lot more runway because it can't produce the power it could otherwise." "I'm fine when I'm in front with racing room, or running alone like in qualifying, but in traffic it's different. I can run two, maybe three miles an hour faster without traffic in front of me. I just couldn't take anyone through the straights. That was pretty obvious out there. Unser's turbo Offy was pulling a lot more horsepower than we were, and when he passed me, well, he just plain blew me off."

"A thousand horsepower? No, not hardly. We figured we had about 430 today with the warm sun. The engine was set for 480. So, if some people think we're pulling a thousand horses, somebody's made quite a mistake somewhere." Granatelli said his turbines were jacked up to 510 horsepower with a turn of the screw for qualifying. "We had to turn it back today so the engines would last more than two and a half hours," he added.

Pollard's sister turbine, with only 800 track miles to the No. 60 car's 2,300, went out with similar trouble on the very same lap. The third, Hill's No. 70, went into the wall on the 112th lap when the handling suddenly, mysteriously, turned sour. "Apparently I have bad luck," Granatelli mused. "It's obvious. The drivers don't deserve this kind of luck. Joe drove a great race. A great race. He didn't deserve what happened. Sometime in the next 24 hours I'll probably really realize what happened. Right now, it's just too soon. It hasn't hit me yet."

With Leonard, it was probably much the same. But the patience and poise slipped a bit when a late comer stormed up and blurted "Joe, have some trouble out there?" "No, I just thought I'd get out and take a rest," Leonard said softly, exasperated. "Were you playing a game, toying with Unser, trailing him like that?" Leonard gritted his teeth. "I drove as hard or harder today than I ever have in my life," he said.

And Andy Granatelli rooted and hoped and prayed harder than ever before, in all probability. And even the two, combined, weren't enough. Andy Granatelli is still racing's hard luck champion.

Fuel Blamed for Turbine Disaster; Leonard 'Flamed Out' on New Blend

The two STP Lotus Turbocars conked out almost simultaneously in yesterday's 500 due to fuel and "gearbox" problems. The disastrous turn of events was unexpected but not unexplainable, because the fuel used in both cars was changed for yesterday's race. The end result was the fuel in some manner caused a malfunction in the Pratt & Whitney gas turbine fuel system, and the engine simply "flamed out."

Opinions were voiced by principals from within the STP racing organization that the fuel didn't lubricate evenly. This would indicate the fuel set up a "wash" condition and created a galling or seizing of the components which make up the engine's fuel system. This accounts for the engine quitting in the Turbocar driven by Joe Leonard.

A J-4 aircraft quality kerosene is the recommended fuel for the Pratt & Whitney powerplant being used in the STP Lotus Turbocars. The kerosene in itself contains properties which lend to lubrication, and thus keep the fuel system functioning smoothly. A different blend or type of fuel was used for yesterday's race, and it apparently backfired from an engineering standpoint.

An American Oil Company spokesman said unleaded white gasoline was used for fuel. Gasoline tends to have a washing effect and removes the lubrication film from moving parts. There was a strong possibility that had Graham Hill's turbine machine still been in the race it, too, would have been sidelined with a malfunctioning fuel system.

Crewmen for Art Pollard told United States Auto Club technical observers that Pollard had gearbox trouble by over speeding the engine to accelerate when the green flag went back on for the 192nd lap. They reported that engine governors controlling the engine shut off the fuel supply but did not elaborate on the fact the Turbocar has no gearbox but utilizes a chain drive system.

S.A. Silbermann, chairman of the USAC technical committee, said he will have an official report on the car this morning. Andy Granatelli, president of STP Corp., said yesterday that the turbines developed 510 horsepower for the qualification runs, but had been set back to 480 horsepower in order to increase engine life. Whether the change in fuel caused a lowering of performance was not revealed, but none of the turbines gave any indication of having the superior speed edge over piston engines that they displayed in practice and qualifications.

Pollard said he began noticing a power fall-off after 150 miles. He never was in contention for the lead. Leonard said he had not noticed any diminishing of power until the engine quit. "Then it was like somebody turned off the key," he said.

The turbines' unfortunate showing was shared almost equally by the Ford Motor Company. Eight of the first 10 cars were powered by turbocharged Offy engines, and none of the turbocharged Ford V8's finished the race. Two of the four cars using this engine, however, were eliminated by causes other than engine failure, but still were not among the leaders when they went out of the race. Al Unser in the Retzloff Chemical four-wheel-drive turbocharged Ford hit the wall, and the debris from his car broke the oil cooler on Arnie Knepper's Bryant Heating and Cooling turbocharged Ford, eliminating it from competition.

Jim Malloy wheeled the Jim Robbins turbocharged Ford for 67 laps before the quick-change gears in the rear end failed and split open the gear casing. Jerry Grant in the Bardahl turbo-Ford went out with an oil leak and Mario Andretti in the Overseas National Airways turbo-Ford dropped out after the first lap with a burned piston.

Dan Gurney finished second with his Olsonite Eagle, powered by a Gurney-Weslake stock block Ford. The engine which uses a 289 cubic-inch Mustang block and special Gurney-Weslake heads, posted the highest finishing position by a stock block engine in the 500 since the pioneering days of the automotive industry.

The victory by a turbo-charged Offy completely blanks out the Ford double overhead cam V8 from the winner's circle on oval tracks this season. The sturdy four-cylinder powerplant now in its third year of development is putting out in excess of 600 horsepower, has good throttle response, and has demonstrated a high degree of reliability.

And this from the Medford *Mail-Tribune*:

Something in Turbine Just Quit Running, Pollard Says

"Something in the turbine just quit running," reported a disappointed and dejected Art Pollard following the Indianapolis 500-mile auto race yesterday. The Pratt & Whitney turbine-engined car No. 20 piloted by the Medford driver conked out after Pollard, running in sixth or seventh place had completed 188 laps in the Memorial holiday classic at Indianapolis, Ind.

The Pollard-chauffeured machine was the third and last of the Colin Chapman-built, Andy Granatelli-sponsored turbine vehicles to bow out of the race.

Pollard declined to use the term, "flame-out" for what happened to the No. 20 car. He said that possibly the fuel pump failed. He reported that the car was "progressively losing power ... running short on power" the last 50 laps it was in the race.

The Medford driver maintained that heat was not a problem – "just a little mechanical difficulty." He said that the car handled "real good" except for being shy on power, until it just quit. Pollard was running 10th in the early going of the race. Two pit stops to check out a problem when the car was not running properly put him well back in the field. He just worked his way back up toward the leaders.

Although the turbine car driven by Joe Leonard quit before the one driven by Pollard, the Medford man had fewer laps in when his car conked. Pollard had 13th place in the unofficial standings while Leonard was 11th.

Sponsor Andy Granatelli said Thursday of the turbine cars that he didn't know what happened. "They just quit."

With his car out of contention late in the race, Art gives winner Bobby Unser a congratulatory wave.

EIGHTEEN

A Champion with the Kids

With a smile on his face and warmth in his heart, Art Pollard loved interacting with children and young adults. It seemed so natural for him, as many have described Art as just being a grown-up kid himself at times. Whether it was with his own children, Mike and Judy, or nieces or nephews, or simply the neighborhood kids, Art always took a special interest in their fun and well-being.

Art celebrating with aspiring young race drivers at the Big2 Quarter Midget Banquet.

1971 – Art, Joe Leonard and Bobby Unser sharing some quality time with kids from the Indianapolis area.

(Indianapolis Star Newspaper)

Away from the track, Art spent much of his time traveling around the country. He spoke at high school assemblies to impress upon teenage drivers the importance of safe driving.

One such example took place in Tombstone, Arizona. It was in February of 1967, when Art appeared under the sponsorship of the Champion Spark Plug Company. A local newspaper article said Art was well-received by the students, whose language he appeared to speak. During his visit, Art was named both the Honorary Mayor and Honorary Deputy Marshal of Tombstone.

Pilot for Astronauts Speaks to Local Students

Art Pollard, Indianapolis 500 experienced racing driver, visited the old silver mining camp Friday last, and while here attempted to impress upon local high schoolers that driving an automobile is a skill that must be learned through study and practice, rather than acquired in the age-old method of a novice turned loose in a forty-acre field and told "get to driving and learn for yourself."

"Know-how, experience, courtesy and a regard for ones fellows, are necessary before any person can become an accomplished driver," according to Pollard, who last Memorial Day drove the famed five-hundred miler, and the balance of the season in a precision machine owned by astronauts Gus Grissom and Gordon Cooper.

Brought to Tombstone under the sponsorship of the Champion Spark Plug Company, Pollard appeared under local auspices of Motor Supply Company, Bisbee.

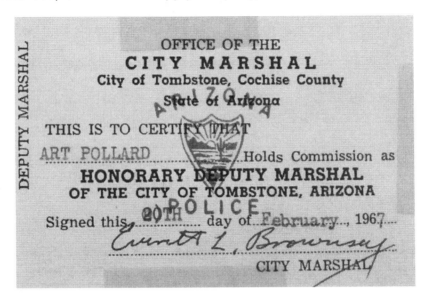

One of eight top-notch veteran speedway pilots carrying a safe-driving message to teenagers across the country, Pollard hails from Medford, Oregon. Having eleven years of motor racing competition under his belt, the personable young man broke into the classic Indianapolis marathon as a rookie last spring.

Well received by local high school students, whose language he appeared to speak, Pollard made numerous friends in the course of the short stay in this historic town. The car number sixteen that he will drive Memorial Day next will have numerous rooters in this famed camp.

In 1968, Art began an extraordinary association with Larue D. Carter Memorial Hospital in Indianapolis. Founded in 1945 as a teaching, treatment and research hospital, and affiliated with Indiana University, the hospital provides in-patient mental health services to both adults and emotionally disturbed children and adolescents.

For years during the month of May, Indy car drivers visited the children in the hospital. Art was one of the most visible among them. He spent many hours with kids, along with serving as host when the children were able to spend a special "day in May" at the Speedway. These kids served as an inspiration for Art.

One such day was described in the *Indianapolis Star* newspaper on May 18, 1977:

Picnic for Kids Draws Racing Greats

It was a kite-flying, chicken-munching, softball-playing, driver-idolizing day for 28 children from the LaRue D. Carter Memorial Hospital who attended the annual Art Pollard Memorial Picnic yesterday in the area behind the Tower Terrace.

The picnic was the fourth honoring the late Pollard, a close friend of the children at LaRue Carter. Pollard, who was killed during practice for the 1973 '500', made frequent visits to the hospital, often bringing other driver friends, sometimes arranging for the children to visit the Indianapolis Motor Speedway to watch the action.

When the buses from Carter arrived at the track, the first activity planned was a softball game which included drivers, children and staff members from the hospital as well as members of the media. Kites filled the sky, and there seemed to be more drivers playing softball and kite flying than driving race cars.

Guests included '500' Festival Queen Kathy Hegg and her court; Bruce Melchert, deputy mayor, and almost enough drivers to fill a field. Busy signing autographs were Pancho Carter, Bill Vukovich, Wally Dallenbach, Larry Cannon, Dick Simon, Bob Harkey, Al Unser, Jim Hurtubise, Bobby Olivero, Chuck Gurney, George Snider, Steve Krisiloff, Tom and Jerry Sneva, John Mahler, Gary Irvan, Roger Rager and Duke Cook, as well as Freddie Agabashian.

The adults, who outnumbered the children about seven to one, seemed to be enjoying the festivities as much as the kids. Bill Vukovich confused everybody by wearing a George Snider T-shirt, and Trevor Sneva, the 15-month-old son of rookie Jerry Sneva and his wife Kay, abandoned his stroller for a better view of the proceedings.

"This is our first time at the picnic," said Kay Sneva, who is settling into the championship circuit with ease. The Spokane (Wash.) residents will make temporary camp here until July, renting a furnished apartment that normally is used as a model. "We were really lucky to find a place already furnished, and there are lots of babysitters handy and other children to play with."

The Jerry Snevas married eight years ago, and when they met "I had never been to a race before. It was winter, and the whole family said, 'You're in for a real treat.' I do love it. It's fun meeting everybody who knows Tom. All the brothers are easy to get to know, and hopefully, there will be two other Sneva boys racing here someday, Jan and Blaine. They're racing modifieds which their dad built."

Although racing was something new to Kay, her husband, who drives the 21st Amendment Liquor Stores Car No. 36, like his pole-sitting brother, was raised on it, and "used to race soap box derby cars when he was little. He and Tom would hire the neighborhood girls to be trophy queens, and they'd round up officials and starters.

"The family album is wonderful. There are all sorts of pictures of Tom and Jerry as kids, sitting at a track, just covered with dirt, their eyes about the only things visible."

Little Trevor has a head full of beautiful blond curls, but not as long as Jerry's were as a toddler. "Jerry and Tom used to have a little push car when they were small and Tom would be the last out of bed, so Jerry usually got to it first. Their mom thought Jerry looked cute in long curls, so she would put a bobby pin in his bangs so he could see when he went out to play. Tome knew all he had to do was get that bobby pin and he could get the car."

As usual, manufacturers were generous, especially STP, which donated carryall bags, T-shirts and hats, and Shurfine Foods, which gave a miniature race car, jacket and decals to each child. Champion, Valvoline, Dayton-Walther, Bryant Heating & Cooling, A.J. Foyt and Johnny Rutherford also sent stickers, balloons and other souvenirs.

In a May 2003 article that appeared in *Indystar.com*, Ruth Holladay wrote:

"It was just a genuine affection between a down-to-earth Oregonian, who came to racing later in life, and Indianapolis kids known as 'very tough cases' in treatment at the state psychiatric facility. On his own, the fun-loving guy his friends called 'Alley Oop' returned every spring, quietly dropping in on the kids in the evening, telling stories, mesmerizing them. A hospital doctor at the time said Pollard showed an amazing 'sixth-sense' for relating to them."

On the day he died, those who knew Art began working on the idea of establishing the Art Pollard Fund at the Larue Carter Hospital. His estate left $25,000 to enable future visits to the Speedway and an annual picnic in Art's name. Attorney Forrest Bowman III and retired sports announcer James A. Wilson were named the fund's trustees.

Following Art's death Fremont Power, a respected journalist with *The Indianapolis News*, wrote a memorable tribute to Art and his involvement with the hospital. These are some excerpts from his article:

"The late Art Pollard was being given the victor's ride around the Milwaukee racetrack on June 8th, 1969, when he suddenly asked the driver to stop. He got out and went over to the fence to speak to a man there he knew. 'Any of the kids from the hospital here?' Art asked. No, just himself, said Dr. Richard C. McNabb, clinical director of children's services at Larue D. Carter Memorial Hospital.

Pollard's inquiry about the children was more than a casual one. He had become enamored of the young patients there and had a talent for relating to them that will probably always impress Dr. McNabb. 'He had the capabilities I try to train into the people I supervise,' the doctor said.

He was able to read the children's 'sensitivities' the doctor remembered. 'Our kids are more perceptive than the average kid. That's what got them in trouble in the first place. They read a person very, very quickly and with them and Pollard it was love at first sight.

This year, Susan Cooper, recreational therapist, was trying to arrange free admission to the track for small groups of Carter children. Mrs. Cooper went to the track twice for appointments that weren't kept. Pollard called her at home, she said, to see how arrangements were going. They weren't. As so Pollard, while trying to get ready for Saturday's shot at the pole, worked on it himself for four or five continuous days. The children, whom Dr. McNab characterizes as 'socially non-functional' got their tickets.

[Pollard] came back every year, with the exception of last year when he was laid up in Methodist Hospital with a broken leg. 'Art didn't appear before them,' the doctor recalled. 'He appeared with the children. And between them there was an instant 'immeasurable chemistry.'

The clinic director remembers one visit when the race film had been shown and a punch and cookies party in the lounge was virtually over. But there was Art, on a couch, with a five or six-year-old on each knee – their arms about him. 'I couldn't tell who was having a better time,' the doctor remembered.

In groups, [Art] was invariably talking to one. 'The others waited their turn,' Mrs. Cooper remembered. Pollard's big brawny arms would be about a child. 'Some of these children can't stand to be touched physically,' the doctor said. 'Pollard never physically reached out to draw a child to him,' the staff remembers. 'He waited until they came to him.'

'It's kind of a sixth-sense, when to cuddle a child,' the doctor said. 'I never saw Art make a mistake. He was able to read children's sensitivities. What happened to him on Saturday is a tragedy for children's mental health.'"

In May 2003, on the 30th anniversary of his death, the hospital's playground was named in Art Pollard's memory by Family and Social Services Administration's John Hamilton. Mike Pollard, his cousin Brad Pollard, and their wives attended the special ceremony, along with 42 kids and dozens of staff from the hospital. The occasion also included the annual Art Pollard picnic.

The playground at the Larue D. Carter Memorial Hospital in Indianapolis.

Pat Pollard and racer Roger McCluskey give kids a garage tour at Indy.

Fittingly, the *Indystar.com* article quoted David Harrison, a volunteer coordinator at Larue Carter:

"We have never generated a lot of friends in the community. People are uncomfortable around mental illness. There is so much stigma. Pollard didn't see stigma. He saw kids. For that, he will always be a winner."

Another example of Art's fantastic rapport with kids took place in the family's Medford neighborhood. Not only was he the talk of the town during the racing season, he gifted the kids with photos, decals and even kid-sized STP crew uniforms. This photo and description on the following page appeared in the *Medford Mail-Tribune* in May, 1966 – just prior to the Indianapolis 500:

Tuning up their Johnson Street Special in preparation for their own big Memorial Day race are these little wheels of the pit crew, properly garbed in regulation track regalia furnished by veteran race driver Art Pollard. The speed suits were sent to the neighborhood aficionados from the Indianapolis 500 track where Pollard, also of Johnson Street, barely missed participation in the big event.

The "petit pitmen," from left to right, are: Lee Stegal, 5-year-old front where tightener; Thomas Gass, 5, fifth wheel expert; Brian Hercher, 4, rear axle adjuster; and Arlo Kane, steering linkage loosener.

The crew, to a man, is convinced neighbor Pollard wouldn't be sitting out the 500 if only he'd taken their 2-hoofpower special through those qualifying laps.

NINETEEN

The 1968 Season Continues

The results from Indianapolis were in the record books, but there remained a long Championship Car season ahead. It would be a busy summer and fall for most of the teams.

On June 9th, it was back to the Milwaukee Mile for the traditional running of the Rex Mays Classic. After Indianapolis, Parnelli Jones had purchased one of Granatelli's turbine "Wedges" and entered the #60 car with Joe Leonard as the driver. Art would be in the #20 turbine for Granatelli.

Roger McCluskey put the G.C. Murphy Eagle/Ford on the pole. Art qualified third fastest, with Leonard directly behind. George Snider was now driving the #11 Gerhardt/Offy for Fred Gerhardt.

During the race, the lead bounced back and forth between several drivers. Art led only one lap, and Leonard led 13. On just the second lap, there was an unfortunate crash that took the life of Ronnie Duman, driving Pete Salemi's Gerhardt/Offy. Duman was the driver who bumped Art from the 33rd starting position for the 1966 Indy 500.

Lloyd Ruby was the first under the checkered flag, followed by Andretti and Al Unser Sr. Art's car retired after 61 laps because of a fuel leak, and Leonard's car was out with suspension issues after just 38 laps. Neither driver scored points.

On June 15th, the Telegraph Trophy 200 took place on the 2.459-mile road course at Mosport International Raceway in Ontario, Canada. The one-day event was broken down into two heat races. Because the Granatelli cars were not entered, Art was scheduled to drive one of Rolla Vollstedt's Bryant Heating & Cooling Vollstedt/Fords. Jim Malloy was in another Vollstedt/Ford entered by Jim Robbins. Joe Leonard had signed up to drive Vel Miletich's Vel's Parnelli Jones Mongoose/Ford.

During practice, Art crashed his Vollstedt car, but then jumped into the cockpit of Jack Adams' Lola/Ford and qualified 13th for the 17-car field. Because of an oil leak, Art only completed 15 laps, and would not compete in the second heat race. Dan Gurney led all 40 laps for the win, followed by Andretti. The pair duplicated this performance in the second heat.

Art drove in several more events during 1968 for his longtime friend Rolla Vollstedt. At the Langhorne 150 in Pennsylvania on June 23rd, Art started third on the grid behind pole-sitter Gordon Johncock and second fastest Wally Dallenbach. However, Art's #21 Vollstedt/Ford dropped out with a magneto problem after completing 41 laps. He scored 18th in the 23-car field. Johncock's Gerhardt/Offy picked up the win.

Art's next contest took place on July 7th on the 2.66-mile road course at Continental Divide Raceway in Castle Rock, Colorado. The Rocky Mountain 150 was an inaugural event for the series. Now back in the #20 STP turbine car, Art qualified 12th fastest. Road racing expert, Ronnie Bucknum, was on the pole in an Eagle/Ford, while second quickest was Bobby Unser driving a Coyote/Ford for Bob Wilke.

After the start of the 57-lap race, Bucknum led through lap 23 when a half-shaft failed on his car. From that point until the finish, A.J. Foyt led the remaining distance to take the win in his Sheraton-Thompson Coyote/Ford. Following him across the line, in order, was Lloyd Ruby, Jim Malloy (Vollstedt/Ford) and Al Unser. Art drove a terrific race for Granatelli, earning a fifth-place finish and an important 150 driver points.

Weeks later, Art was back in the seat of the Vollstedt/Ford for the Indy 200 on the road course at Indianapolis Raceway Park. The one-day event would consist of two, 40-lap heat races. For heat one, Art qualified 13th, completed 38 laps, and finished seventh in the 26-car field. Though Andretti's Brawner/Ford started from the pole, it was Al Unser's Lola/Ford that claimed the win.

The lineup for heat two was determined by the finishing order of the first heat, so Art started seventh in the Bryant Heating & Cooling car. Al Unser led the entire distance to again take the win over Andretti. Art finished this race in the ninth position and was awarded a combined total of 100 driver championship points for the weekend.

On July 28th, it was another two-for-one racing event back at the Langhorne Speedway. The one-mile paved oval would host two 100-lap features in succession. In the first go-around, Art qualified his Vollstedt/Ford ninth in the field, just ahead of Johnny Rutherford's Gerhardt/Offy. On the first lap these two drivers tangled and both cars were eliminated. Still on a roll, Al Unser guided his Lola/Ford to a win in both races.

It was back to the Granatelli team on August 18th for Art, at one of his most successful tracks, for the Tony Bettenhausen 200 at the Milwaukee Mile. During qualifying, Art turned a sensational lap to take the pole position in his #20 STP turbine, setting a new track record with a speed of 119.245 mph. Joe Leonard would share the front row with Art in the #60 STP Parnelli Jones-Beau Vince turbine. The second row featured Wally Dallenbach and Bobby Unser.

Following the green flag, Art led the first 18 laps before he was overtaken by both Bobby Unser and Dallenbach. Art took back the lead on lap 28 for the next 26 laps. Leonard's turbine held the top spot for laps 54 through 90, when Art passed back into the lead position. The race was looking positive for Art until brake problems arose on the 129th lap. Ironically, Leonard's car was also plagued with a brake issue.

In the end, Lloyd Ruby led the final 34 laps in his Mongoose/Offy to grab the win over Andretti and Al Unser. Art led a total of 83 laps, completed 179 laps, and ended up 14th overall. His prize money was $1,039, but he gained no driver points for his effort.

During this era, the Championship Car schedule included about a half-dozen dirt track races for traditional sprint cars. Driver points gained in these events were included in the overall standings at the end of the year. When Art was with the Gerhardt team in 1967, they did not have a dirt car with which to compete. However, according to Phil Casey, they were going to build one for Art to drive in 1968, had he stayed with the team.

Art had gained plenty of experience running sprint cars in his earlier years, so he would have no problems adjusting to a dirt oval. He finally got a chance to show his stuff on Labor Day weekend at the DuQuoin State Fairgrounds in DuQuoin, Illinois.

The Ted Horn Memorial would be 100 laps on the one-mile dirt track. Art was entered in the #31 Don Collins-built sprint car, listed in the records with Dick Simon as the car owner, and sponsored by McClure Plastics of Portland. Recall, Del McClure and Art were longtime friends in the Pacific Northwest. Art qualified 14th in the 18-car field and finished in the same position after crashing out on lap 71. Andretti won the contest in a Kuzma/Offy.

(Author Photo)

A week later it was another race on the dirt at the Indiana State Fairgrounds in Indianapolis. Again in the McClure Plastics machine, Art started 17th and finished 10th, one lap down to winner A.J. Foyt. With his finishing position, Art gained 30 driver points and collected $1,405 from the total purse.

"Every lap was an adventure," Art said following the race. "I lost my brakes after 60 laps or so and it was all over then. I just had to stroke it. Boy, is it galling to sit back there at the rear of the pack. I like to run with the leaders and be competitive. That's the only way."

Don Collins stands next to Del McClure's #31 machine on the grid at DuQuoin. Art qualified the car 17th and finished 10th, one lap down to race winner A.J. Foyt.

(Del McClure Collection)

DuQuoin Fairgrounds 1968. Art talking things over with car builder and mechanic Don "Duck" Collins and car owner Del McClure.

September 22nd was another date for the Championship Cars to return to the pavement for the Trenton 200. Art qualified his STP turbine sixth, never led a lap, and finished tenth after the left rear suspension broke on lap 164. He did gain an additional 60 driver points. Andretti led a total of 170 laps in taking the victory.

The starting grid of the Trenton 200 in 1968. On the pole is Al Unser, Sr. with Mario Andretti alongside. Pollard's #20 is outside of row three with A.J. Foyt's inside.

The teams then traveled to the west coast for another dirt race, which was the Golden State 100 at the California State Fairgrounds in Sacramento. At the helm of the #31 McClure Plastics Offy, Art started the 100-lapper 13th and finished 10th, logging another 30 championship points. A.J. Foyt and Gary Bettenhausen finished one-two.

Art dirt-tracking it through a corner, chased by Carl Williams, at the Golden State 100 at the California State Fairgrounds in Sacramento.

It was back to the Midwest part of the country for the next event, which was Champ Car's inaugural race on the fast, two-mile paved oval at Michigan International Raceway. Art was slated to race the turbine, but that plan went awry when he crashed during a pre-race tire test and eliminated the car from making a qualifying attempt.

Art was unhurt, so he teamed up with Al Unser and car owner Al Retzloff to drive the Retzloff Chemical #24 Lola/Ford. Unser, who was in the team's #5 car, qualified seventh and Art qualified 14th. Unser's car broke a wheel hub on the 47th lap and was credited with 18th position overall. In an unfamiliar car, Art had a spectacular run to finish in the sixth position, earning 101 driver points. Ronnie Bucknum's Eagle/Offy was first at the checkered flag.

In early November, it was time again for the Hanford 250 in California. It turned out to be a disappointing weekend for Art when he was unable to qualify his turbine car due to a broken differential. Teammate Joe Leonard started from the pole in his turbine and finished fourth behind Foyt, Bobby Unser, and Andretti.

Al Unser Sr., Gordon Johncock, Mario Andretti, Art Pollard.

Two more races were left in the 1968 season, and the driver's championship was coming down to a close-knit battle between Mario Andretti and Bobby Unser. At the 'Bobby Ball Memorial' at Phoenix on November 17th, Art would start his turbine on the outside of the front row, alongside pole winner Andretti. Joe Leonard was unable to qualify the second Granatelli car.

Art quickly shot to the front at the start of the race and led the first 13 laps. The caution came out on lap six following a crash involving Andretti and Foyt. A hard charging Al Unser managed to pass Art on lap 14, but Art's turbine regained the lead one lap later and held the position until lap 41. That's when a universal joint failed and put Art out of the running. At the end of 200 laps, Gary Bettenhausen drove to his first series win in the Thermo King Gerhardt/Offy.

The final race of the season, the one that would determine the driver's championship, was held on December 1st. The site was the challenging road course at Riverside International Raceway. The race would also mark the final appearance of Granatelli's storied 'Wedge' turbine cars.

A total of 40 cars were on the entry list, but only 30 would comprise the field. Joe Leonard (#60) and Art Pollard (#20) were hoping to make a good showing for this last race of the STP turbines. Leonard qualified third while Art qualified tenth behind pole sitter Dan Gurney's Eagle/Ford. Title contenders Andretti would start second and Bobby Unser qualified ninth.

A master at road racing, including Formula One circuits in Europe, Dan Gurney would lead all but four of the 116 laps in his drive to the checkered flag. However, the real drama was taking place back in the field with Andretti and Unser fighting for the championship. As a backup measure, a second car driven by road racer Jerry Titus was in the field, in case Andretti's Firestone tire-shod primary car failed during the race.

In the early stages, Leonard was running a strong fourth and Art had moved up to the sixth position. Jerry Titus' #64 car lasted only 27 laps, dropping out with suspension issues. Bobby Unser was methodically working his way up the ranks on his Goodyear tires. Back then, there was also a fierce rivalry between Firestone and Goodyear for bragging rights.

By mid-race, Andretti had been running comfortably behind Gurney, but then calamity happened when his engine failed on lap 59. With his backup car out of contention, Andretti somehow had to keep his championship hopes alive. With Parnelli Jones' blessing and Firestone's urging, a quick deal was made to call in Joe Leonard and put Andretti into the STP turbine. In his biography, Andy Granatelli best explained what happened next:

"Mario whipped the wedge out of the pits just ahead of Art Pollard, who was running comfortably in third place in my remaining Turbocar. He eased up and let Pollard pass. Of course, Andretti had zero experience in the turbine, so he tucked in behind Pollard to learn how to drive a turbine."

"Mario attempted to take Pollard on the inside around the breath-taking sweep of downhill turn nine at Riverside – and slashed into him. In one shattering, ironic blow, both Turbocars were wrecked. The Grand Tour was over."

The actual cause of the accident was never determined. It should be noted that earlier in the year, mechanics found that the turbo car's original inboard braking system was insufficient for short tracks and road courses. The address this issue, they fitted the car with a second set of brakes mounted outboard on the uprights, resulting in eight calipers and discs. It was observed that, even with this setup, it was difficult to finish a race with any brake pad wear remaining.

In the final tally, Art's #20 turbine would finish in 16th (63 laps) position and Leonard's #60 was credited with 17th (62 laps).

Pollard's #20 STP Turbine at Riverside International Raceway in 1968.

At this time of the race, the championship was yet to be decided and Andretti needed another car. Lloyd Ruby had been driving a steady race near the front of the field in his Mongoose/Ford but was called into the pits to allow Andretti to take over the #25 machine. Andretti finally finished the race in third place, but at the same time Bobby Unser had driven aggressively, avoided problems, and he finished second.

Bobby Unser won the 1968 Champ Car season championship a mere eleven points ahead of Andretti, and Goodyear won the tire war. With that, the curtain fell on the season. It had been a magnificent year overall: 28 total races that included nine road course events, six dirt track shows, and the annual Race to the Clouds at Pikes Peak, Colorado. A total of 99 drivers had participated in at least one event.

Art competed in 20 of those races, accumulating 696 points and placed 23rd in the overall driver standings. His average starting position was 9.5 and he had an average finish of 12.5, along with one pole award. Art's total earnings were $17,274.

Also in 1968, Art drove in four USAC Stock Car events driving a 1968 Ford Galaxie for Jim and Jerry's Service located in Milwaukee, Wisconsin. He recorded one fifth-place, one eighth, and a tenth, ending up 18th in the driver standings.

TWENTY

Driving for Andy Granatelli

Andy Granatelli and Art Pollard firmly established their owner/driver relationship in 1968, and that association would continue through the 1969 season.

"Andy spoke very highly of Art," Harvel Pollard remembers. "In his mind, Art was smooth and got the most out of the race car. Granatelli called him a 'charger'. During their leisure times away from the track, Art had a group of guys he would play cards with, and Granatelli would often join in."

Now at the age of 42, Art still felt much younger and kept himself in great physical shape. "Maybe it's because I don't have too many tough miles on me," he said. "I spent a lot of my racing life bashing around the Pacific Northwest, where you don't race very dangerously. You don't earn much money, but you do have a lot of fun."

The turbine car era for Indy-type cars ended at the end of the 1968 season. In brief, the United States Auto Club imposed additional restrictions that essentially removed turbines from competition.

Given that, the never-say-die Granatelli came up with an all-new plan for 1969. According to an April 1969 article in *Car Craft Magazine*:

"Granatelli waited until after the rules committee met in January to see what the latest trends in thinking would be. Sensing that USAC favored a return to passenger car-type engines, Andy selected the Plymouth, as he feels it is one of the best small-block engines around. In addition, the rules governing these engines will be in effect for three years, during which time substantial development work can be completed."

Granatelli's plan was to modify his 1968 Lotus-designed STP turbines to accept the Plymouth power plant and have them ready in time for the 1969 Indy 500. With involvement by Plymouth Engineering and master engine builder Keith Black, the project was based around Plymouth's 340 cubic-inch V8 engine that was de-stroked to 318 inches. These highly developed engines were projected to muster around 525-horsepower. Reportedly, the money for this project came from the fact that Richard Petty left Chrysler in order to run a Ford during the 1969 NASCAR season. The budget Chrysler had earmarked for Petty instead went to the Granatelli-Plymouth project.

The Plymouth 318 cubic-inch stock block engine installed in Granatelli's new race car.

(STP Corp.)

Granatelli was interviewed in March 1969 by Robert Markus of the *Chicago Tribune* newspaper, saying:

"If you want to win the '500', the best way to do it is to take last year's winning car, make a few improvements, build about three of them and then hire the best driver money can buy. Sure, I could run an Offenhauser at Indy this year. And suppose I won with it? What would that prove?

There are hundreds of thousands of racing cars with Chevrolet or Ford stock-block engines, but nobody has ever raced a Plymouth stock-block. Sure, that's one reason I picked it. But I like the engine. I think it will give us solid performance."

In a *STP Press Release*, Art remarked: "I had a great time with the STP Turbocar last year. It was a new and novel racing experience and I wouldn't take anything for it. We all realize the STP Plymouth effort got a late start and is a long-shot effort. The chassis design and the great new wedge body design should contribute much to the car's chances. We don't expect a super-powerful engine, but we do think the Plymouth will provide very dependable power."

Another important aspect of this project that was not really touched on was that it could be a very big marketing opportunity for Plymouth, especially at a time when Detroit's muscle car manufacturers were fighting tooth-and-nails for bragging rights.

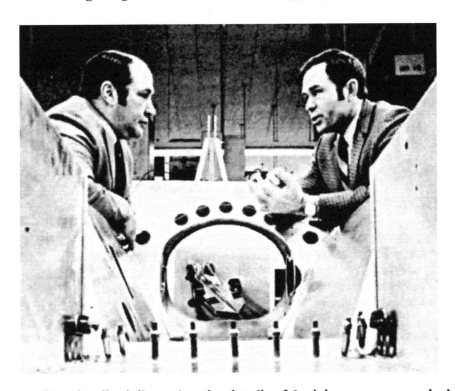

Granatelli and Pollard discussing the details of Andy's new race car design.

(STP Corp.)

Noted race car builder and mechanic, Grant King, was selected to be Art's crew chief, and the two men shared roots in the Pacific Northwest. King was the son of Chinese parents and was born and raised in Victoria, British Columbia. He became obsessed with race cars as a youth while working in his older brother's garage. He subsequently moved to Portland, Oregon and began earning a reputation for roadsters, sprint cars, and modifieds. One of his achievements was working with Rolla Vollstedt in building the first rear-engine Offenhauser to qualify for the Indy 500 with driver Len Sutton.

Noted race car builder and mechanic Grant King.

(Bill Throckmorton Collection)

The first event for the 1969 Championship Car season took place at the end of March at Phoenix International Raceway. In the off-season, Granatelli brought on Mario Andretti as Art's teammate. Because the new Plymouth-powered machines were still being developed, Andretti would be driving a Brawner/Ford (#2) and Pollard would be in the #20 Gerhardt/Offy. Both cars carried STP sponsorship.

Twenty-four cars made up the qualifying field, with Al Unser grabbing the pole in the Vel's Parnelli Jones Lola/Ford. Andretti would start in the fourth position while Art qualified 13th.

Following the green flag, Andretti soon got by Unser and led laps 12 – 27 but exited the race on lap 38 with a failed half-shaft. Art lasted only 27 laps when his car overheated. In all, it was a disappointing day for the Granatelli team. George Follmer led the final 29 laps to come home first in his Cheetah/Chevy.

Next on the schedule was the California 200 at Hanford Motor Speedway on April 13th. Andretti thoroughly dominated the weekend, starting from the pole and leading all 134 laps in taking the win. Art had qualified ninth but went out after 67 laps due to a pit fire and subsequent crash. His finishing position was 15th. After two races, he had yet to register any driver points.

Sadly, this race was marred by the death of James 'Red' Stainton, who was a 38-year-old Fresno mechanic for the Fred Gerhardt team and a member of Art's pit crew. According to an *Associated Press* announcement:

"Art Pollard of Medford, Ore., came into the pit to refuel and his car burst into flames. One attendant, Grant King, was burned and Stainton, finding his coveralls on fire, leaped back into the path of Andretti's car. Both men were rushed off in the two ambulances at the track.

Since the race would not proceed without one ambulance in attendance, the competition was delayed until one arrived. No times were kept as of the result of the break. After the accident, Pollard got back into the race, but slammed into the wall in turn one and didn't finish. He wasn't hurt."

Stainton died two days later with serious head injuries and second and third-degree burns to his head and arms.

Granatelli's radical Super-Wedge, Plymouth-powered racer was lacking the speed to compete in the 1969 Indy 500.

Granatelli's original intention for the upcoming Indianapolis 500 was to debut the new Plymouth-powered car for Pollard, while Andretti would be behind the wheel of a revolutionary four-wheel drive Lotus/Ford. In early practice runs, the team's primary plan went by the wayside. The Fred Gerhardt-built, Super-Wedge Plymouth was found not to be fast enough, so Art climbed into the #20 STP Lotus. He just could not get a handle on the car and on May 17th, he spun the car in Turn Three and simply drove it back into the pits.

On another practice day, things turned worse for the Granatelli team, when Andretti's new racer lost its right rear wheel in Turn Four, sending the car hard into the outside wall. The car was destroyed, and Andretti walked away with facial burns.

Granatelli's new four-wheel-drive Lotus, which was initially the car Andretti was slated to drive in the '69 Indy 500. It was destroyed in a practice accident.

(IMS photo)

At the same time, Art was behind the wheel of the #57 Gerhardt/Offy that was first assigned to Carl Williams. When Andretti's car went out of control, Art was directly behind. To avoid making contact with Andretti, Art expertly turned his car into a 180-degree spin-sliding a total of 280 feet – but did not touch either Andretti's car or the wall. In the aftermath, Andretti refocused on getting his back-up car, a Hawk/Ford, ready for the first day of qualifying.

Another close call for Art took place on the Friday before Pole Day, when he was on the track in the #40 STP Lotus/Offy. Late in the afternoon, the car spun all the way around in Turn One, after something locked up in the rear end. Again, fortunately, there was no wall contact.

A strange thing took place on Pole Day. Leon 'Jigger' Sirois had never qualified for the Indy 500, but was first in line for qualifying. During his run, he had achieved a speed of 161.535 mph before his attempt was called off by his car owner, who felt the speed would not be fast enough to make the race field. Shortly afterward, it began to rain hard and further qualifying was washed out for the remainder of the day. Had Sirois been given the chance to complete his run, he would've been on the Pole. In the days ahead, he made two more qualifying attempts but was unable to make it into the race.

Sunny skies returned to the Indianapolis area on Monday and qualifying resumed the following weekend. A.J. Foyt earned the Pole in his Sheraton Thompson-sponsored Coyote/Ford with a four-lap average of 170.568 mph. Andretti was second quickest while Bobby Unser was third in the Bardahl-sponsored Lola/Offy. An exciting front row!

When it came time for Art's qualifying run, he spun all the way around, again in Turn One, on his warm-up lap. He drove his Lotus/Offy back into the pits without taking the green flag. Under Indy rules, the car was not charged with an attempt. Art went back out later in the day to set the 12th fastest time, securing a starting position on the outside of the fourth row.

Art's Lotus/Offy for the 1969 Indy 500.

(IMS photo)

Once the race started on Friday, May 30th, it evolved into a battle primarily between Andretti, Foyt, and sometimes Lloyd Ruby. After struggling all month, it was a short race for Art. He completed only seven laps when a broken torque gear ended his day. At the finish, it was Andretti the victor after he led a total of 116 laps. Behind him, the other top five finishers were Dan Gurney, Bobby Unser, Mel Kenyon, and Peter Revson.

It was a glorious day for both Andretti and especially Andy Granatelli, who had been trying to win at Indy for 23 years! We have all seen the famous victory lane photo of Andy planting a kiss on Mario's cheek. In one later interview Andretti said, "So when I crossed the finish line to win in '69, it was like a huge weight was lifted off my shoulders. I thought, 'At least I've got that under my belt, and now we move on.'"

The victors of the Indianapolis 500, 1969.

(IMS photo)

TWENTY - ONE

Two Championship Car Wins!

Though Art was a teammate with Mario Andretti during the 1969 season, because each driver was behind the wheel of their own unique race car, there was not much sharing of information that took place.

"The teammate situation was such that we were really two separate teams," Andretti explained. I sold our team to Granatelli and retained Jim McGee and Clint Brawner as crew chiefs, but we were two separate operations. The cars were entirely different, so we didn't have much to share. From that standpoint, it was not the standard teammate situation, if you will. We didn't have a lot of chatting back and forth because we were concerned with our own operation."

A week following Indianapolis, the Rex Mays Classic took place at the Milwaukee Mile in Wisconsin. In addition to Andretti and Pollard, the Granatelli team entered a third car for driver Greg Weld, which was the #57 Gerhardt/Offy. The decision would play a very significant role in the race.

Still driving the #2 Brawner/Ford, Andretti claimed the pole with Jim Malloy and A.J. Foyt right behind, followed by Lloyd Ruby and Art Pollard. Art was driving the #40 Gerhardt/Offy this weekend.

A full report on the event appeared in the October 1969 issue of *Auto Racing Magazine*, written by Indianapolis Motor Speedway Historian Donald Davidson:

Art Pollard of Medford, Oregon joined a select group of forty men when he won the Milwaukee 150-mile USAC National Championship race on the weekend following the Indianapolis 500.

Art's victory made it three in a row for the STP-sponsored cars headed by STP President Anthony Granatelli. But Pollard did not win in the car he qualified. Starting fifth in the 24-car starting field, the driveshaft in Art's STP Oil Treatment Special broke as he was entering the backstretch from the second turn on the first lap. He went into a spin and started a chain reaction accident that was to eliminate 10 cars.

Gary Bettenhausen figured in one of the most spectacular accidents ever witnessed in a rear-engine machine. He ran over the wheel of another car and flipped over four times, landing upside down.

Miraculously, he escaped without injury, which must certainly serve as a tribute to the safety features that are required on USAC Championship cars.

The accident brought out the red flag to halt the race until the track could be cleared of wrecked cars. During this time, it was decided that Pollard should take over the STP car that had been qualified by Greg Weld.

Since the accident had occurred before a single lap had been run, a complete restart was called for. The front two rows, consisting of Indy winner Mario Andretti and Jim Malloy in row one and A.J. Foyt and Lloyd Ruby in row two, lined up as they had originally qualified and, as expected, Andretti led at the start.

On the seventh lap boy Foyt and his teammate, Roger McCluskey, moved by Malloy who was driving the Vel's Parnelli Jones Ford Special that Al Unser was to have driven at Indianapolis prior to his motorcycling accident in May.

On lap 12 McCluskey edged around Foyt and set after the front running Andretti. Ruby pulled into the pits with a fire in his engine compartment. It was extinguished with little damage, but "Rube" was done for the day. McCluskey began to close in on Andretti and was running less than two seconds back at one point.

In the meantime, Pollard, who had to start last since he had taken over the other car for the restart, was moving up. By the 43rd lap he had passed Mike Mosley and was running fifth. McCluskey made a quick stop for fuel, allowing Foyt to regain second spot. Pollard was right on his tail and at 65 laps had bounced Foyt back to third again.

Johnny Rutherford, driving an excellent race, moved by his fellow Texan 12 laps later, but Foyt made a battle out of it and got third spot back.

On the 87th lap Andretti's engine began to sound sick and Pollard closed in fast. On the 89th lap Pollard passed his teammate and assumed the lead. Andretti kept on going but dropped behind first Foyt, then McCluskey. On the 101st lap Pollard lapped Andretti, but then Andretti began to pick up speed and seemed to have solved any problems he had had.

Both McCluskey and Foyt stopped for fuel but Roger stalled and could not be restarted. Andretti moved up as Foyt made his stop and ran third behind Pollard and Rutherford. Mario caught John, and on the 139th lap, just 11 laps from the finish, Mario moved back into second. Rutherford began to slow, and it was determined that he was low on fuel.

Andretti soon had the same problem and both of them coasted slowly into the pits. Andretti's car stalled. They restarted it, but the engine died again and this time it was for good. Rutherford got restarted but Foyt, Malloy and Bud Tinglestad had slipped by. Malloy caught Foyt in the closing stages and took second place. With Andretti stalled in the pits, Pollard continued the final laps at a reduced pace, for he too was low on fuel and the engine was sputtering in the turns.

Pollard made it to the finish line to win the 150-mile race at a record average speed of 112.157 mph.

Andretti finished seventh but remained far ahead in the USAC Championship point standings with 1490 against the 895 earned by Bobby Unser, the defending Champion. Unser was one of the people who were eliminated on the opening lap and therefore went pointless on this day.

Milwaukee Trophy Presentation.

Art savoring his first Championship Car victory with car owner Andy Granatelli.

The STP team was now on a roll with three consecutive wins. Andy Granatelli must have been in seventh heaven by now! Would this steamroller be slowed at the next race, on June 15th, at Langhorne, Pennsylvania?

Andretti set the pace during qualifying and landed on the pole with a speed of 124.649. Bobby Unser would start on the outside of the front row. Art started sixth in his Gerhardt/Offy. Just 28 laps into the race, with Bobby Unser leading, rain began to fall and the race was called. The restart would have to wait until the following weekend.

One week later, the continuance of the race became a duel between Andretti and Bobby Unser, with Unser's Eagle/Ford eventually leading the final 62 laps to the checkered flag. In the meantime, Art drove a terrific race by staying competitive and earning a second-place finish. His Offy was the only other car to complete all 150 laps. Teammate Andretti finished fifth. Though it took two weekends to run, the outcome was that Art earned 240 points and $6,395 in purse money.

Art did not compete in the series' annual stop at the challenging Pikes Peak Hillclimb (won by Mario Andretti in an STP Chevy sprint car for Grant King). The next race was to be on the road course at Continental Divide Raceway. After further development, it was time to try out the new Lotus/Plymouth for Art. Andretti continued in Granatelli's trusty Brawner/Ford.

Nineteen cars made up the field behind pole sitter Dan Gurney and second fastest Andretti. Art qualified a commendable sixth, but it was to be a very short race when his brakes failed after only two laps. Andretti made it to the 33rd lap when an oil leak ended his run. Gordon Johncock's Eagle/Ford was the winner while Gurney finished second, one lap behind.

The next oval track race was at Trenton on July 19th, but it turned out to be a no-go for Art's Gerhardt/Offy. He did not qualify for the race due to a broken driveshaft. On the other hand, Andretti was on a terror and recorded another win in Granatelli's Brawner/Ford.

On July 27th, another pair of heat races were on tap at the road course at Indianapolis Raceway Park. Back in the #57 Gerhardt/Plymouth, Art qualified 14th for the first heat, but finished 25th when a U-joint failed after just ten laps. The win went to Gurney's Eagle/Ford. The second heat wasn't much better for Art, as the car bottomed out on the 16th lap and he finished 16th. Peter Revson grabbed the victory in the Brabham/Repco for owner Jack Brabham. Andretti finished second.

It was now mid-August of 1969 and the series returned to one of its most popular paved tracks at the Milwaukee Mile. Thirty-one cars were entered and 26 made the field. Granatelli entered four cars for this contest: Andretti (Brawner/Ford); Pollard (Gerhardt/Offy); Joe Leonard (Gerhardt/Offy); and Jim Malloy, who would be driving the Lotus/Plymouth.
Andretti qualified in the second slot behind Al Unser while Art's #57 would start tenth. Joe Leonard turned the third fastest time and Jim Malloy would start 19th. Malloy wrecked on lap two of the race and was quickly out of the running. Al Unser led all but 13 laps to take the win. Andretti's car came home fourth and Art finished sixth, five laps down. Leonard was credited with 20th after losing power on the 73rd lap. Art picked up 160 driver points and $2,039 of the total purse.

After a dirt track weekend at the Illinois State Fairgrounds (Art didn't race), the Champ Cars would make their one and only appearance on August 24th at the new facility at Dover Downs Raceway in Dover, Delaware. Opened in 1969, Dover Downs was a dual-purpose facility that accommodated both horse racing and motorsports events. The very first racing event on the one-mile asphalt, high-banked oval occurred on July 6th. It was the NASCAR Mason-Dixon 300 that was won by Richard Petty. The track was nicknamed 'The Monster Mile'.

Granatelli's entries for the Delaware 200 were the same as at the previous race in Milwaukee. The one exception was that Pollard and Malloy would now each be driving a Gerhardt/Plymouth. Art would be in the #57 and Jim was driving the #20.

Bobby Unser's Eagle/Offy secured the pole with an amazing speed of 155.259 mph. Roger McCluskey's Coyote/Ford, owned by A.J. Foyt, was second quickest and was followed by Andretti. Art grabbed the tenth starting position, just in front of Leonard and Malloy. Unable to qualify was veteran Lloyd Ruby, who received facial burns when his Offy crashed during practice and the Texas driver was hospitalized.

From the green flag, McCluskey led until lap 34 when he was passed by Andretti, who would point the way for the next 19 laps. Driving for car owner Parnelli Jones, Al Unser's Lola/Ford then shot to the front until he lost a wheel in the fourth turn and made contact with the guardrail on lap 128. On the 137th lap, Andretti made contact with another car and wound up against the infield fence.

Art stayed in the front mix throughout the race and narrowly avoided both the Unser and Andretti incidents. He inherited the lead after Unser was forced out. The Plymouth stock-block engine was finally showing its full potential, enabling Art to stay ahead of

Gordon Johncock's Gerhardt/Offy. Art led the remaining 72 laps for his second checkered flag of the season!

At left is Art's Dover-winning Gerhardt/Plymouth on display at the Speedway Motors Museum of American Speed in Lincoln, Nebraska. At right is a full-page Champion Spark Plug advertisement announcing Art's win.

(Speedway Motors Museum of American Speed and Pollard Family Collection)

Though only ten cars were running at the end, it was a terrific victory for Art, Granatelli, and Plymouth. The victory was worth 400 championship points and earnings of $10,690. Historically, this would be the only Championship Car race that a Plymouth-powered car would ever win. An *Associated Press* report described the day:

Back in February, Pete Hutchinson, a Harvard arts graduate, started a crash program to build a Plymouth stock block engine for the United States Auto Club's championship racing circuit. The aim was to get Plymouth into last May's Indianapolis 500. That goal failed, but Hutchinson's development program paid off Sunday when veteran Art Pollard drove the experimental car to victory in a 200-mile race at Dover Downs.

It was Plymouth's first victory ever in a category outside of stock cars, and it was Pollard's second victory of the year. He completed the 200-mile trip over the highly banked Dover oval in 1:36.01 for an average speed of 122.261 miles per hour.

The race, witnessed by 17,000, was marred by three spectacular wrecks plus another that occurred during a morning practice session. Two drivers, veteran Lloyd Ruby and Wally Dallenbach, were hospitalized. Ruby, 41, was burned about the face when his Turbocharged Offenhauser crashed during practice. Dallenbach, 33, was cut and burned about the face when his car hit the wall at the 114th mile of the race.

Al Unser was leading the race when he lost a wheel in the fourth turn and crashed into the guard rail. Moments later, Mario Andretti collided with another car on the backstretch and wound up against the infield fence. Neither he nor Unser was injured.

Pollard narrowly missed being involved in both the Unser and Andretti mishaps. Second place went to Gordon Johncock, while Roger McCluskey was third, Mike Mosley fourth, Gary Bettenhausen fifth, Rick Muther sixth and Johnny Rutherford seventh.

The next race for Art was in early September on the one-mile dirt track at the Indiana State Fairgrounds – the Hoosier Hundred. The Granatelli team consisted of Andretti driving a Kuzma/Offy, along with Pollard and Greg Weld, both in a King/Plymouth. Qualifying found Weld earning the pole with a speed of 104,046 mph, followed by Andretti in second and Art third quickest.

Following the start of the race, Art lasted only five laps before retiring due to handling issues. Andretti led the field until lap 54 when Foyt passed for the lead in his Meskowski/Ford. A.J. then led all the way to the checkered flag. Weld crossed the line in fifth place, just ahead of Andretti.

September 14th was another visit to the road course for two heat races at Brainerd International Raceway in Minnesota. The Granatelli entries were Andretti, Pollard, and noted road racer Sam Posey, each in a Lotus/Plymouth. The day's first 34-lap heat was won by Johncock in an Eagle/Ford, and Andretti finished fourth. Neither Pollard nor Posey fared well and didn't finish a single lap due to mechanical issues, which kept them from running in the second heat. Dan Gurney won that race, ahead of Johncock and Andretti.

The Trenton 300 was next up on the schedule, with 34 cars entered. Andretti qualified the Brawner/Ford sixth, Art qualified 11th in a Gerhardt/Offy, and the third STP machine was the Lotus/Plymouth in the hands of Malloy, who qualified 14th. Through much of the race, the lead bounced around between Bobby and Al Unser, Foyt, and Dallenbach. Finally, Andretti drove into the lead on lap 142 and led the remaining 200-lap distance to earn another victory for the season. Art completed only 136 laps but was running at the finish for the 14th spot. Malloy's car was also on the track at the finish to record 18th place, though credited with just 63 laps.

In late September, there was one more scheduled dirt track race in Sacramento – the Golden State 100 – for Andretti, Pollard and Weld from the Granatelli stable. Weld qualified the #60 King/Plymouth on the pole while Andretti would run the #2 Kuzma/Offy from third on the grid, and Pollard would steer the #80 King/Plymouth from the fifth position. Al Unser led all 100 laps for the win in his King/Ford. Weld finished 12th after completing 94 laps. Pollard came home 14th, ten laps down to the leaders. Andretti lost oil pressure after 83 laps for a 15th place finish.

The last road race for the Championship Car year was on October 19th at Seattle International Raceway in Kent, Washington, which was a challenging 2.2-mile course featuring elevation changes. This was also the first-ever Champ Car race held in the rain.

In qualifying, Dan Gurney won the pole with his Eagle/Ford. Andretti would share the front row with his Brawner/Ford. The STP Lotus/Plymouths were represented by Sam Posey (qualifying ninth) and Art Pollard (qualifying 14th) in the 19-car field for heat one. Art finished next-to-last after a crash on the seventh lap. Andretti scored another win by leading all 45 laps, and Posey finished a lap behind in the eighth position.

With his #57 car repaired in time for the second heat race of the afternoon, Art completed 40 laps of the 45-lapper before he spun off-course to finish 12th overall. This time around, it was Al Unser's Lola/Ford that led all the laps to pick up the win. Andretti and Posey finished second and third, on the same lap as Unser.

The 1969 season was drawing to a close with just two races to go: Phoenix and Riverside. In the Bobby Ball 200 on November 15th, Granatelli drivers were Andretti in the Ford, Pollard driving the Offy, and Malloy in the Plymouth. Their starting positions were second (Andretti), eighth (Malloy), and 14th (Pollard). Al Unser was on the pole and led all but seven of the 115 race laps. Andretti and Bobby Unser made contact on the 73rd lap and both were eliminated. Art's car lost a right-front wheel on the 90th lap and he finished 19th. Jim Malloy had the best run of the day for Granatelli with an eighth-place finish.

The final race of the season on the road course in Riverside, California drew 40 entries, but ten cars either withdrew or failed to qualify. Among those drivers that didn't make the field were Foyt, Dallenbach, Bettenhausen, and Dick Simon.

By now, Andretti had already locked up the driver's championship by a wide margin over the Unser brothers. Even so, he qualified his Brawner/Hawk quickest in the 30-car field. The second fastest of the STP team was George Follmer in the #40 Lotus/Plymouth, followed by Sam Posey's #20 Lotus/Plymouth in tenth and Art's #57 Gerhardt/Plymouth in 15th.

Once the green flag fell, much of the race was a three-way dice involving Gurney, Andretti, and Mark Donohue. Posey's car lasted only seven laps when his engine went sour and he was credited with a 25th place finish at the end. Pollard completed 92 laps but was running at the checkered flag and came home in 16th. Follmer was also on the track at the finish after being scored with 101 laps and 14th place. Andretti took the lead for good for the final four laps to record his ninth victory of the season.

It was a stand-out year for Andy Granatelli and Mario Andretti. Not only did they both accomplish a victory at the Indy 500, but Andretti won the driver's championship a full 2,245 points ahead of second-place finisher Al Unser.

Mario Andretti and Art Pollard having a discussion.

1969 turned out to be Art Pollard's most successful season in his relatively short career in the USAC Championship Car Series. He competed in 19 of the 24 races on the schedule, winning two of them. He recorded three top-five and four top-ten results, leading a total of 133 laps. In season-end standings, Art placed 12th overall in a total field of 72 drivers who recorded points.

In a wonderful article published in the August 1969 issue of *Auto Racing Magazine*, Andy Granatelli spoke personally about Art:

Art Pollard – As I See Him

He's content only when he's running up front with the leaders.

"Life begins at 40" may be a trite, time-worn expression, but it fits race driver Art Pollard to a "T". At a time when most professional athletes have retired, or are thinking about it, this native of Medford, Oregon was just getting started. Getting started, that is, in big-time racing. Pollard was 40 on May 5, 1967. Twenty-five days later he started in his first Indianapolis 500-mile race.

Art, a graduate of the hardtops and the modifieds in his native Oregon, actually went to Indianapolis first in 1966 – when he was only 39. He qualified a rear-engined Offenhauser car at 157.985 mph but was bumped on the final day of qualifying by Ronnie Duman. He did drive in seven Championship races that season and his best finish was a fourth in the Milwaukee 100. He was 23rd in the National Championship standings.

The next year things were different. He qualified a turbocharged Offenhauser again, but this time at 163.897. He's not a bit superstitious, this fellow, because his 13th starting position didn't faze him. He was running third when he made his first pit stop and looked like somebody the front-runners would have to reckon with. But a spin on the northwest curve and a penalty lap for a push to restart dropped him to an eighth-place finish.

This 40-year-old rookie proved to be a real comer, not just an over-age (for race driving) newcomer who was looking for some new kicks. Pollard finished 11th in the standings, even though he missed eight races because of a broken leg suffered during a tire testing program at Trenton, New Jersey.

He qualified one of the celebrated STP-Turbocars in 11th spot in 1968 at Indianapolis, despite almost zero time at practice in the car. He raced his way to fourth place by the midpoint of the Memorial Day classis and held fourth until a tiny fuel pump drive shaft failed just a few laps from the finish. When the car quit, he was within shooting distance of third-place Mel Kenyon and second-place Dan Gurney.

Pollard drove nearly every race on the United States Auto Club's Championship Trail in 1968, most of them in the STP-Turbocar. Hard luck dogged him nearly everywhere he went. He led the first Milwaukee race until he was black-flagged. His brakes failed at Castle Rock, Colorado, and he was running in contention at the time too. At Milwaukee it appeared that it was Pollard's and the Turbocar's day. He won pole position for the 200-miler and won that coveted spot with a new track record speed. Pollard jumped ahead of the field and for a time it looked like a runaway. Then the back luck hit – brakes again. He led it for the first 135 miles on the State Fair Park one-mile asphalt oval.

Then came Trenton. He qualified fourth and ran second for a time, but suspension problems knocked him out of the park that day. He and Mario Andretti shared a new track record at Phoenix and Art led the race for 45 laps. It was a new problem this time. A universal joint gave away.

He qualified 11th at Riverside, the concluding Championship race of the season – run on the famed California road course. Pollard whipped the Turbocar into third spot and was running strongly in that spot until Andretti in a sister Turbocar smashed into his Turbocar and put him out of the race.

When it came time for the 1969 season, Art Pollard was the first driver chosen for the STP team. He was picked to drive the STP-Super Wedge powered by a Plymouth engine, a novel experiment in major league racing. The chassis was basically the same one he drove in 1968 when it was powered by a turbine but now adapted, naturally, for the Plymouth engine. But he was willing to take the chance. He knew that the chassis design and the great super-wedge body design would contribute much to his car's chances.

Art Pollard could best be described as steady, cool and thoughtful. He neither looks like nor drives anything like his 42 years might indicate. He's a charger when the right time comes. Pollard is a stocky 5 feet, 11.5 inches tall. He weighs 195 and has dark, curly hair, free of the gray which sometimes slips in at his age. How has he kept his youth? "Maybe it's because I don't have too many tough miles on me," he says with that typical Pollard grin. "I spent a lot of my racing life bashing around in the Pacific Northwest where you don't race very dangerously. You don't earn much money, but you do have a lot of fun.

Pollard, who has been married 23 years to his wife, Claudine, and has a son, Mike, 21 and a daughter, Judy, 19, still has time to have fun even though he spends a full year racing. Off the track he is an expert water skier and bowler (with a 170 average).

I'm sure he'll agree that the famous ride in 1968 at the Speedway in the STP-Turbocar really catapulted him to fame. When he took his first ride in it, one headline writer wrote: "Ride in turbine really turns Pollard on." "It was really impressive," he said after his first ride in the Turbocar. "It's just like driving a passenger car." Pollard impressed more than himself when he took the famous No. 40 for a first ride around at 163.5 mph. "It's amazing," he said. "It's really super."

What made the turbine so competitive? "It just makes driving at Indianapolis easier. Actually, it isn't the turbine but the four-wheel drive and the engineering and the chassis. It's different to drive too. You have to anticipate the throttle. There's a lag there. It's probably more psychological because of the instant response with a gas engine. You have to get on the turbine much sooner. If you wait too long, you bog down."

But the rules-makers outlawed all that. Actually, they cut down the "formula" for turbine engines to the point that it was not feasible to run them at Indianapolis or on the Championship Trail. That's why we switched to Plymouth, hoping that we can develop a winning combination before this season is over. By the way, it should be noted, in view of Pollard's remarks, that the four-wheel drive is going by the boards too after this season.

Pollard drives dirt cars and stock cars with the same kind of determination that he exhibits at Indianapolis and on the Championship Trail. He's a proud man who hates to run at the rear of any racing pack. He hadn't too much experience on the dirt, I remember, when he qualified for the Hoosier Hundred, a rich race on the Indianapolis Fairgrounds track. He never was in contention for first or second or third, but he was out there working himself and his car like crazy. Pollard was trying desperately to get around another car and into ninth place. It was a show race fans will never forget. You would have thought he was racing for the $25,000 first prize.

"Every lap was an adventure," he said later after the long grind. I lost my brakes after sixty laps or so and it was all over then. I just had to stroke it. Boy, is it galling to sit back there at the rear of the pack. I like to run with the leaders and be competitive. That's the only way."

His own summation is about the way I'd describe him as a race driver – he's content only when he's running up front with the leaders. He's been that way, I guess, since he first started driving hardtops in Roseburg, Oregon in 1955. After only two years of driving, he won his first title, the local hardtop championship. Art moved up to modifieds in 1959 and won the Oregon championship. Then it was super-modifieds. He won the Northwest title in 1960 and 1961. Sprint cars were next. He won every race he was able to finish in 1962.

He won many big modifieds and super-modified races throughout the West in those years. But he thinks winning the Western States Modified title at Fresno, California in 1961 and winning at least two super-modified races in eight cities throughout the Western States in 1961 and 1962 were the highlights of his early career.

Pollard is one driver who wasn't in a particular hurry to get to Indianapolis. He kept driving in so-called minor league races in the West until 1965 when he got his first break on the Championship Trail. His first Championship race was in the Milwaukee 200 in 1965. He finished an amazing fifth at Trenton later that season and by then was on his way.

Art is more than a race driver. A couple of years ago he was hired to go out across the United States to "preach" safe driving to high school kids. He was one of a team of seven or eight race drivers who traveled from city to city appearing at high school assemblies. They'd show a movie which dealt principally with race driving at Indianapolis, but which also told a story about good highway driving habits. He was an instant hit with the kids. He spoke their language, and because he was a "500" driver they knew that he knew what he was talking about.

Art Pollard is a rare exception in many ways. He can be both tough and gentle. He can dress as fancy as any "city slicker," but at work, in the pits or in a race car, he's as tough as nails and isn't interested in impressing anyone unless it's with some super speed on the racetrack.

Does life really begin at 40? It did for Art Pollard.

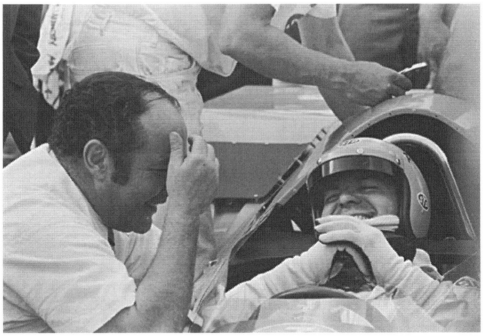

At the end of the year, Art parted ways with Granatelli. It was time to look ahead and plan for the upcoming season, which was right around the corner. An opportunity loomed for Art to become a partner in a new team that could make its debut at the 1970 Indianapolis 500.

TWENTY - TWO

The Pollard Car Wash Team

It would be an entirely new endeavor for Art in preparation for the 1970 Championship Car season. After several years being the 'hired-gun' for other team owners, he partnered with John Newcomer, President of Race-Go, Inc., of Indianapolis to form a new team. A press release dated March 13th, 1970 described the optimistic business plan:

"A team of three red, white and blue racing cars will be entered in the 1970 Indianapolis 500-Mile Race Classic by the Art Pollard Car Wash Systems, Inc. 'Art Pollard of Medford, Oregon, will be our number one driver and our first area of responsibility will rest with having Art in the race. Once Art has qualified, we will then seek and additional driver,' Newcomer said.

The cars are being built by Grant King, and Grant will also serve as the Chief Mechanic. King has been building race cars for over twenty years. The cars will be powered by a new turbocharged Offenhauser engine with an anticipated horsepower of 800.

'Motor racing will truly be the sport of the seventies as football was the sport of the sixties. Sponsoring the racing team, headed by Art with Grant as Chief Mechanic, will really put Art Pollard Car Wash Systems on the racing map. Art was most successful last year and with the new innovations we have built into our cars for 1970, I am confident that we will have a very good year.'

This marks the first time in racing history that a car wash equipment manufacturer has sponsored a racing car on the USAC Championship Trail, and I believe it is indicative of the exposure that racing will receive in 1970,' Newcomer told the gathering of Mid-Western press representatives at the Essex House Hotel.

Race-Go, Inc., who purchased the cars from Grant King, was organized only two months ago by Newcomer, Al Warne, President of Acme Builders of Indianapolis, and Roger Isch of Fort Wayne, Indiana."

Not much is known about John Newcomer today, or whether he had any motorsports experience prior to linking up with Art and the other partners. Another press release issued about the same time merely stated:

"Newcomer has been associated with various aspects of the sport for the past several years and is currently engaged in investment activities. Newcomer is from Tucson, Arizona and now resides in Indianapolis."

John Newcomer and Art with the new Kingfish/Offy, designed and built by Grant King. The Race-Go partnership was brief.

In a handwritten note to his cousin Harvel in early March of 1970, Art wrote: "Thought I would mail you our press release. It's going to be a pretty good team this year. My bosses are making me a partner in the wash business it seems. I've got my same crew as last year so I'm pretty happy. We open at Phoenix on the 28th of this month. You can catch it live on TV. You'll have to check your local TV listings for the station. The first seven races will be televised live. Tell the kids and Mary Lou 'Hi' and I hope to see you after Phoenix."

As Art mentioned, the first race of the new season was the Jimmy Bryan 150 at Phoenix. Qualifying found the Granatelli/Andretti/STP team picking up where they left off at the end of 1969 by putting the #1 Brawner/Ford on the pole. Al Unser's Colt/Ford, wearing its new 'Johnny Lightning 500' sponsorship colors, would share the front row. Bobby Unser and Lloyd Ruby qualified for the second row, and Art's run in the #10 Pollard Car Wash Gerhardt/Offy earned a seventh place starting position.

The talk in the paddock was that the car to beat belonged to Al Unser, who proved everyone correct by passing Andretti for the lead and dominating the last 136 laps to grab the first checkered flag of the season. In the early stages of the race, there was a multi-car wreck on the front straight when Nick Dioguardi spun. In the melee, Gordon Johncock's car caught fire and the race was red flagged for 30 minutes to clear the mess. Fortunately, no drivers were injured.

After the restart and through the middle stretch of the race, the most exciting battle was for second place, involving Andretti, Pollard, and Bobby Unser. Andretti dove into the pits with a dropped valve and subsequently dropped out of the race on lap 78. That moved Art into second place, but still a long way behind Al Unser. By now, Lloyd Ruby had moved up behind Bobby Unser, and the battle continued.

Art's fine drive in his new car came to an end on lap 104 when his turbocharger let go as he was approaching the first turn. He moved into the upper groove, did a slow spin coming into turn two, but managed to keep the car off the outside wall. Bobby Unser and Ruby went on to finish second and third while Art was credited with an 11th place finish and earned 30 driver points.

The next race, April 4th, was on the road course at Sears Point Raceway in Sonoma, California. For reasons unknown, the Pollard Car Wash team did not field an entry. The race was won by Dan Gurney, ahead of Mario Andretti and Al Unser.

Late in April, Pollard's team took two cars to New Jersey for the Trenton 200, with the second car assigned to driver Greg Weld.

Weld's racing background was in USAC sprint cars. In 1963, he won the prestigious Knoxville Nationals, and in 1967 was the Sprint Car Series National Champion. His years in the Championship Car series were from 1965 through 1972, with 36 career starts. Weld was inducted into the National Sprint Car Hall of Fame in 1998. He also founded Weld Wheel Industries, which produced forged alloy wheels for both race and street cars. In 2008, Greg Weld passed away due to a heart attack at age 64.

At Trenton, Art qualified the #10 Pollard Car Wash Kingfish/Offy 12th, while Weld positioned his #93 Gerhardt/Offy in tenth. It would be a short race for both cars as Art dropped out after 22 laps with ignition problems and Weld's day ended on lap 48 with a blown engine. Their combined earnings only came to $2,105. Lloyd Ruby won the race in a Laycock/Offy.

SHOWING THE area in the side of the race car where fuel cells are installed to veteran driver Art Pollard is Firestone Fuel Cell representative Ed Edmonds. Pollard's car has a cell on each side of the driver and carries 75 gallons of fuel. The tough, rubberized fuel cells prevent fuel spillage and fires in the event of an accident.

end

PR-70-171

FIRESTONE NEWS SERVICE

And now, the Silver Anniversary of the Indianapolis 500 would consume the month of May for the Pollard Car Wash System team. The driver and car combination would be the same as it was at Trenton: Art in the #10 Kingfish/Offy and Weld in the #93 Gerhardt/Offy. In the days leading up to the first qualifying weekend, the favorite for both the pole and the race was Al Unser's Johnny Lightning 500 special, which had been on a roll.

Art cruising through the garage area at Indianapolis in the Grant King-built Kingfish/Offy.

On Pole Day, Al Unser answered with a four-lap average of 170.221 mph and earned the top spot in the field in the Colt/Ford entered by Vel Miletich. Johnny Rutherford and A.J. Foyt would share the front row. Before rain shortened the day's runs, Pollard's Kingfish/Offy performed very well. He qualified sixth fastest and would start the '500' outside of row two, alongside Roger McCluskey and Mark Donohue. On another day, Weld made the field in his Gerhardt/Offy and would start 28th.

The Race-Go Team at the 1970 Indianapolis 500 – Art Pollard's #10 Kingfish/Offy and Greg Weld's #93 Gerhardt/Offy.

(IMS photos)

On race day, rain delayed the start for a bit, but the track soon dried and the field got underway for the parade and pace laps. As the cars were coming off Turn Four for the green flag, a radius rod on Jim Malloy's racer (starting from the ninth position) broke and sent him spinning. The other drivers skillfully avoided Malloy's car, but the incident caused a short red flag.

Upon the restart, Rutherford shot into the lead but was quickly passed by Al Unser. Greg Weld's machine fell out after just 12 laps because of a broken piston. During the ensuing laps, Art worked his way up to the third position and was charging hard, but then a piston in his car let go on the main straight, cutting short his hopes for a good finish. Al Unser went on to win the first of the four victories he would record at the Brickyard, with Donohue finishing second and Gurney third.

It was a disappointing month for the Pollard Car Wash team, with Art finishing 30th and Weld 32nd. Their combined earnings were just $28,000. In 1970, the cost of a competitive Champ Car was about $50,000, or the equivalent of about $311,500 in today's world.

Al Unser Sr. earned his first Indy 500 victory in 1970 driving a Colt/Ford – known as the 'Johnny Lightning Special.' Al would go on to score three more victories in the 500 during his long racing career.

(IMS photo)

One week after Indy was the Rex Mays Classic at Milwaukee. It was just a one-car effort for Art and his team. He qualified the Kingfish/Offy 12th fastest while Andretti won the pole in the STP-sponsored McNamara/Ford for Andy Granatelli. Art's car lasted 119 laps until an oil leak took him out of the running for an 18th place finish. Now a teammate to Al Unser, Joe Leonard's Colt/Ford was the race winner.

Soon after, the Pollard Car Wash Team disbanded and the partners went their separate ways. Art would finish out the 1970 season driving for two other car owners.

June 28th featured another road course at Continental Divide Raceway in Colorado. For this event, Art was driving the #21 Vollstedt/Ford, which qualified 21st in the 23-car field. He managed to get in only two race laps when the car overheated. Mario Andretti edged out Swede Savage for the win.

TWENTY-THREE

1970 - The Second Half

Following the demise of the Pollard Car Wash System Team, Art began driving for Dayton, Ohio steel foundry executive George Walther. His son was racer David 'Salt' Walther, who over the years competed in the USAC, CART, and NASCAR series.

Salt Walther competed from 1970 through 1981 with 64 combined career starts, including the Indy 500 from 1972 - 1976, and again in 1978 and 1979. He is best known for his fiery crash at Indy in 1973 when, upon the start, his race car was launched into the air, spewing 80 gallons of fuel as it sailed upside-down into the fence along the front stretch. The car burst into flames and the aftermath claimed eleven race cars and injured numerous spectators.

Walther was badly burned over much of his body and suffered several broken bones. He was given a five percent chance to live. Fortunately, he survived to race again but always concealed left-hand finger injuries by wearing a black glove. Following his racing career, Walther had a troubled life. He died in 2012 at the age of 65.

Art Pollard's first drive for the Walther Team came on the Fourth of July on the fast, D-shaped two-mile oval of Michigan International Speedway. In qualifying, Art was 15th fastest in Walther's #77 Morris/Ford. George Morris was a respected ex-driver and mechanic who had previously been involved with Ted Halibrand in building the Shrike Champ Car.

During the race, tire wear appeared to be an issue. Number two qualifier Mario Andretti had a tire failure nine laps into the race. Then Al Unser, who started fourth, had the same problem on the 28th lap. Neither car continued. It became Art's turn with tire ills on lap 50, which forced him out of the running with a 17th place finish. Pole sitter Gary Bettenhausen drove to victory in the Thermo King Gerhardt/Offy for Fred Gerhardt.

Art sat out the next two races, and then returned to the cockpit on August 23rd at Milwaukee for the Tony Bettenhausen 200. He qualified Walther's #77 Morris/Ford tenth in the field of 26 cars, completed 171 laps and was running at the finish to end up 11th. Al Unser was having a stellar season. From the pole, he led all 200 laps on his way to victory lane.

Next on the schedule was the inaugural California 500. In what was to become 'The Indianapolis 500 of the West', the new Ontario Motor Speedway (OMS) was constructed on an 800-acre parcel of land across from the Ontario International Airport, 40-miles east of downtown Los Angeles. The track was designed to be a replica of the Brickyard, but with a few differences: the surface was one lane wider and the two short chutes were banked, enabling OMS to offer slightly faster speeds than at Indy.

Built at a cost of about $25 million, the multi-purpose facility included an infield road course and a drag strip. OMS also pioneered a private "stadium club" with annual memberships and corporate suites. The track also featured crash-absorbent retaining walls and safety fencing, plus a computerized timing and scoring system that, in real-time, kept track of the race status.

The expansive Ontario Motor Speedway made its debut in 1970. It became known as 'The Indianapolis 500 of the West.'

Because this was to be the first-ever Championship Car race at the facility, it came as no surprise that a total of 40 cars were entered. Seven of those failed to qualify or were withdrawn. Art was driving a second car for Hayhoe Racing Enterprises. A developer of upscale country club and retirement communities, Jim Hayhoe had a lifelong interest in racing and attended his first Champ Car race in 1951. In his second attempt as a car owner at Indy in 1968, Ronnie Duman finished sixth in the Hayhoe Racing Enterprises Hayhoe/Offy. Over his many years as an entrant, Hayhoe's drivers also included Roger McCluskey, Bruce Walkup, and Jimmy Vasser.

The car that Art would be competing with was the #64 Quickick-sponsored Scorpion/Ford. His teammate would be McCluskey in the twin #11 car. The product of Clint Brawner and Jim McGee, the Scorpion was constructed at Brawner's shop in Phoenix, Arizona. A well-seasoned constructor and mechanic, Brawner had produced the car that Mario Andretti drove to win the Indy 500 in 1969, as well as that season's USAC championship. From 1965 through 1969, Andretti had amassed 27 wins in Brawner-designed cars.

For the 1970 race at the Brickyard, Brawner had obtained sponsorship from Hayhoe for his newly designed Scorpion. McCluskey qualified the car on the inside of the second row but logged only 62 laps of the race due to suspension failure. In the next race at Milwaukee, McCluskey drove the car to a second-place finish behind Joe Leonard. The Scorpion definitely had a winning potential!

In qualifying for the California 500, spectators were thrilled to witness popular Lloyd Ruby take the pole position in a Laycock/Offy. Dan Gurney and Johnny Rutherford would round out the front row. The Hayhoe team didn't do so well, as McCluskey would start the race in 24th and Pollard was way back in 32nd, sharing the last row with Carl Williams and Jim Hurtubise.

Harvel Pollard and his family lived not far from the Ontario Speedway, so it was convenient for them to visit with Art and watch the race in person. "After a practice session," says Harvel, "Art came up in the grandstands and gathers our whole family. We get in his Pontiac station wagon and he drives it out on the track for a lap, narrating all the way. We're going around the oval and he's telling us how fast the race cars would be going, talking his way through the turns. After one lap I thought we were coming into the pits, but Art said we were just getting up to speed, so let's take another lap. A station wagon full of kids going around the track! Art was always so good with kids."

In those days, youngsters were not allowed in the pits, and that included Harvel's sons Brad and Mark. On another occasion, Art said to the boys, "When I come around here in this station wagon, you guys are going to jump in the back seat and lie on the floor."

As Harvel recalls, "I'm sitting in Art's Pontiac along with Mario Andretti and one of the Unsers. We pull up and Andretti opens the back door, and the kids jump in and onto the floorboard. Andretti and I are sitting in the back and have our feet on the kids. Art drives into the pits like there was nothing up. As soon as we get to the garage area where his race car is parked, Art says to the boys, 'Now listen, when I come around and open that car door, you guys are going to see my race car. You run over and get in that car as fast as you can!'

Harvel continues, "So the door opens, and the boys jump out and run to Art's race car. He put helmets on the boys so they wouldn't be identified. They had a ball, and Art was lovin' it!"

Harvel's son Brad offered his recollection of the time. "I remember when they snuck my brother Mark and me into the pits by putting us on the back floorboard of Art's station wagon. Mario Andretti was sitting in the back seat and put his feet on us. Once inside the pit area, Art told us to get out of the car and run over to his race car, put on a helmet, and pretend we were race car drivers. Honestly, once I got into the car and put the helmet on, I thought, 'Oh, this is it for me! From that point on, all I wanted to do was be a race car driver."

In preparing for the race, the teams had several areas of concern – the southern California heat, strong winds, and fuel mileage. The Granatelli team installed extra-large radiators on the cars of Andretti and Follmer. They were planning a three pit stop fuel management strategy when most of the other teams estimated they would have to stop four times for fuel.

On race day, a crowd approaching 175,000 filled the grandstands for this new 200-lap event. Once underway the lead jumped back and forth for most of the race, but Al Unser's car appeared the strongest. In the meantime, Art worked his way to the front at a steady pace, aided by the fact that there was a lot of mechanical attrition amongst his competition. Art's teammate, Roger McCluskey, fell out after just 26 laps with a broken valve.

Nearing the final stages of the race, Andretti dropped out on lap 182 with engine problems. Four laps later, and with a commanding lead, the rear-end pinion gear on Al Unser's car broke, ending his hopes for a win. That moved NASCAR veteran Lee Roy Yarbrough, driving a Brabham/Offy, into the lead for five laps until his engine failed.

Art had worked his car into second place, and then to the lead on lap 192, but with a tire going down. He managed to hold off a charging Jim McElreath, driving a second Coyote/Ford for A.J. Foyt, for the next four laps. Art's failing tire proved too much of a handicap, enabling McElreath to make a late pass and drive to victory, two seconds ahead of Art.

The oldest driver in the field, Art Pollard had driven an inspiring race to finish second from his last row starting position. His effort earned 800 driver points and $74,900 in prize money for the team. Finishing third was Dick Simon's Vollstedt/Ford. There were just eight cars running at the end of 500 miles. "Art should have won that first race, but had a flat tire right at the end," Art's cousin Harvel recalls. "He had it won!"

Art did not compete in the next three races on the schedule, which were all dirt track events in Illinois, Indiana, and Missouri. On October 3rd, he was back with the Walther Team at the paved oval in Trenton, New Jersey. The winner that day was Al Unser, who led all but five laps in the race that was red flagged after 176 laps due to rain. Art's Morris/Ford started in the ninth position and finished sixth.

The final time Art would drive for Walther was at the annual Bobby Ball 150 at Phoenix in late November. This was the last race on the 1970 Champ Car schedule. He qualified the #77 car 15th but was the first one out of the race due to a dropped valve on lap 30. Road racing standout, Swede Savage, led just the last lap to earn the victory over Al Unser and Roger McCluskey.

In 18 races, Al Unser drove to victory ten times in dominating the season-long championship. He finished a full 2,870 points over his older brother Bobby. Jim McElreath was third in the overall standings. Art had a satisfying year while driving for several teams and finished eighth on the championship ladder. He drove in ten races and completed a total of 897 laps, with an earnings' total of $99,296.

As a footnote to Art's 1970 racing season, he drove in eight races in the USAC Stock Car Division under the Pollard Car Wash sponsorship. Using a Chevy Camaro, his best finishes were a second on the road course at Sears Point in California, and sixth place run on the half-mile oval in Kaukana, Wisconsin.

TWENTY - FOUR

Life Changes

In 1970, Art married a second time, to Patricia McFall. Pat grew up in Fowler, Indiana, but met Art while living in Lafayette. Pat did not know much about racing when they were first introduced. As she described, "A pilot friend and his family, that I had worked with previously as a flight attendant, invited me to a race at Indy. Afterward, someone had a party and we were introduced. I had no idea if Art was a driver, crew member, or simply a fan."

"We really were in-tune," described Pat. "Surprisingly, because of the difference in our age, you would not think that. But we really did think alike and just seemed to be in-tune with everything. You have an idea in the back of your mind that racing is a dangerous sport, but it's just like anything else in life," Pat commented. "If something bad is going to happen, it will happen to someone else."

"Art knew of the dangers, but he didn't dwell on them," Pat continued. "He had terribly fast reflexes. He was in the very high percentile. He worked out and went to the gym. I remember when we were in Denver for a race. We flew out on Granatelli's plane, and Andy had arranged a tour of the Air Force Academy in Colorado Springs. We got to the gym there, and Andy asked Art if he could make it up a climbing rope. Art said, 'Yeah, I think so.' He actually made it all the way up, just the way you're supposed to – with your legs out front and just using your forearms. When Art got back down, Andy said 'I would give a million bucks if I could have your body.'"

Art never hesitated to make Pat the main focus of his life, both in and out of the racing scene. As she noted, "I really loved the fact that, considering I was much younger, Art asked my advice as though I had lived as much life as he had. At one point he asked me to take over, saying 'You're going to be my business manager for all those speaking things.' He'd get calls all the time from people who wanted him to speak at this or do that. I'd have a hard time telling them how much it would cost, so we sat down and figured out what he should charge. He said, 'Now, you handle it.'"

Pat continued, "So when the first person called, I told them how much Art would charge for a speaking engagement. We talked about it for a little bit and then I got off the phone. Art asked who it was and then said, 'Oh, I want to do that one for free.' Because he liked people so much, business management wasn't his strong suit."

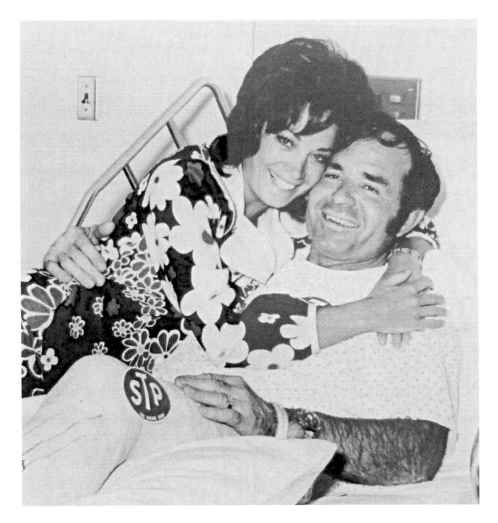

1972 – Pat Pollard visiting Art's hospital room after breaking his leg at Indy.

Pat remembered another situation in Art's hectic schedule. "In the month of May, we had about three days when we weren't speaking at a luncheon or dinner. Art was so good about making me a part of everything. One time, Andy Granatelli asked Art to fill in for him speaking – I think it was for the Golden Gophers in Minnesota. Art said he would, but they would have to provide a ticket for me. We became close friends with Neil Larson, a Minnesota car dealer, who made the arrangements for that engagement. Everywhere we went, we made friends."

Naturally, many of those friendships that Art and Pat maintained were with others within the close racing community, including Johnny and Betty Rutherford. "We had a really good friendship with Bill and Joyce Vukovich too," she said. "They lived in California and had just one son, Billy Junior. One time we were at their house for dinner, and when it came time to leave, I searched high and low, but could not find my purse anywhere. Sure enough, the next day Joyce called and said she'd found my purse. Billy had hidden it in a dresser drawer because he didn't want us to leave. He grew up to be such a nice, nice young man. He died in a racing accident and it just made me sick, because I knew what a special young man he had become. I just really thought the world of him. He was such a sweetheart."

Pat also recalled their times with the Unsers, though she and Art didn't run around much with them as much as they did with others. "I did get to know their wives pretty well," said Pat. "I remember one time – I think it was in Colorado-and Al's wife Wanda and I were sitting in the infield just watching the cars go around. Their little son ('Little Al') just started screaming and we figured out he was standing on an ant hill. He was only four or five years old, and ants had climbed down his pants. We jerked his pants down to get those ants out of there, and that was traumatic. I'd never before seen anyone having ants biting them. He was just screaming bloody murder!"

"Mel Kenyon was very caring about everybody," Pat reflected. "One time when Art crashed, he was kind of stuck in the car. It was during practice. Art asked Mel to come and tell me that he was okay. I wanted to chat about it, but Mel said he had to get back in his car, saying "I need to get back on the track.' Mel's just a very caring, great person."

As much as possible, Art and Pat traveled just about everywhere together. "So much of the time we'd have to fly," Pat said, "but we did enjoy just driving on road trips. I can remember when we and Clint Brawner [the legendary Indy crew chief] were towing a race car. He and Art sat in the back seat playing cards while I drove. I said, 'I can't believe you're letting me tow this expensive car'. They said, 'Well, you're in the hot seat too, and will suffer the same consequences.'"

"We had so much fun and were so compatible," says Pat. "Another thing that I had fun holding over Art was after he won his first Champ Car race. He was presented a bicycle along with a trophy. I thought I should have it, but he said he needed it to ride in the pits, but I could have the next one. Well, the next race he won, he was presented with a beautiful red Raleigh 'Chopper', and it was all mine! I was the envy of all the kids in the neighborhood when we went biking. I still have it, and now they are starting to reproduce my collector bike."

Pat continues: "That was the race with the photo of car owner Andy Granatelli with Art after the race. Art told the crowd that Andy was the only one that could French kiss him through the side hole in his helmet. They had a good relationship."

Along with everyone else that knew him, Pat knew how strongly Art cared for children everywhere. "How much he loved kids!" she noted. "He would just tease them and play with them all the time. Back in the day, we borrowed the Winnebago from the STP group and drove around Indiana. We picked up all my nieces and nephews and took them for the weekend. Of course, they thought they'd died and gone to heaven. Art loved doing that kind of stuff. It was just the best thing for him, and they loved him."

"I asked Art once about his life and he said he felt his life had been like cake, with good family, friends, and career – and that I was the icing on the cake. I've never forgotten that."

Pat has been married to her second husband, Dave Arslanian, for over forty years. They became a couple when Dave began his football head-coaching career at Snow College, a junior college in Ephraim, Utah. From there, he spent 16 years on the coaching staff at Weber State University in Ogden. For seven years he served as an assistant coach, and then was the Wildcat's head coach for the next nine seasons. In 1998, Arslanian became the head football coach at Utah State University for the next two years. Pat and Dave are now retired and live between their homes in Ogden, Utah and Goodyear, Arizona.

TWENTY – FIVE

Having Fun Away from The Track

As motorsports writer Robin Miller remembers, Art was an overall great organizer – whether it be small STP uniforms and stickers for the neighbor kids in Medford, escorting groups of children from the Larue C. Carter Hospital around the Indianapolis Speedway, or simply weekly poker nights for his friends and competitors at his Indianapolis apartment.

One event Art helped organize took place in-between the 1970 and 1971 racing seasons – a charity basketball game at the Indiana State Fairgrounds. (The first edition of this event took place in October of 1968). The fun-filled evening was described in the February 1971 edition of *Stock Car Racing Magazine* by writer Jim Kohlmeyer:

You Call This A Sport?

Some people call the sport basketball, but it certainly didn't look like it. One of the funniest things to ever happen to the roundball sport took place recently at the Indiana State Fairgrounds Coliseum here when the United States Auto Club 500 All-Stars fought the PERT (Press, Entertainment, Radio and Television) team to a deadlocked 170-170 tie game.

Following the trend of the two previous games, the third annual USAC Benevolent Fund Game that raised approximately $8,000, was just a basketball version of television's "Laugh-In" with the players doing about everything except playing basketball. The 170-170 score is somewhat misleading since both teams playing for a week wouldn't be able to score that many points. Only a handful of the players on both teams looked as if they had ever seen a basketball before in their lives.

Drivers Roger McCluskey, Johnny Rutherford, Wally Dallenbach, Johnny Parsons, Jr., Bill Puterbaugh, Art Pollard, Chuck Arnold, Steve Krisiloff, Al Loquasto, Cy Fairchild, Bruce Walkup, Ralph Liguori, Gary Bettenhausen and former two-time Indy 500 winner Rodger Ward represented the USAC All-Stars.

Handling the coaching duties for the drivers was USAC Technical Supervisor Frank DelRoy. Adding able assistance and beauty were water girls Linda Vaughn and June Cochran of the Hurst Performance Corporation.

Headlining the PERT team were former Harlem Globetrotter Hallie Bryant and former Indiana Pacer Jerry Harkness. Bryant and Harkness are both Indianapolis radio announcers. Coaching the PERT outfit was Wayne Fuson, sports editor of the Indianapolis News. Helping out as water girls were Union 76 Racestoppers Ann Romeo and Bonnie Leigh. Indianapolis 500 Chief Starter Pat Vidan and auto racing writer Dave Overpeck of the Indianapolis Star officiated the wild and wooly affair.

The driver-press game began in 1968 as a benefit for Bob Hurt, who was paralyzed while in a qualifying accident at the Indianapolis Motor Speedway that same year. The first game was a huge success so both the United States Auto Club and the Indiana Pacers decided to make it an annual affair with the money going to the USAC Benevolent Fund. Sid Collins, the voice of the Indianapolis 500, called the play-by-play action of the "Hee-Haw" contest. Providing the ultra-sharp uniforms for both teams was the J.B. Hinchman Company of Indianapolis.

1971 – The third annual USAC Benevolent Fund game. In the lower right photo, Art Pollard is going in for a lay up over two defenders. He was always a great athlete.

(Stock Car Racing Magazine photos by D. Lynn Justis)

At left is Art experiencing a different type of cockpit. Right photo shows that Art always had the time for a fan's autograph.

TWENTY - SIX

1971 - The Jim Gilmore Team

Jim Gilmore was the Michigan-based owner of television stations and car dealerships who, from an early age, was fascinated with mechanical projects. In his youth, he built miniature, motorized race cars that could achieve speeds upwards of 50 mph. He was also involved with the construction of the Gruff, the first radio-controlled model airplane.

Jim Gilmore's first visit to the Brickyard came in 1966, and he was immediately lovestruck with the racing bug. Over the next several years, Gilmore sponsored cars for Gordon Johncock. Later, Gilmore would become the noted sponsor for A.J. Foyt. Jim Gilmore was inducted into the Michigan Motor Sports Hall of Fame in 1989. Unfortunately, he was killed in an auto accident on December 31st, 2000.

Jim Gilmore

During the 1970 Champ Car season, Gilmore was impressed by the performance shown by the Clint Brawner/Art Pollard combination. He decided that he would sponsor the team's Scorpion/Ford in 1971 for the full season. While Art would be driving the 1970 car, a second new chassis was commissioned for driver Jimmy Caruthers. Caruthers hailed from Anaheim, California and his family name was synonymous with midget car racing. His father Doug and brother Danny were well-known competitors in that arena. Jimmy won the 1970 USAC National Midget Series Championship over Dave Strickland by a mere 12.48 points.

The 1971 season began with an international flair on February 28th. The two-heat event was on a 2.874-mile paved track in Rafaela, Argentina known as the Autodromo Ingeniero Juan R. Bascolo. Twenty-seven cars made the long journey south, but not the Gilmore team. Al Unser continued his winning ways by driving to victory in both heats. Lloyd Ruby finished second to Unser in both races.

Back on home turf in the United States, the second race of the season was the Jimmy Bryan 150 at Phoenix International Raceway. Art qualified his #8 Gilmore Racing

Scorpion/Ford eighth, but on the ninth lap of the race he spun in turn three and impacted the guardrail. The damage was too much to continue and he finished in the last position.

The Gilmore team traveled to New Jersey in late April for the Trenton 200 with a single car for Art. He qualified 18th in the field of 26 cars while Bobby Unser placed his #2 Olsonite Eagle/Offy on the pole. The 134-lap race was won by Mike Mosley in a Watson/Ford. Art drove a smart race to finish sixth, six laps down to the leader. The result gave him 160 points and $2,887 in winnings.

Indy 1971 – Art was unable to qualify the #8 Scorpion/Ford, so switched to the team's #64 car and placed it on the inside of the 11th and final row. He completed only 45 laps before a dropped valve put him out of the running.

The long month of May at Indianapolis ended in disappointment for Art and the Gilmore team, which had entered two cars. Art was unable to qualify the #8 Scorpion/Ford, so he switched to the #64 car and managed to place it on the inside of the 11th row. Once the race started, Art completed 45 laps before a dropped valve put him out of the running. The result was a 26th place finish. For the second year in a row, Al Unser was the victor over Peter Revson and A.J. Foyt.

1971 – Art Pollard, Mike Mosley, Al Unser Sr. and Cale Yarborough (laying down)

A 1971 magazine ad for Jim Gilmore Enterprises.

Things went better the following weekend at Milwaukee, where Art had driven to his first Champ Car win in 1969. For the first time, the Gilmore team placed two cars in the starting lineup: Art's #8 Scorpion/Ford would start 15th and Jimmy Caruthers would start the #64 car in 20th.

The race itself was dominated by a duel between Joe Leonard and Al Unser, each driving a Colt/Ford for owner Vel Miletich. At the checkered flag, it was Al Unser the winner once again with Leonard directly behind. Art had a nice run and finished in the fifth position, three laps down, but gained another 150 driver points. During the race, Caruthers spun but was able to continue and came across the finish line in 12th.

On the Fourth of July weekend, the series christened a new racing facility – Pocono Raceway – in Long Pond, Pennsylvania. The super-speedway was unique in that it was a three-turn track with long straights that enabled cars to reach a terminal speed upwards of 210 mph. The layout, which became known as 'The Tricky Triangle', was unfamiliar territory for all the drivers. The event weekend was sponsored by the Schaefer Beer Company and was viewed as the third track in Champ Car's 'Triple Crown' of racing, sharing that honor with Indianapolis and Ontario speedways. Thirty-three cars would make up the field.

During qualifying on the 'green' track, Mark Donohue won the pole with a speed of 172.393 mph in Roger Penske's Sunoco-sponsored McLaren/Offy. His front row neighbors were the Unser brothers. Art Pollard would start the Gilmore #8 car in 25th position while teammate Caruthers was further ahead in 20th. The field's average qualifying speed was 165.499 mph.

Art is watching practice at Pocono Raceway in 1971. In the race, his oil tank ruptured on lap 171, putting him out of the running.

(Gapinski Collection)

From the start, Donohue's car was clearly the quickest, but the big leads he built were interrupted due to pit stops and caution flag periods. In all, the race saw 16 lead changes. At one point, Art's car faltered and came to a rest on the inside shoulder at the beginning of the front straight. A wrecker was dispatched to pick up his disabled machine, but Art waved it off and pushed the car all the way back to the pits in order to stay in the race. It was a valiant effort and the car was eventually restarted, but on lap 171 his oil tank ruptured and the car was retired.

In the closing laps, Donohue was closely hounded by Joe Leonard's Colt/Ford. Leonard passed for the lead on the 191st lap but was re-passed by Donohue on lap 194 and the Penske car stayed ahead and captured the win by just two seconds over Leonard. There was a lot of attrition during the race and only 14 cars were running at the end, including Caruthers, who finished 12th for the Gilmore team. Art's final placing was 16th, with $6,199 in earnings but not driver points.

The second race in July was the Michigan 200 on the wide, high-banked tri-oval. Bobby Unser's Eagle/Offy took the pole with a speed of 193.444 mph. The next two fast qualifiers were Donohue and Andretti. The Gilmore team brought just one car, the #8 for Pollard, and he qualified 22nd in the 26-car field. Barring cautions, some were predicting this could be the fastest race in Champ Car history.

The early leader was Bobby Unser, but he was passed by Donohue on the 16th lap. Bobby Unser's engine failed on the 35th lap and Donohue drove to victory by leading a total of 75 laps. Billy Vukovich, Jr. drove an outstanding race in the Sugaripe Prune Brabham/Offy to finish second. It was another bad day for Art, as a crash on lap 54 left him in the 16th spot at the finale.

The ultra-competitive Milwaukee Mile hosted the next race on August 15th, the Tony Bettenhausen 200. Again, it was just Art's #8 that was entered by Gilmore Racing and he qualified in the eighth slot. Bobby Unser was experiencing a good season thus far. He started the race on the pole and led 191 laps in taking the win over A.J. Foyt. Art's bad luck continued with a dropped valve on the 138th lap and he wound up in 16th place.

One year earlier at the Ontario Motor Speedway, Art was on his way to an almost certain victory. But with just five laps to go, a deflating tire slowed him, allowing Jim McElreath to pass for the lead and the win. The 1971 'California 500' was again held on Labor Day weekend and 36 cars were entered for the 33-car grid. Gilmore Racing had just one car, that being Pollard's #8 Scorpion/Ford.

Mark Donohue secured the pole position with Roger Penske's McLaren/Offy by turning a fast time of 185.004 mph. Second fastest was Bobby Unser, followed in order by Peter Revson, Swede Savage, and Johnny Rutherford. Art clocked in eighth quickest.

During much of the race, the lead alternated between the Unser brothers, Donohue, and Foyt. Crashes during the event eliminated Savage, Bud Tinglestad, Bobby Unser, Greg Weld, and George Snider. Fifteen other cars fell by the wayside with mechanical failures, but Art's car was running well for a change. He stayed out of trouble and methodically worked his way to the front of the pack.

Joe Leonard's Colt/Ford inherited the lead from Al Unser on the 161st lap when Al's car developed gearbox problems. Leonard led the remaining distance and drove into victory lane. For the second year in a row, Art crossed the line in second place. He was one lap down to Leonard but one lap ahead of Gary Bettenhausen in third. Art's splendid finish was worth 800 points and $71,287 in winnings.

It was back to the east coast for the Marlboro 300 at Trenton Speedway. The original date of September 26th was a rainout, so everyone had to simmer until the following weekend. Bobby Unser was on the pole and Pollard's Scorpion/Ford would start from the ninth position. Just before the half-way point of the race, the Gilmore car broke a valve and Art finished a dismal 20th. Bobby Unser was the winner, leading all but ten laps. With his third-place finish, Joe Leonard locked up the 1971 driver's championship despite winning only one race.

The final event of the season came at Phoenix, and it would also mark Art Pollard's final run for Gilmore Racing. He qualified 16th and finished ninth, two laps down to winner Foyt. Of the 26-car field, only ten were running when the checkered flag was waved.

The 1971 season had been shortened to just 12 races, versus 18 the year before. In the final standings, A.J. Foyt finished 695 points behind Champion Joe Leonard. Billy Vukovich, Jr. experienced a successful season with a third-place ranking in the standings. Art drove in a total of ten races, with two top five finishes and four in the top ten. He ended the year 11th overall in points and earned $105,151.

Following the end of the season, in early December Art joined other members in the racing fraternity on a goodwill tour of U.S. military bases in Vietnam.

In December of 1971 Art joined others from the racing fraternity for a goodwill tour of United States military bases in Vietnam. From left in the back row is Ray Marquette, Art Pollard, General Creighton Abrams, Richard Petty, Butch Hartman and Captain Fettes. Kneeling in the front row is Wally Dallenbach and Don Garlits.

In his book, *Tales from the Drag Strip*, Don Garlits described the group's experience:

"Back during the Vietnam War, President Nixon asked a bunch of racers around December if we'd go over to Vietnam and visit some of the kids who were fighting and weren't going to make it home for Christmas.

So, I spent 16 days rooming with Richard Petty in Saigon. I'll tell you, it was something I'll never forget when we had to helicopter out to where the troops were in the field. We took fire as we flew over the jungles, and we returned machine gun fire with the Viet Cong. Luckily, we were flying high enough that they couldn't hit us, but we could hit them."

TWENTY - SEVEN

1972 - Back with Granatelli

The 1972 Championship Car schedule was comprised of ten events on seven paved ovals: Phoenix, Trenton, Indianapolis, Milwaukee, Michigan, Pocono, and Ontario. As in the past Phoenix, Trenton, and Milwaukee would each host two races. Beginning in 1971, dirt track events were no longer included in the series' championship.

In March 1972 a group of racers were invited to a reception at the White House. Here, noted car owner and promoter J.C. Agajanian and Art are meeting President Nixon.

Twenty-four cars turned out for the first race, the Jimmy Bryan 150 at Phoenix. Art Pollard was to drive a Scorpion equipped with a new, A.J. Foyt-designed engine based on the turbocharged Ford Indy V8. Art's #11 was listed under the ownership of the 'Quality Racing Team,' an enterprise we could find no facts about.

Art qualified the car 21st, but on lap 118 Johnny Rutherford's oil cooler let go. Art slipped on the greasy track and crashed in the first turn. His day ended with a 14th place finish while Bobby Unser won the event just ahead of Mario Andretti.

Art did not compete in the next race at Trenton. The following event on the schedule was the Indianapolis 500, and Art would be given another opportunity to win the biggest race of his dreams with Andy Granatelli's STP team.

The 1972 running at the Brickyard would go down in history as 'The Year of the Wing'. One year prior, the McLaren team discovered a way for a large rear wing to become an integral part of the car's bodywork, thus complying with USAC rules. The wing provided tremendous downforce and much faster lap times. The concept was allowed in 1972 and virtually all teams adapted the technology into their new cars. A total of 88 entries were accepted for this year's race.

Art's new mount for the 1972 running of the Indianapolis 500. It was fast right out of the box.

Beginning with the month's first practice runs, things looked promising for Art and the STP Oil Treatment #40. On May 7th, he became the 13th member of the 180 mph-plus club by posting the seventh fastest lap of the day. His car had just arrived at the track that morning and, after being inspected and tuned, Art recorded a speed of 180.252 mph within just a few laps. The pole speed for the 1971 Indy 500 was 178.696 mph. As practice continued in the days ahead, thanks in part to the new rear wing, the field's lap times continued downward.

Pole Day on Saturday the 13th was, for all intents and purposes, rained out until 5:50 p.m. Three cars made attempts in that late hour, but none was able to complete a four-lap run. Pole qualifying was rescheduled for Sunday.

The following day started out dry and the track reopened for practice at 9:00 a.m. At 10:21 a.m., tragedy struck when Jim Malloy, driving for the Gerhardt Racing Team, was searching for even more speed. The car suddenly cut sharply to the right and veered nearly head-on into the outside retaining wall in Turn Three. Malloy never regained consciousness and passed away four days later. Jim was a popular driver from Colorado and, like Art, graduated to the big leagues after a very successful career in the CAMRA series. During that era, Malloy and Pollard were both tough competitors to each other on the track, but good friends otherwise.

Jim Malloy – Denver's popular driver and good friend and competitor of Art's.

(Colorado Motorsports Hall of Fame)

Following that terrible accident, rain once again closed the track until 2:30 p.m. Billy Vukovich, Jr. was at the head of the qualifying line and on his first lap, he officially broke Peter Revson's record in 1971 with a speed of 185.797 mph. Unfortunately, Vukovich crashed in Turn One on his second lap. He was uninjured but the car was finished.

Mike Mosley was next up, but his car stalled on the backstretch of his fourth and final lap. It started raining once again and activities were halted for another hour. Around 4:15

p.m., Joe Leonard became the first driver to complete a full qualifying run, setting new one and four-lap records. Mario Andretti was the next car on the track and bested Leonard's speed. With one hour to go before the track closed at 6 p.m., Bobby Unser wowed the fans with a record-setting four-lap average speed of 195.940 mph. He shattered the 1971 record by over 17 mph!

A total of 12 cars secured starting positions for the race. Pollard's Lola/Foyt was tenth fastest. But due to earlier rain delays, there were still six cars eligible to make attempts for the Pole. Their opportunity would come the following Saturday, May 20th.

Prior to his practice accident, Art had qualified 10th quickest on the first day of qualifying. That would position him on the inside of row four at the start of the 1972 Indy 500.

(Glenn Binegar photo)

On May 16th, Art's hopes for the upcoming race – and subsequent events – were dashed in an instant during a practice session. A right rear hub broke, causing the wheel to come off, and he crashed hard into the outside wall. Though Art always kept himself in great physical shape, the impact left him with a badly broken leg. The car was destroyed, forcing the Granatelli team to bring out a backup car. Wally Dallenbach was hired to replace Art, but due to the car and driver change he would have to start the '500' in the 33rd position.

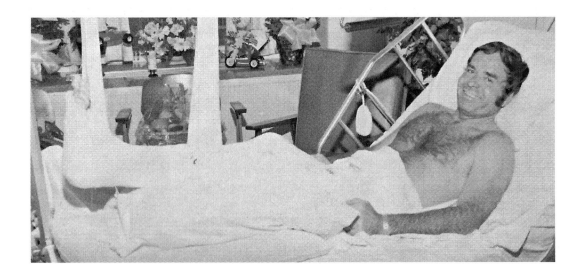

On the third day of qualifications, five of the six drivers eligible for the Pole made their runs. Bobby Unser held onto the first position, Peter Revson was second fastest, and Mark Donohue was third. For the first time since 1940 and 1941, the same three drivers were on the front row in consecutive years.

Come race day on May 27th, Al Unser was hopeful to win the race for the third year in a row. The field's average qualifying speed was 162.962 mph, or about five miles-per-hour faster than 1971.

Bobby Unser led the first 30 laps, and during the 500 miles, while other leaders were Gary Bettenhausen, Mike Mosley, Jerry Grant, and Mark Donohue. There were five cautions during the day. Donohue led the final 13 laps to take his first and only win at the Brickyard in Roger Penske's car. Dallenbach, subbing for Art, came from the back row to finish 15th and was running in the end. He had completed 182 laps.

In 1972, Mark Donohue drove to victory at Indianapolis for car owner Roger Penske.

(IMS photo)

Art spent the summer recuperating from his leg fracture, sitting out single races at Michigan and Pocono, along with the two events at Milwaukee. Wally Dallenbach drove the #40 STP entry at Michigan (finishing second) and at Pocono (finishing 14th).

Despite his injury, you couldn't keep Art away from the track while he was recuperating.

Art was able to get back in the saddle in time for the annual California 500 at Ontario. He only managed to qualify the #20 STP Lola/Ford on the inside of the last row of the 33-car field. His teammate this weekend was Dallenbach, who qualified the #40 Granatelli machine 32nd. Jerry Grant's Olsonite Eagle/Offy was on the pole with a speed just shy of the 200-mph mark.

The 200-lap race was tainted with a total of 11 caution flag periods. In the early laps, two of them were caused by jack rabbits on the backstretch. Two more came later when rain moistened the track surface. The race victor was Roger McCluskey, who led the final 40 laps. One lap behind, second and third place went to Mike Hiss and Billy Vukovich, Jr. Primarily due to mechanical attrition, just ten cars were running at the end. Art had a competitive drive by finishing seventh, gaining 300 driver points. Dallenbach was forced to drop out on the 109th lap with a broken valve.

The next race was at Trenton in late September. Granatelli's STP entries were the same as at Ontario, with Art in the #20 car and Dallenbach in the #40. Bobby Unser would start from the pole. Dallenbach qualified 13th, with Pollard in 16th.

The 200-lap contest was extremely competitive, with 14 lead changes involving seven drivers. Bobby Unser secured the lead for the final time and led the last 69 laps for the win.

It was another solid weekend for the STP cars, with Dallenbach coming home seventh and Art finished ninth for his second consecutive top ten finish.

Staying with tradition, the final race of the 1972 season was back at Phoenix in early November. Joe Leonard had already clinched his second consecutive Championship and was not entered. However, there remained a close battle for the runner-up spot between Vukovich, Jr. and McCluskey.

Following qualifying, Donohue was on the pole and shared the front row with Andretti. Granatelli's Lola/Foyt cars would start ninth (Pollard) and 19th (Dallenbach). Andretti led the first 53 laps of the race and then exchanged the lead with Bobby Unser, who would stay in front for all but one of the remaining laps. Dallenbach's car lasted only six laps before being sidelined with a broken throttle. Art was running at the finish, though 18 laps down to the leader, and finished 11th to tally an additional 30 points.

With the season now completed, Billy Vukovich Jr. finished second in overall points to Leonard and Roger McCluskey finished third. Due to his leg injury Art was only able to compete in four races but finished in the top ten in two of them. His season ended with a 20th overall rating, earning just $19,021.

TWENTY - EIGHT

A Historian's Perspective

As the Chief Historian of the Indianapolis Motor Speedway, Donald Davidson holds what may be one of the coolest full-time positions in all of motorsports. As a youngster growing up in England during the 1950s, he developed a strong interest in Grand Prix racing. He also began studying oval track racing in the United States and, in particular, the Indy 500.

Donald Davidson is the long-time Chief Historian at the Indianapolis Motor Speedway. His gift of remembering even the smallest of details is amazing.

(IMS photo)

Because video coverage of racing in that era was still in its infancy, Davidson turned to books and other publications about auto racing. Described as having the gift of "Selective Retentive Easy-Access Memory", he began memorizing the results of every Indianapolis 500 since 1911.

Davidson's first visit to Indianapolis came in May of 1964, and he made himself known to longtime Indy radio announcer, Sid Collins. Being able to recite the record of every driver who had ever competed at the Brickyard, Davidson amazed everyone within earshot. As a result, Collins invited Davidson to make a guest appearance during the broadcast of the 1964 race.

The next year, Davidson returned to Indy and was welcomed into the radio network staff. Shortly after the 1965 running of the "500", he was hired by Henry Banks to work as a statistician for the United States Auto Club. Davidson held that position for the next 31 years.

1964 – Donald Davidson's first visit to the Indianapolis Motor Speedway. Here he is posing with Chief Starter Pat Vidan.

(IMS photo)

In 1998, Davidson became the full-time Historian of the Indianapolis Motor Speedway. During his career he has also written, or was a contributor, of many books and articles about auto racing and the Indy 500. As his schedule permits, Davidson serves as a guest speaker at trade shows, civic, and social events and award ceremonies. In 2010, he was inducted into the Auto Racing Hall of Fame at the Speedway. In 2013, he was also inducted into the Richard M. Fairbanks Indiana Broadcast Pioneers Hall of Fame.

Davidson chatted about Art Pollard's legacy at the Speedway: "At that time, most drivers would show up at Indy when they were in their mid-to-late 20s, but Art was in his late 30s," said Donald. "He was always very bright and breezy. It just seemed like he was light on his feet and always smiling. Art had a very sunny personality."

Donald recalled that Art was always wide-eyed and grinning. "I never saw him angry or never heard of him being angry. He was never throwing hammers into the wall," Donald laughs. "Art and Robin Miller used to pal around a lot. When they were driving somewhere, Robin would have the radio on and Art knew all the songs. He seemed younger than he was."

"Art was a great ambassador for the sport," Donald observed. "He was a very good speaker, a good spokesman, and representative. He would do the talks and, quite early on, established his relationship with the Larue D. Carter Memorial Hospital in Indianapolis. I forgot the details on how that came about, but there was a boost to get the drivers down to visit the kids at the hospital. Art was so struck by what he saw there, that he took it upon himself to round up other drivers. I know he sometimes had difficulties. He would do this on Wednesday of race week, and it was very difficult to get drivers to obligate to do."

"I know Gordon Johncock did this a couple of times and there was, at least on one occasion, where he was the only other driver to show up. But Art was unfazed by that. There was a picnic he paid for and he set up some kind of trust. And they're still doing it!"

Donald spoke more about the Larue D. Carter Hospital, which is located about two miles from the Speedway. "I finally did that myself about two years ago," he said. "The guy called and said they were having a hard time getting a driver and asked if I could come visit. I asked, 'Well, who have you been getting?' The man told me 'last year they had Mario Andretti'" And then Donald said with a laugh, "I didn't have too much difficulty going over. I think that's amazing because it's been 40 years that they've been doing this. The thing is perpetual in Art's name."

Donald also remembered that he and Art gave several talks together, including an appearance at a local event for kids known as the "Pinewood Derby." "We were the judges and directors of competition, and we had to pick the best cars. He was great with both the kids and adults."

"When Art had the accident in 1972 and broke his leg after he qualified for the race, I actually got several talks when people called up and said to me, 'Hey, Art Pollard was going to be our speaker', so I did a few of those."

Donald's keen memory flashed back to when Art first started competing in the Championship Car Series. "I think it was the summer of 1965. Pollard's USAC debut was at Milwaukee, and then Trenton. It was the car Len Sutton had driven as a new car in 1964, and then Billy Foster was running it in 1965. Billy Foster had gotten a new car, so Pollard came in."

"Honestly," Donald recalled, "We'd say 'Who the hell is Art Pollard?' We'd never heard of him. It's another CAMRA guy [Canadian American Modified Racing Association]. He finished fifth at Trenton, so we thought 'golly, this guy is for real.'"

In July of 1972, when Art was still in a leg cast, there was the "Michigan 200." Donald had an interesting story to share about that weekend. "There was a little independent outfit that was going to televise it. Jim Wilson, a local sports reporter, was going to anchor it. I was the color man and Art was the driver expert. The broadcast position was at the top of the grandstands and there was no elevator, so we had to go up steps. It was sort of a contorted arrangement, so the further up you went the steeper the steps. We're getting near the top and it was an effort."

Donald goes on, "Here's Pollard on friggin' crutches, and we would stop every now and then to take a break. He never complained! I remember thinking, 'that guy, now that's amazing! This is difficult for him to do, but he would never complain.'"

TWENTY - NINE

Starting the 1973 Season

Now fully recovered from his broken leg, Art was ready to pursue a possible championship. Moreover, he still held the lifelong dream of standing in the winner's circle and enjoying a swig of milk at the Brickyard. He had the backing of thousands of friends and fans in the Pacific Northwest.

The Champ Car schedule for 1973 was extended to 16 paved oval races, and two of those would be held at the two-mile track at Texas World Speedway in College Station, Texas. The track was built in 1969 and included several road course configurations. It was a fast arena, similar in layout to Michigan, but with steeper banking in the turns.

The first race of a new season is always exciting for the teams, drivers, and fans because many new cars are making their debut. In early 1973 most of the major team and driver combinations were the same as the previous season. Art was back in the familiar #20 Lola/Foyt owned by Andy Granatelli and sporting the Day-Glo orange colors of the STP brand, He qualified the car 11th in the 26-car field. Bobby Unser put his Olsonite Eagle/Offy on the pole with the jaw-dropping speed of 212.766 mph.

Bobby Unser led the first 30 laps of the race before he pulled into the pits with a broken piston and was finished for the day. Art's car only made it to the 32nd lap before suffering a broken front hub that ended his chances. He would be credited with a 19th place finish in his last drive for Granatelli. Al Unser took the checkered flag in front of Gary Bettenhausen and Mike Mosley.

The next race on April 15th was a two-heat event called the Trentonian Split 300 at Trenton, New Jersey. There was not an entry by Granatelli, nor did Art compete. He was making plans for the 1973 running of the Indianapolis 500.

Like so many other drivers, Johnny Rutherford and Art Pollard were fierce rivals on the track, but the closest of friends in their leisure time. Johnny recalls one special weekend in 1973 on the way to Indianapolis: "We had taken a little vacation to New Orleans," Johnny remembered. "My wife, Betty, and I, along with Art and Pat and another couple from Minnesota all had a great time. I had become good friends with Pete Fountain [the famous New Orleans-based jazz clarinetist]. We went to see him and, of course, it was a packed house at the hotel he was playing at. He [Fountain] got us seats, it was a great show, and we all had a good time. Al Hirt [another great jazz musician and trumpet player] had been to the

Speedway and had his own place. We went to that and just had a great time. Art and Pat were a great couple and had not been married long. Art was a funny guy. He was fun to be around and a jokester."

"Of course, from there we went to Indianapolis to get ready for the month of May," Johnny said.

Johnny Rutherford after winning his third Indianapolis 500 in 1980.

(IMS photo)

THIRTY

A Sixth Attempt at the '500'

With a new team and the latest technology, Art Pollard was enormously optimistic when preparing for the 1973 Indianapolis 500. His car owner was Bob Fletcher of Arizona.

Fletcher's business enterprise was Cobre Tire Company, a Phoenix-based enterprise that supplied tires for the big earthmovers used by mining and construction companies. Fletcher was providing Art with a brand-new Eagle/Offy, along with a second car for Jimmy Caruthers.

In a letter to his cousin Harvel, Art wrote: "I'll have my new Eagle and also Ron Falk and my other guy, Bruce Anderson, to work on the car. We have an engineman to handle both cars. Fletcher wants to go first class so I think we can really do something. Sure hope so. They will be called Cobre Special. Cobre is Spanish for copper. Fletcher does a lot of business with the mines in Arizona. So, he has to connect some way I guess. They couldn't make it in time for Trenton. But I'll be ready for Indy. On time this year."

The first days of May found Art fine-tuning his new Eagle. With each day came more speed as he was becoming comfortable with the car. On just the third day of the month, the #64 Cobre Firestone Special turned a fourth quickest lap of 182.002 mph. Teammate Caruthers' #21 car was just behind at 181.268 mph.

Art was super-happy with how things were progressing. "When he got to Indianapolis," said Harvel Pollard, "Art called and said he had gotten me a subscription to the daily Indianapolis paper so I could follow the news leading up to the race. He told me, 'Hey, I have a chance. You know, this is the best car I've ever been in. It came out of the box fast.' He was really, really tickled."

In another letter dated May 3rd, Art's wife Pat wrote a short note to Harvel's family: "Art is busy as ever at the track. He has 15 speaking dates so far for the month of May, and more coming each day. He has been on the track only a couple of times to shake the car down, but says it feels great. His second time out he ran what he qualified at last year (183 mph) and said it was like nothing. He is due to run today, but the weather has been very windy, so I doubt there will be much heavy running. Several of the guys are getting up into the lower 190s, but all the speeds should start jumping in a couple of days."

Pollard and Caruthers upped their speeds the next day. Art clocked a lap of 189.194 mph and Jimmy ran a 187.149 mph lap. Art's birthday was May 5th, and he received a great gift from his crew – a car that gave him a key to the prestigious "190 Club" at the Speedway. Art was seventh fastest that day with a speed of 192.700 mph. In previous days, Gordon Johncock and Johnny Rutherford had also surpassed the 190-mph mark. Swede Savage, driving the STP-sponsored Eagle/Offy for owner Pat Patrick, remained the quickest of the month with a lap of 197.802 mph. When Mark Donohue won the Pole in 1972, his four-lap average speed was 195.94 mph.

"Art was so up," Pat (Pollard) Arslanian remembers. "His car was running great and he was faster than most. So many cars don't get to start at the front and he just felt so positive about the way the car was running. His mechanics were very happy too."

Art said of his new Eagle/Offy, "Hey, I have a chance. You know, this is the best car I've ever been in. It came out of the box fast."

As was his custom, away from the track Art kept a busy schedule. His primary mission was supporting the resident children and staff at the Larue D. Carter Memorial Hospital. Art was also a popular guest speaker at several functions taking place in Indianapolis during the month of May.

Art's close friend, motorsports journalist Robin Miller, said, "Art enjoyed talking as much as he did driving, and he was a master of the after-dinner speech." And whenever possible, Art loved hanging out with his racing buddies and was described by Miller as a master of organization. Robin wrote: "Race drivers are, as a group, almost impossible to organize – be it at or away from the track. But Pollard possessed a knack for getting on the phone and making things happen. He began a weekly Thursday night poker game at his apartment that saw Johnny Parsons, John Mahler, Cy Fairchild, Billy Vukovich, Art's friends and neighbors lose money from 7:30 p.m. to 1:30 a.m. and enjoy themselves. Then on

Tuesday and Thursday morning, Pollard would get up and begin rousing Parsons, Mahler, Merle Bettenhausen and myself to go down to the Athletic Club and work out."

Pat also recalls those days in Indianapolis. "He was just such a friendly guy that everybody liked him," she said. "They would gather at our house to play cards one night a week. Guys like Billy Vukovich and Johnny Parsons would come over and play cards. Robin Miller was always there. Because we didn't have children the guys could have a good time and not interrupt anyone's bedtime."

It wasn't always a friendly card game when it came to having fun in the Pollard household. "They got into racing those little slot cars and they all had their own cars," Pat recalled. "They'd do this or that to their cars so they could be faster than the other guys. It was funny to watch them – they were like little kids."

Art and fellow competitor Roger McCluskey.

THIRTY - ONE

May Twelfth, 1973

Fifty-three entries had been received for the 57th running of the Indianapolis 500, all vying to qualify for the field of 33 cars. There was an abundance of anticipation and excitement amongst the teams, the fans, and the media in the time leading up to Pole Day on May 12th. Would they witness the first official 200 mph lap at the famed Brickyard?

Inclement weather had interrupted the quest for speed during the second week of practice. Mario Andretti ran a lap just under 193 mph on Thursday, May 10th. Thus far, it had been a relatively safe month. There had been only three incidents during practice that involved contact with the outside wall, and none that caused injury.

Pole Day on Saturday dawned with sunny weather and mild temperatures. Teams were attending to the last-minute details on their cars, and spectators were streaming through the Speedway's main entrance. A crowd upwards of 250,000 was expected to fill the grandstands and infield for qualifications.

The track opened for practice at 9:00 a.m. and some drivers were preparing to go out on the course for some last-minute tuning and to check on the track conditions. Art Pollard was among them with his Cobre Firestone Special. Robin Miller recalled sitting with Art on the pit wall early that morning and was surprised when Art said he was going to take the car out during practice. "You're good," Robin said to Art. To which Art replied, "I think we can trim it out and get a little more out of it."

Art's longtime friend and competitor, Dick Simon, recalls making a friendly wager with Art early that morning. Between them, the one who posted the fastest qualifying time that day would be treated to a steak dinner in the evening at St. Elmo's Restaurant, which was a favorite Indianapolis hangout for racers during the month of May.

"Art rode into my garage on a bicycle that morning and was the most positive I have ever seen him," Dick remembers. "We made the bet about St. Elmo's – that was the place you go where you have shrimp cocktail. If you had a cold, you could walk out of there with clean nostrils or no cold."

"A couple of girlfriends and I went up and taped blankets on the top row of the grandstands, so we'd have seats right above the pits," Pat (Pollard) Arslanian remembers. "I'm very organized, and that was one of the things I did. I was sitting up there chatting with my friends when, all of the sudden, people below were turning to me and saying, 'Pat, Pat, Art wants you.'"

"And sure enough, there is Art standing at the fence looking up at me. He motioned me to come down there where he was. He didn't want anything but to give me a kiss. That was it. Here he is getting ready to qualify and all the things the crew has to worry about, and he's thinking of me. He was at the height of his career. On a day like that, a driver motioning to his wife, who was on the top row of the stands, to come down there as if he had something important to tell me. It turned out to be very important."

Pat returned to rejoin her friends and watch Art while he got in a few more laps of practice before official qualifying began. Art had just turned a lap a tick over 192 mph when suddenly, at 9:37 a.m., tragedy struck.

Art's car veered into the outside wall just prior to Turn One. The impact ripped off the right-side wheels. Still moving at a high rate of speed, the car careened across the track and continued spinning through the infield grass of the short chute between Turns One and Two. As the car slid back up to the track apron, it flipped 360-degrees and finally came to a rest in the middle of Turn Two. The car was heavily damaged after it had covered a distance estimated at 1,450 feet from the first point of impact.

"When the yellow came out, I knew within seconds that it was Art," Pat said, "because he didn't come around where he had been the lap before. Everybody's saying, 'who is it, who is it?' I told my friends that it's Art. He's not where he should be. Sure enough, it was."

The track safety crews arrived at the scene in an instant, smothering the flaming wreckage with fire retardant. Art was slumped in his cockpit, unconscious, but still alive. He was carefully removed to the waiting ambulance, which sped to the infield medical center. From there, Art was rushed to nearby Methodist Hospital in the track's new cardiac ambulance.

Art's friend Johnny Rutherford remembers, "I was the first one by the scene of the accident where he crashed. It was horrendous and I could tell it was not good. I went out in qualifying later and set a new track record. Going through Turn One on one of the four laps, the car snapped on me. The back end jumped out and I caught it. It was a quick input on the wheel to the right, and it came right back – but it only happened that one time. I've often wondered if maybe that was what Art may have experienced."

Approximately one hour after the accident, Art Pollard was pronounced dead. He had suffered internal lung lesion due to flame inhalation, a broken leg, a fractured right arm, third-degree burns and a severe spinal injury.

To this day, Pat (Pollard) Arslanian struggles with her memories. "I hurried to the infield hospital. Somebody picked me up in a golf cart and took me to the hospital. When I got there they were working on him. They assured me and said I should just wait. [While waiting at Methodist Hospital] I stood in the hallway, and then somebody opened the door and I could see they were not working. They were just standing back, so I knew then. Within a few minutes, the doctor came out and said, 'Would you and your family come into the room with me?'"

The pride of Roseburg and Medford, Oregon had driven his last lap. A proud family man, a well-respected competitor, a humanitarian, and a friend to all, was gone. He had just turned 46-years-old one week earlier.

The beloved Tom Carnegie had been the "Voice" of the Indianapolis Motor Speedway since 1946 and was known for his deep, rich delivery over the track's vast public address system. As he had so sadly done over those years, he once again had to publicly announce a competitor's death. This time, it was for Art Pollard, and the news cast a pall over the remainder of the day's qualifying sessions.

Pat was unable to get to a phone before the general media reported Art's accident and subsequent death. "All I asked was if they'd give me time to call his family in Oregon," Pat recalls. "Somebody from the hospital released the news, but I was not able to get in touch with anybody."

On the west coast, daughter Judy (then 23-years-old) and son Mike (25-years-old) heard this shocking and unwelcome news on radio and television in the early morning hours.

As Judy related, "There is no good way to get the horrible news that your dad has had an accident and died. From the time I was a little girl, I never thought it would happen to him. He did everything so well. Racing families never think it will be their loved-one. We just don't!"

"It was hard, and I still miss having him in my life," adds Judy. "It's hard, but I find tremendous solace in my faith and the fact that I had such a loving dad. I was lucky, even if I had him less time than I wanted. He died living his dream, doing what he loved; and it was a privilege for him to race at that level."

Mike Pollard was working as a steel fabricator for Fred Gerhardt in Fresno, California. He turned away from the flatbed truck he was working on when the radio news mentioned his father's name. Mike couldn't believe what he was hearing. "Back then, the 'Wide World of Sports' televised the qualifier, but they did radio updates every thirty minutes," Mike said. "Once I got the news, I called the hospital, but by then he had passed away."

Bob Pollard and his wife, Diane, were also living in California at the time. "We were listening to the radio broadcast of the activity at Indy when they announced that Art had crashed and later passed away in the hospital. The original comment we heard on the radio was 'Veteran driver Art Pollard was killed at the Speedway this morning.' Our mom, Bobbie Pollard, called after the announcement, asking if what she heard was true. It's a shame she had to hear about Art over the radio, but that's the way things happen when a sporting event is being broadcast."

As Harvel Pollard remembers, "One of the fellows I coached with for a number of years wasn't feeling well that day. I got up early and went to visit him. After a while, I told my friend that I had to get back home to watch the time trials. As I was driving along I had the radio on, and that's when I heard about Art's crash. His death hit my family very hard, and to this day we miss him. He was so funny, kind, and always put other people first."

In an interview with the Bakersfield newspaper, Harvel recalled that he last saw Art just two months prior to the accident. "It was raining at Ontario, so he came up here and stayed with us for a couple of days. He was a sentimental guy," said Harvel. "He always enjoyed coming back to this area and seeing things that reminded him of his childhood. He would drive around Delano and take pleasure in pointing out things that he remembered, like a tree that his father had planted."

Harvel continued the interview saying, "We would get together and talk and I would ask Art how much longer he planned to keep racing. And he would answer with, 'how much longer do you plan to keep coaching?' His point was that he was doing something he loved and felt that he could still do it, so why quit?"

Harvel said that Art still felt hopeful of becoming an Indy champion, and giving it about two more tries before getting some land in Oregon to settle down to a simple country life.

Harvel noted that despite what some people think about those 'daredevil' race car drivers, that was not Art. "He was not daring at all," said Harvel, "but very smooth and mature. The only time he ever drove fast was on the racetrack – but never on the highway. He did a lot of speaking in schools on highway safety."

"Art was the most even-tempered person I ever met," Harvel told the newspaper reporter. "He was philosophical about everything and took life in stride. He was a tough competitor but when the race was over, it was over with him and he never had any alibis or regrets."

Although interested in many sports, Art's favorite was football. "He even came over the night before a big race at Riverside to see one of our playoff games with Fullerton at Anaheim," Harvel recalled.

Harvel's son Brad clearly recalls his reaction upon hearing the news. "I was eating breakfast at the kitchen table. My mom was listening to the radio and she was crying. I asked what happened, and she said Art was fatally injured. I was still young enough not to understand what that meant. I asked, 'is that bad?' and she said, yes, it was. I was devastated."

The news was spreading to Art's family and friends in Oregon and California. Art's high school buddy and racing pal, Don Caskey, said, "I was out in the field on my tractor, and my wife Shirley came out and told me Art was killed. He was too damn young."

There have been many theories regarding the cause of Art's accident, but those are not to dwell on today. Doing so would not change the outcome. Championship IndyCar owner, Pat Patrick, talked about that day in a May 2013 article in *USA Today* by saying, "Very sad, about as sad as you can get. I still feel bad about it."

At the close of the Speedway at 6 p.m. on May 12th, 1973, a total of 24 cars had qualified. Johnny Rutherford became the Pole winner with a four-lap average of 198.413 mph. There is no doubt that the celebration that evening was very much subdued. Rutherford dedicated his record-breaking run to his close friend, Art Pollard.

In the days to come, Art's wife Pat was flooded with support from everyone in the racing community, especially those who were closest to Art. "I sat in my bedroom with Art's mechanics and I thanked them over and over," said Pat. "They felt so badly, because they felt something had broken on the car. I told them he was happier this month than I've ever seen him, because his chances were so good. It meant a lot to me that Art had enjoyed it as much as he did there at the end. Somebody called to say they saw something fly off of that car. It never mattered to me what it was, or how it happened, because that would not change anything."

Pat continued, "Johnny and Betty Rutherford were very supportive, as was Clint Brawner and his wife, Kay. Tire people like Don and Emily Roble were really good to me. We were very good friends with Robin Miller. He worked the night shift at the *Indianapolis Star* newspaper. Every night when he got off work, he'd bring me a milkshake or something, knowing that I wasn't sleeping. I'd lost quite a bit of weight after Art passed, and with that help from Robin, I started putting the weight back on. Robin and Art were very close. Robin was really someone that got me through the late nights."

In conclusion, Pat reflected on the relatively short time she and Art were a loving couple. "I think it was wonderful that we had the relationship that we did. He put me on a pedestal and that was it. It didn't matter where he was going or what he was doing, I was always foremost on his mind. I did appreciate that."

From the *Indianapolis Star* newspaper:

Sadness Grips Indy

INDIANAPOLIS, Ind. (UPI) – Memorial services were scheduled here tonight for racing veteran Art Pollard who was fatally injured Saturday morning during practice at the Indianapolis Motor Speedway.

Pollard, who kidded younger members of the racing fraternity because he was a fast-moving grandfather, died in Methodist Hospital here and about one hour after his car lurched into the wall coming out of the first turn and virtually disintegrated in a fireball. The mangled machine, which had been traveling over 190 miles per hour on the lap before impact, bounced into a grassy portion of the racing apron, then flipped and came to rest upright on the racing surface.

Doctors said Pollard, Medford, Ore., who celebrated his 46th birthday a week earlier, died from head and other injuries and from flame inhalation.

His racing career dated back to 1955 when he began driving hardtops in Roseburg, Ore. He also was a regular member of the Champion Highway Safety Program team, traveling around the country speaking to teenagers and visiting high schools and other youth organizations for lectures and demonstrations.

He was a much sought-after speaker for dinners and banquets and was keen on physical fitness and usually worked out daily.

But most of all, he was considered a gentleman by his fellow drivers, the news media and the fans.

Pollard Services Tomorrow Night

Funeral services for race driver Art Pollard, killed in practice yesterday morning at the Speedway, will be at 8 p.m. tomorrow night at Farley Speedway Funeral Home.

Friends may call after 10 a.m. tomorrow at the funeral home. The family has requested contributions may be made in Mr. Pollard's name to the children's ward at LaRue Carter Memorial Hospital here.

Burial will be at McMinnville, Ore. Survivors: the widow, Mrs. Patricia Pollard; a son, Michael Pollard and a daughter, Mrs. Judy Dipple, and his mother, Mrs. Artle Pollard of McMinnville, Ore.

Artle Lee Pollard Jr.

May 5, 1927 – May 12, 1973

THIRTY - TWO

A Race to be Forgotten

In retrospect, many believe that the 57th running of the Indianapolis 500 was doomed from the start of May. The loss of Art Pollard on Pole Day was just a portent of things to come.

On race day, May 28th, a steady morning rain delayed Tony Hulman's command to the drivers to "Start Your Engines!" until three in the afternoon.

Right at the start, a grinding crash on the main straight brought out an immediate red flag. Salt Walther's car veered into the outside wall, made contact with Jerry Grant, and flew into the catch fence. Ripping apart on impact, fuel from Walther's car spewed into the packed grandstand, ultimately injuring at least eleven spectators. The car then flipped back onto the racetrack, upside-down, and continued spinning and spraying fuel. At least ten other cars became involved, several with extensive damage. Walther suffered severe burns, but other drivers suffered only minor injuries.

Aside from removing all the debris from the racetrack, the catch fence needed major repairs before the race could be restarted. Before that task could be completed, rain began falling once again, thereby requiring a postponement until 9 a.m. the following day.

A bit of rain was falling on Tuesday morning, which held up the start until 10:15 a.m. Officials announced that the race would start from scratch and the single lap on Monday would not be scored. In a pre-race meeting with officials, angry drivers complained, among other issues, that the pace lap speed of 80 mph was too slow for a rolling start. It was agreed that the new pace lap would be upped to 100 mph.

Finally, the field began their warm-up laps, but the troublesome rain again brought things to a halt. By mid-afternoon, with no relief from the weather, the race was postponed until the next day.

With more rain on Wednesday morning, the mood around the track was gloomy. By now thousands of fans had returned home, either to return to their weekday jobs or simply fed up with all the delays. Eventually the sun did appear, and the track-drying effort began in earnest. The race was able to begin shortly after 2 p.m.

The first quarter of the race was uneventful, but there was a high attrition rate. Bobby Unser's car appeared to be the class of the field. On the 57th lap, Swede Savage pitted for 70 gallons of fuel and a right-rear tire. Two laps later, while exiting Turn Four, his car appeared to twitch and Savage lost control. Still at full speed, the car veered across the track and violently impacted the inside wall nearly head-on. The car appeared to explode into pieces amidst a plume of flame and smoke. The cockpit area (with the driver still strapped inside) finally came to rest near the outside retaining wall, still engulfed in flame. Once removed from the wreckage by the track safety crews, Savage was immediately rushed to Methodist Hospital with serious burns and other injuries. Unfortunately, he passed away on July 2nd.

Popular and talented racer Swede Savage also lost his life at Indianapolis in 1973.

(Motorsports Tribune photo)

During all the bedlam, a crew member for Graham McRae (Savage's teammate), sprinted up pit lane toward the crash scene. Armando Teran was struck by a speeding fire truck and succumbed to his injuries later that afternoon.

Following another long delay, the race was restarted with Al Unser in the lead, but mechanical woes continued to sideline the remaining cars. Gordon Johncock took the lead on the 73rd lap after Al Unser's engine blew. By the halfway point of the race, only 11 cars were still running, with most many laps down to the leader. On lap 129, a light rain began to fall and the caution flag appeared. Four laps later, with the rain increasing, stewards declared it an official race with Johncock the winner.

Because of all that transpired during this month of May, this Indianapolis 500 will never be celebrated. The traditional victory banquet was cancelled. Reportedly, Gordon Johncock left the track to visit Swede Savage at the hospital. Later that evening, Johncock and his crew had a muted victory dinner at a fast food restaurant.

One positive to come out of the event was sweeping, safety-related changes for the near future. A car's fuel capacity fell from 75 to 40 gallons, rear wing sizes were reduced, and turbocharger pop-off valves were introduced in order to reduce horsepower. Additionally, major safety improvements for both drivers and spectators alike were made both at the Speedway and elsewhere.

1973 Indianapolis 500 winner Gordon Johncock.

(IMS photo)

THIRTY-THREE

A Racer Returns Home

Art's final trip back to his beloved Oregon was just as he would have wished for. On a mild spring day on May 17th, 1973, he was laid to eternal rest at Evergreen Memorial Park outside the city of McMinnville, nearby his parent's gravesite.

Art was laid to rest near his parent's gravesite in McMinnville, Oregon.

(Author photos)

Officiating at the service was Milt Anderson of the Church of Christ, that of Art's mother Bobbie, who survived her son. Art's father, Art Sr., had passed away earlier. Art's pallbearers were Ron Falk, Bob Green, Neil Larson, B.B. Cochran, Vic Lewis, Ed Harvey, Mel Goldstein, and Bud Van Osten.

Bill Smyth, representing the United States Auto Club, delivered the eulogy. In part, Smyth noted: "Art was an affirmative thinker and a man of action. Art's ready smile and quick wit were outward proof of his philosophy. From his visit to troops in Vietnam to the speeches at high schools and churches, he carried a vital message of courage and determination."

Motorsports journalist Robin Miller was on the staff of *The Indianapolis Star* newspaper at the time of Art's death and went on to become one of the nation's best-known writer and commentator for Indy car racing. Perhaps more importantly, Robin and Art were very close personal friends. Art's passing was one of the worst moments of Miller's career.

The day following Art's fatal accident, Miller wrote a touching tribute that appeared in the *Indianapolis Star*. Herewith, with Robin's permission, are some excerpts:

"When a race driver is killed on the track the first thing everybody says is, 'That's too bad, he was a hell of a guy.' In the obituary the next day, his past performances are listed and any other worthy achievements are mentioned.

Yesterday Art Pollard left us. Not Art Pollard the race driver, but Art Pollard the human being.

This is a personal eulogy.

I'm 23 years old. Art was 46 just last Saturday. But we had as much in common as any two people I know. We had a lot of good times together and in the three years I knew him, he showed me why he was different from most. At 46, he was just hitting fourth gear.

For one, he was a grandfather but as youthful as any when it came to standing on a gas pedal. His other uncommon feature was that Art Pollard actually cared, gave a damn if you please, about a bunch of people in this world. Whether you raced against him, dined with him, laughed with him or barely knew him, Art Pollard came across as more than an autograph, hand shake or wave.

In the pressurized world of professional auto racing most drivers, understandably, have too much on their minds to stop and chat with everyone who calls their names. But Pollard made time for nearly anybody.

Whether you were a Boy Scout, a crippled child, a pushy mother demanding an autograph or a drunk wanting to talk to 'that old guy,' Art Pollard tried to become a part of your world at least for a couple of minutes. He spent hours and his own money on the children at Larue Carter Hospital here in Indianapolis. He saw to it they spent one day in May with him at the Speedway each year. And if you don't think that means a lot to people, you are mistaken.

But as competitive as he was, he was always vibrant, even-tempered and hardly ever moody. After he helped me get started racing last summer, he told me never to burn any bridges in dealing with people. 'You've got to keep the right attitude all the time. When somebody spins and causes you to wreck, don't fly off the handle and try to get back at them, 'cause sooner or later you're going to make a mistake too,' he used to say.

Most of all, Art Pollard never seemed to age. Last summer we went to a concert to hear the Carpenters and he knew almost every song they sang. He always dressed with style too.

But his mental frame of mind was truly a wonder. A year ago, he suffered a broken leg in a crash after qualifying for the race. That crash probably would have made a lot of guys 35 quit. But Pollard was a tough cuss. Two hours after they put the cast on, he was scheming on how to get it off in time for the Pocono 500. He finally succeeded and ran strong at Ontario.

This May had all the signs of being his best since he drove Andy Granatelli's turbine in 1968. He had a '73 Eagle, two good mechanics and a new sponsor. All during practice he'd been one of the fastest. He kept telling me, 'Man, when things start out smooth and organized like this operation, you know you're going to do well.' He was running 191-plus when he crashed. The burns and broken bones he could have survived, but it was a spinal injury that took his life.

So now he's just another name in the Speedway record book, with an asterisk for being dead. They say, 'Well that's too bad but you got to keep on living.'

But I can't help feel a part of me and a lot of other people went away yesterday."

THIRTY - FOUR

Racing in Art's Footsteps

Art's son, Mike, adored his dad throughout all his life, and the two held a special bond. Much too soon, Michael Allan Pollard passed away unexpectedly in August 2009 at 62-years of age. The cause was complications of chemotherapy treatment he had just begun for early esophageal cancer. Prior to his death, Mike reflected on what it was like to grow up in a racing family:

"I was introduced to racing by the age of three, when Dad raced the little ten-foot hydroboats down the Umpqua River in north Roseburg. By the time I was six years old, Dad was racing micro-midgets inside the Roseburg Fairgrounds Pavilion. In the mid-fifties, Dad got his first hardtop racer, and as they say, the rest is history.

As a young boy growing up with your father, a race car driver, everyone in school thought that was the coolest thing. As a family, we traveled the whole Northwest going to different places so Dad could race. Quite a thrill for a young boy, especially since Dad won just about every race he competed in. Everyone used to race for second place because they knew who was going to win.

We lived in Roseburg until I was in the ninth grade, then we moved to Medford. I played football, baseball, and basketball from the fourth grade on. I remember Dad always had the time to help and practice with me in whatever sport I was playing. He taught me to water ski by the age of ten. In high school I would water ski, competing in the slalom course, and also speed skiing. It was quite a thrill to water ski at 90 mph! During the high school years, I also did some go-kart racing. I graduated from Medford High in 1965 and went to Southern Oregon College for three years, where I also played basketball.

I have always been very competitive at everything I have competed in. After completing school, I played in city-league softball, volleyball, and basketball. I competed in a free-throw contest against the world champion during half-time at a Fresno State basketball game. I made 92 out of 100 free-throws. The champion only made 86 of 100. I started bowling at the age of eight, and by the time I was an adult I was carrying a 205-pin average.

As far as my own car racing goes, at the time I guess I enjoyed watching Dad more, rather than doing it myself. I always seemed to have a fast street car though, from my 1965 Chevelle, to a 1930 Ford two-door sedan, with a 327 cubic-inch Chevy engine. I built that with my best friend. I eventually graduated to Corvettes, the first being a 1977 and then a 1992.

Through the Corvette club in Sacramento, I became involved with the open-road racing that is held in Nevada each year. Rodger Ward (ex-Indy champion), was the promoter of these events. One is called the Pony Express Run, which is an 83-mile race from Battle Mountain to Austin, Nevada. The other is called The Gamblers Twin 50, beginning in Elko, Nevada. The State of Nevada will close off the state highway for a year to hold the race. The first year I participated in the 110-mph bracket. From there, I also ran in the 120-mph and the 130-mph classes. The "need for speed" never seems to leave.

Mike Pollard with his Corvette.

There will always be so many great memories of Dad's racing career, but going as a family to Indianapolis in 1967 and 1968 will always be the highlights. Watching him win the Rex Mays 200 in 1969 on *ABC's Wide World of Sports* was pretty cool also.

There is a special reason for me putting #64 on my Corvette. On May 5th, 1973 (Dad's birthday) we talked and he told me, 'This year, I have a shot at winning. This is the best and fastest car I have ever had at the Speedway.'

My Corvette is the best and fastest car I have ever had. Every time I strap the helmet on I think, 'I have a shot at winning this year.' I will never forget that conversation.

The thing that is probably the most remarkable is that, 30-years later, wherever I go, people are still talking about Dad. What a genuine first-class man he was. He always had time to talk to people and there was never a bad word ever spoken about him. God Speed Dad!"

At right, Mike Pollard proudly displayed his Dad's portrait at the Indianapolis Motor Speedway Museum in 2000. Sadly, Mike passed away in August of 2009 at the age of 62.

Art's cousin, Harvel Pollard, and his wife, Mary Lou, raised three children - Laurie, Brad, and Mark – in Bakersfield, California.

Brad was born in 1959 and growing up he displayed the athletic talents of the extended Pollard family. He competed in football, in addition to becoming the first high school pole-vaulter in Kern County and Fresno State University. While at Fresno State, Brad also earned wins as a snow ski racer in slalom and giant slalom.

"Art was my dad's cousin, but we were so close to him that we always considered him 'Uncle Art'," said Brad. "Art had a profound effect on us growing up. He was always so kind and generous with his time and smiles. Art was really very, very good with us kids."

Even as a youngster, Brad was smitten with auto racing by closely following Art's involvement with the sport. "I didn't know much about Art's earlier racing days, but as I got old enough, probably seven or eight years old, he started racing at Indy and that was a big deal. That's when his career started taking off."

"I was too young to go watch Art race at Indy. My dad was a teacher and football coach, so we didn't have a lot of extra money to go back for the '500'. But we would certainly watch the race on TV, that's for sure."

Brad remarked, "Art's kind generosity and his ability to always be a people-person was such a special thing. We just loved it when he would come around the house. And when we were at the race track he would always make us a complete part of the team."

Brad was 13 years old when Art had his tragic accident. "When Art passed away, my dad told me I was never going to race anything. That made me eventually sneak into racing myself."

When he was 17 years-old, against his dad's knowledge and wishes, Brad drove a Fiat Spyder in a Sports Car Club of America (SCCA) autocross in Bakersfield. "I don't remember if I was any good at it," said Brad, "but I knew it was something I wanted to continue doing if at all possible."

Fourteen years passed before Brad climbed into the cockpit of a real race car. It was a Formula Ford at the *Jim Russell Performance Driving School* at Sears Point, California. In looking back, he says, "I always knew that I wanted to race and be just like Art, and this class confirmed it. It is hard to gauge if you're good enough at something to pursue it professionally. My instructors said I had a level of natural ability that needed to be developed. I spent the next four years trying to get into some kind of car, but with no luck. I was just too busy working, and racing proved to be too costly."

Harvel Pollard's sons Mark and Brad.

After moving to Utah, Brad was able to actively chase his racing dreams. He found that shifter karts were a relatively inexpensive way to hone his skills behind the wheel. "It took some time, but I eventually got better," he said. "To be any good at something that physically demanding took seat time, which is what was best about karting."

Following another move to Texas, Brad learned of *The Motorsports Ranch*, in Cresson, Texas. The ranch, established in 1996, pioneered the concept of a country club for enthusiasts of sports cars, race cars, and motorcycles. "I never knew something like this existed," he recalled.

It was during this time that Brad discovered the Formula Mazda Series. The Formula Mazda (FM) is an open-wheel racer that is adaptable to both road courses and oval tracks. Under the sanction of the SCCA, the FM is a 'Spec' racer where all cars are virtually the same, though minor adjustments are allowed depending on the track and conditions. This may be one of the best forms of racing because it provides a level playing field for the drivers.

Brad's best year in the series came in 2002. He won Formula Mazda's Southwest Division and National Division championships by capturing 11 poles and 14 victories in 21 races.

Success in Formula Mazda launched Brad into the Infinity Pro Series, which then was just one step below the top echelon of Indy Car. In 2003, he competed in two races for the Sam Schmidt Motorsports Team. The following year, Brad drove in six events—three for the Kenn Hardley Racing Team and three for Sam Schmidt Motorsports. Despite only running half of the season's schedule of 12 events, Brad finished 11th in the driver standings with an average finish of 7.5. His sponsor was Xbox, but the ride came to an end when the company decided not to move forward with their motorsports involvement.

Brad Pollard and his Infiniti Pro Series Team at Indianapolis.

Brad noted, "I was really bummed that my racing career ended, but I started late. I was 43 years old when I got into Formula Mazda. If I had been 18 it probably would've been better."

"When I started racing," Brad said, "I met drivers like Johnny Rutherford, Al Unser, Sr., Mario Andretti, and others that were Art's competitors. They would come and tell me how much a gentleman Art was, and how he was great to be around. I was actually racing against some of the older driver's grandkids, such as Marco Andretti and Al Unser III.

"When I was racing, I recalled how Art treated the fans," Brad recalled. "As a driver, you're sometimes sitting in an autograph line and they open it up for only one hour. There were fans that were unable to get their autographs in that time, so I and a couple of drivers would go out beyond the fence for those people. I knew that's how Art was. He would go and talk to the fans and make them feel special. I told myself that no matter how high in the ranks I got, I'm going to carry that forward. The reason we're there was because of the fans."

Inspired by his Uncle Art, Brad Pollard made it a point to spend time with racing fans.

"I couldn't imagine life without a famous racing uncle, and I wanted to be a race car driver so bad. So, it was really, really tough news hearing of Art's death—and I'll never forget that."

"Dick Vermeil and his wife Carol are my Godparents", Brad added. "You can imagine the kind of life I've had. I have Art, and I have Coach Vermeil. I grew up thinking, 'Well, you just go to the Indy 500 and win. You don't think anything but the best."

"I would love to go vintage racing", said Brad. "I want to go buy and rebuild one of Art's old cars and take it out on the track. I would do that in a heart-beat."

THIRTY - FIVE

Remembering Art Pollard

To this day, the memory of Art Pollard holds a special place in the heart of both his fellow competitors and loyal fans throughout the country.

Johnny Rutherford explained, "Art was a gentleman and fun to be with whether he was serious or joking. He was sharp, and it was a really sad situation when he lost his life at the Speedway. He had worked hard to get where he was. It will be good to see Art come back for a little while in this book."

"As a man, Art was very pleasant and a jolly individual," said **Mario Andretti**. "He was one of the good guys in our game. He had a career in the lower ranks for so many years, and it took him a long time to get the breaks. I think Rolla Vollstedt played a part in that."

Regarding Art's fatal accident, Mario reflected, "Oh gosh, it was something you think you're prepared for, but it's lurking out there. Why does it happen to the nice guys? As you know, motor racing has always been a close-knit family, even though we try to tear each other apart on the racetrack."

To which **Dick Simon** added, "Art was phenomenal, and probably one of the best individuals I've met in my entire life. He was a true sportsman, a very strong competitor, and wouldn't hurt a fly. He was that kind of guy. He was very courteous as a driver, but very strong and aggressive on the track – but with respect for the other driver."

"Art was a very, very likable person," said **Bobby Unser**. "He was everybody's friend. Art was such a nice guy, that everybody liked him. He was just a good human being and I don't remember him saying anything bad about anyone."

"Remember," Bobby continued, "Art Pollard didn't make it to the top echelon of Champ Cars until he was in his forties. Art didn't quite make it to the top. He didn't drive for a super-team. All of us guys that really came to success, some way or another, we ended up with really good teams."

Al Unser, Sr. described Art as a formidable competitor. "Art Pollard was just a good racer," remarked Al. "He would race you, but he was clean and fair. He behaved on the track and would never pull any shenanigans on you. If he was having a bad day, and you came up behind him and he wasn't handling as good as you were, he would let you go."

"He did have times, like all of us, that everything was going his way," Al continued. "But weird things happen, whether it's the car's fault or your own. That's the thing that made Art as good as he was. He was a very fair man on the racetrack and that carried through to his personality. If he was having a bad day, he'd never come over and say it was Joe's fault or Henry's fault. He'd just say, 'well, that's racing.'"

"Art was a very fine man and a good family man," Al stated in conclusion. "We used to run around quite a bit together at the races. He was just a neat guy. Art always said he started racing too late. He wished he had started racing earlier in life."

Jack Timmings, Art's old friend and fellow racer from the early days, offered his thoughts: "The day the news came out that he got killed was really a sad thing. I guess Art would be like a brother to me. And the way he got killed, I wasn't happy about that. I was amazed, first off, why he didn't go to the big-time earlier. I asked him about that once and he said he wasn't ready for that yet. That was his answer. In all my years of racing, people like Art were the highlights. If I never made a dime in auto racing, the people that I met were the thing. There was a lot of camaraderie."

Jack Timmings in his heyday.

(Ralph Hunt Collection)

Jack Timmings was one of the last remaining of the Pacific Northwest racers that jumped into the sport following the end of World War II. Even now, at age 90, Jack remains as sharp as a tack when talk turns to his own racing exploits and those of his friend and fellow competitor, Art Pollard.

I first met Jack at the World of Speed Museum in Wilsonville, Oregon. There, he was being reunited with Cliff Nelson's Ranger Special, which is one of the cars Jack raced during the 1950s. Days later, I was able to have a more comprehensive visit with Jack in his retirement home in Oak Grove, a suburb of Portland. It was a most enjoyable "walk through time" and he shared some of his favorite memories of that era of racing. Jack was a truck driver by trade; married and the father of three children.

"I grew up in Portland and went into the service like everyone else," Jack began. "Then in 1947, I started as a pit man on the old roadsters. I got hooked up with Willard Anderson, who was the owner of the car, and Darmon Moore, who was the driver. I worked for them for a couple of years, and then started driving after Moore got out."

"We raced at tracks all over. Besides Portland, I ran at Roseburg, which was a quarter-mile dirt track. We ran at Eugene, a half-mile asphalt track. Salem – that's where the old hot rods started running. Yakima, Aurora Speedway, and Centralia up in Washington."

"When I first met Art, he was running hardtops down in Roseburg. He had a pile-of-junk car that weighed a ton, but when he started coming up to Portland he had two partners – one was Ken Glass. Art did so well because of his driving abilities that he later bought a car that Rolla Vollstedt built, which really worked well."

"One year that I ran so hard against Art, the car I was driving was originally built by a guy named John Feuz. It was a pretty good car that had a Willys body and frame. Bill Hyde used to drive the car for John. It originally had a Studebaker V8."

"The guy that I drove for was Norm Bertrand. Norman was one of those guys who really couldn't afford a car, but he bought it anyway. He had a leased engine from a guy named Mike Goodell. Anyway, he was going to drive it, but it scared him to death. He asked me if I would drive the car until he got used to it. I said 'fine' and that's how we got running."

"Success-wise, Norm Bertrand's car was one of my best rides. It finally got wrecked badly at Eugene. Eugene Speedway, as we used to say, had two 40-watt light bulbs on the backstretch. It was dark. Anyway, the car got wrecked."

"My car and Art's car would run neck and neck. One day at Portland Speedway we ran side-by-side for 18 laps on the half-mile. One thing I wanted to say about Art was that he was a hell of a race driver, but he was also a nice guy. God, he was a nice guy! Oh boy, he could do things with a car that other guys could only dream about. I let him drive Norm's car one time, just to try it out early in the morning. I thought he was never going to quit. His comment was, 'Your car has more horsepower but mine handles better', which was true."

Jack shifted gears to talk about his time driving Cliff Nelson's Ranger Special, especially on the dirt half-mile at the Portland Meadows horse racing track.

One of the cars Jack Timmings raced was the 'Ranger Special', powered by a World War II PT-19 trainer plane.

(Author photo)

The component that made the Ranger Special so unique was its engine, which had previously powered the World War II-era PT-19 trainer planes used by the military. Ranger Aircraft Engines was a division of the Fairchild Engine & Airplane Corporation. At about a 441 cubic-inch displacement, the air-cooled, five-carburetor Ranger engine was large in size but produced only 200-horsepower at roughly 2,000 rpm. What made the engine so desirable for racers was the 375 lb.-ft. of torque it produced, along with its light weight.

"The Ranger was built for Bill ("Wild Bill") Hyde," Jack recalled. "But at some point, he and Cliff got into an argument about something – I don't know what it was. I was joking with Cliff and told him, 'I'm going to drive your car for you up in Pendleton, Oregon'. He said, 'Yeah, okay.'"

"I forgot all about it until I got a call down at work, and they said some guy named Cliff Nelson wants you on the phone. He asked, 'What are you doing at work? We're supposed to be going to Pendleton.' So, to make a long story short, I got off work, we went up to Pendleton and we finished second in the Ranger. That's when I started driving the car."

"They [Cliff Nelson's team] ran two sprint car races at Portland Meadows that I know of because I drove in both of them. In the first one, we just flat ran out of tires at 85 laps with the Ranger. I had no idea what position I was in but going down the backstretch I noticed these pieces of string hanging off the right front tire. I couldn't figure out what it was. Well, it was the cords of the tire!"

"I went to pull it in, but Cliff waved a very big brass hammer and pointed me back out. The next time I came by they held up this big blackboard that said 'P2', so I just kind of backed out of it a little bit and finished second to Len Sutton in Rolla Vollstedt's car. It was funny because I'd never seen the cord come out of a tire like that. At 120 miles-per-hour, I wasn't anxious to run more laps with that condition."

"There were a lot of Ranger-powered cars. There were a couple of them from Seattle that were laid down flat and put in a roadster-style body. The Ranger Special had about the same horsepower as a good-running Ford Flathead V8, but when they rebuilt those things, they took an eighth-inch off the base and that upped the compression. The one I drove for Jim Hartman later on – they advanced the cam a couple of degrees. They have a complete dual ignition. They advanced one magneto over the other one, which gave them a longer spark. That was the fastest car I ever drove."

I beat Art on the dirt at the Madras, Oregon fairgrounds. I got out front and Art came up alongside me, because I could hear his engine. I didn't know it was Art at the time, but I caught a glimpse of him. I kinda' pulled a dirty trick on him. I threw the car extra hard as I was going into the corners and really got on the throttle. It filled him with so much dirt that it went into the carburetor and the car quit running on him. So I beat him there."

"But as far as running against Art race after race, I always finished second to him. Another thing about Art was that you could run six inches from him at full speed and you'd never have to worry about him. Len Sutton was an excellent driver, but Art was just about that much better, having run against both of them."

1950 – Jack Timmings at the Portland Meadows track.

(Ralph Hunt Collection)

I asked Jack if he could recall any serious incidents he had during his racing career. Of course, back in his era, driver and track safety played second fiddle to the actual competition. Jack remembered, "Once at Portland somebody was dropping water, and he [the driver just ahead of Jack] wasn't experienced enough to look for it. I could see water on the pavement, and I was kind of astraddle of it in the corner. I don't think he [the driver ahead] saw it."

"His left rear wheel hit that water and he spun so quickly. I was right behind him and I nailed him head-on. The collision took both cars into the south rail. His car went up in the air. And dumb old me, I hadn't thought about what goes up, must come down right on top of me. Something hit me in the back – I think it was a wheel – but when I came out of the fog that old Ranger was on top of the fence and it was still running, so I had to shut it off. It took me a while to come back to earth. It knocked the crap out of me and that was the end of Harold Sperb's car."

"In the old hardtops, I caught a steering wheel and broke my face all to hell and spent a couple weeks in the hospital. At Salem, things went bad on the backstretch and I rolled, breaking my arm. I've got a plate and four screws in there right now. It doesn't bother me much, but it's weaker than my other arm."

Jack Timmings passed away in 2017 at age 90.

(Author photo)

"After I quit racing, I went for probably 20 years with nothing going on, but then a guy had a Nickel Ad and wanted to start a four-cylinder class. I got in touch with my youngest son and we went to a meeting in St. Helens [Oregon]. So, I built a car I'd say was something like the old hardtops. It had a tubular frame with a Volkswagen Rabbit body. It turned out my youngest son was unable to drive it, and I was really disappointed because we'd built the entire car. My oldest son said, 'I think I can drive that car for you,' so it went from there. We also had a session of about three years of drag racing. All-in-all, I spent about 50 years of my life in auto racing."

"I did get to drive a former Indy car one time in Calistoga, California. It was an old Maserati that Les Anderson had owned. I don't want to be quoted, but I believe it finished sixth at Indy. It had an Offy in it then. A guy I later drove for, Jim Hartman, bought the car and put a Ranger engine in it. We went to Calistoga with no sleep. I won my heat race, I won the semi, and I finished sixth in the main event. Jim still wasn't happy."

"I like to watch the Indy races, but I don't care much for the road races. I like the circle tracks. It used to be that you'd do you own work on the car. Nowadays, you just buy the parts, and that holds true for all kinds of racing."

"One of the last times I spoke with Art was when our truck broke down going south when I was on a sleeper team. We laid over in Medford. Art was home, but in the hospital with a broken leg. I heard that he was in the hospital, so I made it a point to go see him."

Del McClure is one of the most respected sprint car owners in the Pacific Northwest, but his racers have made their mark at tracks throughout the United States. Over many decades, Del's drivers have included the best that the Pacific Northwest has had to offer, including Art Pollard and Mike Bliss.

"I was really surprised when Art was killed at the Speedway," said Del McClure. "He'd been back there and ran so many cars deliberately fast enough that he would spin out. We were all used to it, and then to have something like that happen to him, it was like 'Well, that was Pollard again running it so fast just to see what the car would do'. I have no idea why he crashed. At the time, I thought it was a mechanical problem, and I still think that."

Originally from Milwaukie, Oregon, Del now resides in nearby Molalla. Today he spends much of his time in the large workshop behind his home. This space is filled to the rafters with all forms of tools, machinery, engines, wheels, tires, and racing memorabilia.

Del began his involvement in racing soon after his military discharge at the end of World War II. "In the Navy I was in the machine shop, but I ended up with the responsibility for refrigeration on a ship," Del explained. "I think it was only two holds forward and two holds aft, but four levels tall. Each one of those had a refrigeration unit where they dropped supplies in and out. That turned out to be quite a responsible job because we had all the good stuff, like meat and ice cream mix for all the admirals. So, we couldn't have any problems."

"When I got out of the Navy and had my mustering-out pay, I went straight to the Portland Speedway," he recalls. In the beginning, he tried his hand at driving but that was only for a very short time. Since then, Del has always been involved as an owner of open-wheel sprint cars.

"In 1951, I had a 1939 Pontiac that wouldn't tow my race car out of town," he laughed. "Between my work and what we took in, I bought a plane ticket and went to Detroit. I fellow I knew, Tom Neal, had gone to the General Motors Institute and told me how to go look around there and buy a car out of their parking lot. I had $3,700 and ended up with a '51 Cadillac 62 Series coupe that had about 4,000 miles on it. I drove it home and used it to tow my race car."

In 1954, Del founded McClure Industries, which continues to this day in providing specialized carts used in laundries and hospitals. "The only reason I started the company was to go racing," he says. "It worked out."

We raced until about 1955, but you couldn't make any money racing anymore," Del explained. "Costs had gone up and purses were going down. For a while after the war at the Portland Speedway, not only would they fill the whole grandstand, but they'd let spectators out in the infield. But that wasn't happening anymore. During the war, people didn't have any outside things like racing, so there was a built-up demand. As other entertainment came along, the demand for racing diminished. It's like damming up a creek. The whole country was dammed up."

"We ran five nights of midgets up here and people were making good money," Del remembers. "But in Los Angeles, there were guys running seven nights a week and sometimes twice in a day. If you stop and think about it, two to three thousand dollars would buy a pretty nice house. If you ran seven days a week and were making $200 a day, you were making a lot of money."

Del remembers when he first hooked up with Art Pollard. "Everything we did with Art was through Don [Duck] Collins," Del explained. "At that point, what we called 'hardtops' was the hot tip. Art had built one and ran it around the Northwest for two or three years. It wasn't the most powerful one out there, but he won a lot of races with it. And that's where he got established."

"Art was easy to get along with," Del remembers. "He was a good mechanic and innovator. The #31 car would get dirt up around the clutch linkage where the throw-out bearing was, and it froze on the shaft. After we qualified next to last for the Hoosier 100 and got ready to race, we pulled back on the clutch handle and it wouldn't move. Don Collins grabbed hold of it and tore it off. The rules were, you've got to start your car and drive off, or you couldn't race."

"So anyway, Pollard says to Collins, 'Calm down here. I want you to start the car up just like you always do and get the rest of the guys behind the car and push it, just as hard as you can. When I think you're going fast enough, I'm going to blip the throttle and dump it in gear'. It worked – that's the kind of guy Art was," says Del with a smile.

In early 1968 Art Pollard began his association with Andy Granatelli. "You heard the story about Granatelli hiring Art away from us when we didn't have a car ready?" Del recalls. "It's really simple. Art was running our #31 sprint car and he'd run about tenth in the last half-dozen races. At that time, we could only afford to run Sedalia, Springfield and Duquoin [home of the Hoosier 100] in the Midwest. They always had those races in about a five-week period. Then we came back here to the West Coast to run at Sacramento and Phoenix."

Del continues, "Well, Granatelli knew that our car wasn't anything near what he had and so did we. But we got enthused to build this other car because we finished well in the Hoosier 100. Foyt won it and we could still see him on the track. In other words, we weren't that far off. We thought if we had a decent car, we could do something. So, Don Collins started building a new car that winter. He never got anything done on time, but he did beautiful work."

"When it was getting time to start the new season Pollard didn't have a ride, but nobody knew it," says Del. "Granatelli wanted him, so he paid him something like $20–30 thousand dollars. I don't know exactly because I wasn't there for the transaction. That was enough money for Art to live on, and he sent the other half home to his family. They lived a year or so on the Granatelli money. As I understood it, Pollard was Granatelli's test driver and they plugged him in anywhere they needed him. They didn't hire Art just to drive that turbine car. He was on a retainer."

Del reflected on Pollards driving style. "Art was pushing hard all the time, trying to find a hole to drive through the field. The difference between he and others is that they would try to *make* a hole. Art would find someone who he thought would slip a little bit, and then he'd get up there and show them his car a few times. I never recall him lagging behind until everything got straightened out. He was always charging but was using his head while he was doing it. Art was a hard driver, but you also have to be smart if you're making your living that way."

"Art was on a different deal than most people, if you look into it", says Del. With Granatelli, he was on a retainer and a percentage. Drivers made their own deals. Art was from the days that if you were a good enough race driver, you got paid for it. It isn't like now, where you've got to pay for it."

1968 – Art Pollard, Duck Collins and Del McClure at the Hoosier 100.

(Del McClure Collection)

Art – ready to rumble in McClure's #31.

(Del McClure Collection)

Today, Del McClure is an active participant with the West Coast Vintage Racers. Throughout the summer, the organization and its members hold events at tracks in Oregon, Washington, Idaho and British Columbia. Del's current car is a 1970 Nance chassis powered by a contemporary GMC six-cylinder with a customized injection system. Nicknamed the 'Poorman's Offy', the car was driven by veteran all-around racer Mike Bell of Portland.

Del also owns the Don Collins-built #31 sprint car that was first built in 1958 and driven competitively by Art Pollard and others until 1968.

Del McClure's #31 sprint car now restored with its original Hemi engine.

Vintage racers – Del McClure and Mike Bell with Del's 'Poor Man's Offy'.

(Author photos)

Jack Corley includes Art Pollard as a good friend and fellow competitor from the past. "When Art first came up to Portland to race, he was friendly and I was always talking with him," Jack recalls. "One time he must've been following behind me on the track, because he came up later and said, 'You're having a little problem, huh?' I said yes and he asked, 'Where's your tape measure?' He then added, 'When I'm at the Portland Speedway I run the front end straight-up – no stagger. You should try it.'

So, he got a wrench and we set my front end up that way. It made a world of difference. He was such a good mechanic. Art liked to work on somebody's car and then drive right by them in a race. I think he want guys to run against him. Art had the knack of knowing when to get on the throttle. You have to learn that the hard way. He saved equipment and kept it off the wall, and never busted up the car."

Despite a recent mild stroke, at the age of 88 Jack Corley is still going strong. Known these days as the owner of Jack's Specialty Parts in Gresham, Oregon, Jack is among the large group of old-time racers in the Pacific Northwest. His large shop, where he has a considerable inventory of American car parts dating from the 1930s to the 1970s, also serves as a local racing museum with a vast collection of old photos, posters and automobilia.

Jack Corley, still going strong at age 88.

(Author photo and Ralph Hunt Collection)

Jack grew up in the Gresham area and has spent his entire life in Oregon. Like many of his high school friends he was a car fan, with first a 1938 Chevrolet and then a 1941 Chevy which he hot rodded. After graduation, he got a job in a service station owned by Armund Millen, a local racer, and he began helping Millen at the races. Jack then spent a couple of years in the Marine Corp. and was released from active duty in 1950. Before leaving on active duty, he put his '41 Chevy up on blocks.

Around 1952, Jack was offered a ride in Armund Millen's '46 Ford six-cylinder stock car. "I ran it in a few races, but I couldn't afford that," Jack recalls. His first race was at the Hollywood Bowl in Salem. So he turned to drag racing, joining the Ramblers Car Club, and raced his '41 Chevy at locations such as Scappoose, Madras and Aurora. "Some of the guys went up to Arlington, but I never went that far," said Jack. He was also a member of the Columbia Timing Association.

In 1956 Jack bought his first midget racer powered by a Ford V8-60. "A midget came along and I could afford that," he says. I continued to upgrade it over the years until I could afford a Kurtis. That was a rail frame but Gordy Livingston built me a body so it would look more like a modern midget. Following that I bought Harvey Lawrence's Kurtis midget with a Ford V8, but I bought and Offy engine and put that in it.

According to an article written by Portland historian Albert Drake, Jack has owned 16 midget racers over the year. One year he owned six and raced four of them. He drove one car and hired drivers to run the other three. Corley drove thousands of miles on a racing circuit that stretched from northern California to Washington and Idaho, and as far away as Calgary and Edmonton. "I never really had a real good year because my job as a traveling salesman kept me out of town a lot," says Jack. "I think the best I did was an eighth or ninth place in the overall standings, but I had a number of wins."

Jack Corley in his racing heyday, primarily racing in midget cars.

(Ralph Hunt Collection)

During his racing years, Jack's full-time job was being a factory representative calling on automotive warehouses. He worked for the Niehoff Ignition Company for twenty years and later for Republic Gear Corporation and Republic Parts. One of his clients was the Oldsmobile dealership Art worked for in Medford, so Jack would visit with him regularly. Jack recalls, "I spent lots of time in Medford. [Racer] Jim Roberts, who had a big saw repair shop in Eugene, also came down. The two of us would get together with Art after work and maybe have a few beers together. I got to rub elbows with those guys."

Despite his very busy schedule, Jack also started a business called Jack's Specialty Speed that he operated out of his basement during the years he was racing. He sold racing tires, fuel, helmets and other racing supplies. Each time he went to a race track he'd load his truck with items he could sell to his competitors. It was a good business and helped to pay his expenses.

His full-time job also gave him the opportunity to get inside many old parts houses and as early as the mid-fifties, he began purchasing obsolete parts in quantity. As Jack pointed out to Albert Drake, no one was interested in collecting old automotive stuff then. He and his friend, Jim Davis, would visit Ford dealerships on Saturdays and buy NOS (new old stock) Ford parts that had been on the shelves for 15 years or more. Corley wanted the V8-60 parts for his midgets, and Davis would buy the rest. They extended their search into other parts houses and dealerships.

Nowadays, Jack mourns the things that got away. "I threw a lot of stuff in dumpsters," he remembers. "Things for Auburns, Cords and even Duesenbergs. I didn't know anyone who had one. They weren't really desirable cars at that time and lots of parts went to the landfill. In addition to the V8-60 stuff I was accumulating primarily ignition and brake parts that I was selling. And whenever somebody had a sign or something interesting, I'd take it home and put it in my basement."

Out in Gresham today, Jack's Specialty Parts on Cleveland Avenue is a rather large building that also houses one of his old midgets, his Hemi-powered '32 Ford Highboy and an old pickup truck. His cars are not for sale but he will be happy to sell parts for your old domestic vehicle – perhaps one that was brand new when Jack got into the automotive game.

The last race Corley competed in was in 1973. "I went through my first divorce and that erased my money.

Jack believes the last time he saw Art was at Sacramento or Phoenix when the USAC teams were on their west coast swing. "I knew Grant King, Jim Malloy and his brother pretty well. I saw Art with Mario Andretti an awful lot."

Jack Corley was shocked to hear of Art's fatal accident. "I just never thought it would happen to him. I knew getting involved in racing you would have that chance, but I never thought it some of those guys would die that way. They were too sharp, had good experience and the best equipment, but those things still happen."

Jack's long list of racing-related activities include his 'Corley's Caravan' contributions in the *Racing Wheels* publication, his long-tenured involvement with the annual Old-Timers Racing picnic held in July at Blue Lake Park, plus his weekly participation at the Friday Breakfast Club at Bill's Steak House in Parkrose.

Harry Brown was born in the Eugene, Oregon area in 1933 and, through racing of course, became a friend of Art's about 20 years later. His 'Fuzzy' nickname came across during his high school years. "My friends thought I should have a different name than Harry," he explains.

Harry admits he really didn't mess around with cars very much in high school He got by just driving his dad's family sedans. When he graduated from high school, he was handed the keys to a '49 Ford sedan from the family stable.

He acquired a taste for racing by going to the midget car races at the Eugene Fairgrounds with his dad and cousin. Harry remembers that it was "just a dirt oval with hay bales around it. I was just a kid but I liked it."

At one point, Harry had two friends with a '37 Ford coupe that they would mess around with. "We were running it on a football field – I was driving and a tie rod broke," he chuckles. "I went up into an earthen bank. Thankfully, I was wearing a helmet."

Harry 'Fuzzy' Brown.

(Author photo)

"I was too young to race in those days, but got a chance to run the last race of the season in 1954 and finished fourth in the B-Main."

Harry served on active duty with the U.S. Air Force, followed by time in active reserve. Returning home, he got into the family business of raising fryer chickens – and continued his interest in racing. He became a part-time driver for two to three seasons. "I started working in plywood at Georgia-Pacific in Springfield and my work schedule was varied, so I had to take time off to race."

"We raced at Eugene, Roseburg, Salem, Portland and Madras, which was just a dusty old horse track, but never out of state," recalls Harry. "Many guys asked me to drive their cars just to see what I thought."

Top Photo (from left) – Car owner Cecil Hickson and his driver Fuzzy Brown.

Bottom Photo (from left) – Bob Etchison, Fuzzy Brown and two unidentified competitors.

(Harry Brown Collection)

Harry first met Art Pollard at Roseburg. "A guy had a nice Chrysler-powered car. I started on the pole but all the faster guys were behind me. I led for awhile but then I heard a fast car coming up behind me – of course it was Art. It took him a few laps to get around me, but then I got spun into the infield by another car but still finished fourth in the race." Harry said about Art, "You could watch and see him avoid something that was coming up to happen. He was always prepared and was very easy on his equipment. He had a well-organized crew that would gather around the car on Wednesday nights to prepare for the upcoming weekend."

Harry met his future wife Joyce at the Eugene track. Due to his difficult work schedule, Harry eased out of racing, but for awhile maintained a racing car. "It seemed like a full-time job working on the car and I felt like I was being selfish to the family, so he ended that activity but stayed somewhat involved with the local racing scene and at one time was the Secretary-Treasurer of the Lane County Modified Stock Car Racing Association, remembering that "I made checks out to Art at the end of a race weekend."

Harry became a mail carrier in Springfield but continued to closely follow Art's career. "When he got to Indy he invited me to join his crew there, filling a 'gopher' role, but I just couldn't get the time off from my job. Art was so good and it was a sad day when he was killed. [Racer] Jim Roberts best man at my first wedding. He and his wife and I attended Art's services in McMinnville. Today at age 86, Harry makes his home in Central Oregon at Crooked River Ranch.

Clyde Sullivan of Portland was one of the legions of fans that followed Art's career, starting with those early years in Oregon. His basement is filled with photo books, newspaper clippings, and other artifacts that describe the many facets of the local racing history. In all those years, Art was Clyde's favorite driver to follow.

"We used to go to about 30 races a year, and that's a lot," says Clyde. But we would find out where Art was racing, and that's where we'd go. There was no reason not to like Art. He was clean-cut, friendly and jovial. In all the years I watched him, he never wrecked anyone that I recall. You wouldn't find anybody that said anything bad about Art. Fellow drivers admired him and the fans loved him. That pretty much sums up Art Pollard."

Clyde was amazed at Art's driving ability, no matter the track or type of car. "Years ago, Clyde recalled, "They used to have a 200-lap modified hardtop race at the Portland Speedway at the end of the year. They drew big, fast cars out of Seattle. Art's there with just a Roseburg-legal hardtop, but it just didn't seem to fit in with the other cars. But Art was passing everyone on the outside. That's where he made his moves. I seem to remember they made him tear the engine down after the race. It only had a two-barrel carburetor."

"I once took my cousin to a race in Eugene, and he was really impressed with Art. Art won the trophy dash. Afterwards, he suddenly took a little comb out of his pocket and combed his hair before he got to the trophy girl. I said, 'Look, he's combing his hair so he can be nice and neat.'"

Upon hearing of Art's tragic accident in 1973, Clyde said, "I just couldn't believe it. My dad even called me, and he didn't know too much about Art. My friends who were racing fans also called when I was on my way to work. It was just a sad day, and racing was never quite the same after that. He was my favorite. There just will never be another Art Pollard. He was a special guy."

Many words have been written by those who regarded Art as their friend and hero, despite the fact they never had the opportunity to meet him in person. When Art was at the peak of his career, some of these folks were just a young age, but rooting for him from the grandstands. In one tribute to Art, the *Pacific Racing Association* said:

"Mostly because he was 40 years-old before he raced at Indy – he was regarded as the 'old man' on the USAC circuit. One of his most amazing qualities, however, was how youthful he was in both thought and spirit. Because he was relatively young when he was killed, he never really did get old. It's interesting to look through the photo history of his racing career at how little he really did age from the time he started racing until his death.

Perhaps his most admirable quality was his ability to take a moment of his time and make everybody he talked with feel important. He really was an extraordinary individual blessed with many rare qualities and talents. His reflexes, coordination and courage were probably God-given, but he was a kind and decent guy because that's the kind of guy he wanted to be. He seldom, if ever, used profanity. He almost never got angry and he was cool under pressure.

Art Pollard was a credit to the sport of auto racing to everybody who lives here in Roseburg, and particularly the membership of the Pacific Racing Association. He is our most famous son and, whether you were privileged to know him or not, you can take pride in the fact that Art was one of us.

Our promise to Claudine, Mike and Judy, who all knew him best, is as long as there is a Pacific Racing Association, Art Pollard will never be forgotten, both for the kind of guy he was and for his contributions to the sport we all love so much."

Another such example is a note that Art's daughter, Judy received in May of 2015, from Bart Fisher:

"I grew up just north of Indianapolis in what was a small town at the time, Carmel. I started getting very interested in racing at about the age of eight or so, and Art Pollard became my first 'favorite' driver. Mom and Dad took me to my first 500 in 1969 (though I wish to this day I had been there to see your father driving #20 in 1968). We sat in the infield for the first two years and then they surprised me with grandstand seats for 1971. I was thrilled because now I could really see the race and your dad.

They re-ordered the seats every year, and Dad and I went to Pole Day in 1973 and walked down Georgetown Road toward Paddock B because I wanted to be closer to the start/finish line area. I remember it being a beautiful day. As we walked up the steps and came out where we could see the track, I was so excited to see your father's car be the first one I saw in practice. As I pointed (like a 14-year-old 8th grader, which I was) I yelled, 'Look Dad! There goes Art Pollard!!!

I watched, ever so briefly, until I could not see the rear of the car and then within a couple of seconds the yellow came out. The PA system (with Tom Carnegie) announced it was your father and I remember the entire Speedway going silent. About an hour later they came back on the PA and told the terrible news. We stayed for a little while and then decided it didn't feel right, so we went home.

P.S. My dad met your father at a signing (I think in Chicago) back in the later part of 1968 or early 1969 and he signed a black and white photo of #20, going down the backstretch, personally to me. I had broken my leg playing little league football earlier that year and it meant so much to me for your father to do that. Unfortunately, it has been misplaced. So, the last time I was at the IMS Museum I went upstairs to the photo archives and got this one. It isn't quite the same, but I am proud to have it." - *Bart Fisher, Palm Beach Gardens, Florida*

Another remembrance that Judy received in May of 2015 came from Lee Roy Stegall, Jr.:

"Hello Judy, I'm sitting here watching Indy qualifying. Always makes me remember the excitement here on Johnson Street, in Medford, during the lead-up to Indy. Art used to always send us stickers and such. One of my favorite memories is getting my picture taken in his 1967 racer when they came through town. We also were on the front page of the paper in our STP uniforms Art sent us. Art was always kind to us kids, so were you and Mike. I just wanted to share that." - *Lee Roy Stegall, Medford, Oregon*

A great tribute to Art came in an article written in 2012, by journalist George Phillips for the *oilpressure.wordpress.com* website. With George's permission, herewith are some excerpts:

"My memories of 1973 are not good ones. In fact, I relate only bad things with that year. It was 1973 that I entered the ninth grade. The Vietnam War was still being waged, Watergate was beginning to heat up and there was an energy crisis that created long lies at the pump and short tempers. Polyester, bell-bottoms and bad sideburns were rampant. All in all, 1973 was a bad year any way you looked at it.

Seemingly lost and forgotten in all of the mayhem is that fact that another great driver was lost in the month of May – veteran driver and crowd favorite Art Pollard.

I would be lying if I said I remembered Art Pollard from his rookie yea at Indianapolis. I don't. Some remember him as he driver who began his career at Indianapolis at age forty – much older than most. However, I knew exactly who he was by 1968. I've said before that as a ten-year-old kid in 1968, I thought that the Day-Glo orange, wedge-shaped Lotus 56 turbine-powered cars were about the coolest-looking things I had ever seen. I still do.

Although he had set fast time in one of the practice days, Art Pollard seemed to be the forgotten man. He was a second-year driver that found his way into a great opportunity. Even though he had finished eighth as a rookie the prior year, he was overshadowed on his team by the pole sitter and former winner. He had done a solid job in placing his car on the fourth row, but he was 'that other guy.'

For 1969, Pollard remained with Granatelli's team with Mario Andretti as his teammate. Again, the solid Pollard was overshadowed by the star power of a teammate. Andretti's troubles at Indianapolis with the new Lotus prior to bringing out the Brawner/Hawk are well documented. Pollard had an equally rocky month, yet his problems remain merely a footnote. After qualifying on the fourth row for the second year in a row, Pollard's race was over after only seven laps with mechanical difficulties, while his teammate ended up in Victory Lane.

The following week at Milwaukee was a different story, as Art Pollard won his first USAC Champ Car race. At Langhorne a couple of weeks later, Pollard finished second. He earned his second victory of the season in August at Dover. It seemed after all the time he toiled in relative obscurity, yielding the spotlight to his more famous teammates – Art Pollard's time had finally arrived.

Art Pollard had a fast car for Indianapolis in 1973. On May 5th, his forty-sixth birthday, Pollard turned a lap of 192.700, the seventh-fastest time of the month so far. His daughter recalls a phone conversation with him that day. 'He felt it was his year for the pole, and he was optimistic it might be his year for a win. He was confident that he had the car that could do it.'

Pole Day was Saturday, May 12th. During the morning practice session, Art Pollard slammed into the Turn One wall. He passed away about an hour later. That afternoon, his close friend Johnny Rutherford qualified on the pole. After the run, Rutherford dedicated his run to his fallen friend.

While none of us that followed the sport back then have forgotten that dismal race, it seems that the loss of Art Pollard has dimmed in recent memory. Perhaps it was because his accident occurred in practice – not during the race. Most remember that race as one marred by rain, an aborted start and a terrifying crash that eventually took the life of Swede Savage. It saddens me that the life of a very good man who also lost his life that month is now remembered by so few.

Art Pollard ran in the Indianapolis 500 only five times. I am fortunate to be able to say that I was present for everyone. He was never a superstar. He was usually not even the star within his own teams. Yet, he was always a solid driver whose accomplishments always seemed to go unnoticed. Perhaps he began his professional career too late, and for sure it ended too soon.

His stats on the professional circuit are not eye-popping, but he had the respect of his fellow drivers – sometimes even called the 'driver's driver' – and was a fan favorite. Art Pollard always took extra time with fans. I have read and heard nothing but countless tales where Art Pollard would go out of his way to carry on long conversations with fans and never seemed too impressed with his celebrity status.

Quite simply put – Art Pollard was a gentleman. It is sad that he is still overshadowed. - *George Phillips, Nashville, Tennessee*

A professional racing photographer, Rex Miller, offered his recollection of Art in these personal notes:

"Art may have been the first driver to see the 'trap door' that we used to get the car and driver shots with the 1000mm (super-telephoto) lens just coming out of Turn 3. (Trap door is a hole cut in the fence and then folded back up after pictures are taken).

I was working with the 1000mm lens, checking for lighting and accuracy during the morning (race day start situations). I was trying to be very discrete, since this was the first few days of the trap door that Don (a photographer from UPI) had created (without IMS's knowledge).

I was at the fence. Art came out to the turn to watch a teammate practice and watch others handle the bobble in Turn 3. He had already been out and was in his driver uniform. The observer stand was just down-track from me. He finished observing what he came to see, and then wanted to see what I was doing. We had a great chat. He laughed about the trap door and checked the view that I saw from the 1000mm lens.

It was just us and roar and fumes for about ten minutes. As Robin Miller said in his eulogy, and has been said by others, Art was 'kind, generous, friendly, outgoing, persistent, honest, gentlemanly, optimistic, competitive, even-tempered and vibrant.' These words describe a few of the qualities of this exceptional person who was also a great race driver. He liked and understood people and he gave of himself to his fans and friends.

That is exactly what I experienced in a ten-minute friendship. Later that day, no more than three hours later, I felt cheated because of a crash on the other end of the track. I hurt deep inside because I wanted more – not just more time with Art, but time for Art. He was not just a man in a driver's suit." - *Rex Miller, Muncie, Indiana*

I would like to include this poem that Pat Pollard wrote, through her husband Art, expressing her thanks and love for the many compassionate people who lent their support following Art's passing:

I am in the land of happy, as all of you must know.
Please remember this of me, as I was glad to go.
My wife has known the love that few will ever know.
I now must place her hand in God's; together we shall watch her grow.
For none could know a love like ours, that grew each passing day.
Without a joyous feeling, each and every year in May.
My family – yes they're my pride, weep not for me, you see, I'll still live at your side.
You friends who made my life so full, thank you for your thoughts and deeds. Please know that I did not feel needs.
For none could better what I've had, or what you've meant to me.
I know that's why I'm sailing now, this sea of tranquility.
Remember please, the joy and laughter that we've known and happiness I've always shown.

For the past several years, the World of Speed Museum in Wilsonville, Oregon has hosted a very special Art Pollard Day in early May. As a tribute not only to Art's racing career, the museum recognizes the many contributions he made to the welfare and enjoyment of young and sometimes trouble youth. The museum provides a number of family-oriented activities throughout the day, along with a talk and slide presentation by Judy (Pollard) Dippel. She shares her personal memories of her Dad and answers many questions from the audience – young and old alike. A humble man, Art Pollard would be proud of this presentation.

At left is Judy (Pollard) Dippel hosting a presentation of her Dad on Art Pollard Day at the World of Speed Museum. To the right is Judy with her husband Mark and one of their grandchildren, Eli Kinman.

(Photos by the author and Steve Veenstra)

Above, Judy is with car owner Del McClure. She sits in the cockpit of Del's #31 sprint car that Art drove for him in the late 60s. Below are a few of Art's racing items on display at the museum.

(Author photos)

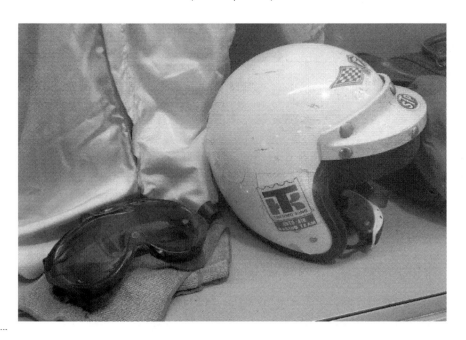

ACKNOWLEDGEMENTS

There are so many caring people who assisted me with this effort, in one way or another, that it would be difficult to acknowledge all of them. To those that I may overlook, a big "Thanks!"

However, there are a few that I would like to mention, beginning with Art Pollard's daughter, Judy Pollard Dippel. From the beginning, Judy has been extremely supportive and always willing to help in so many ways, both as a loving daughter and a published author in her own right. As this is my first book, Judy was also invaluable in proof-reading and advising me on the mechanical aspects of publishing. I am truly indebted to her!

Along with Judy, I would also like to pay tribute to the other members of Art's family – especially his brother Bob, cousin Harvel, and Pat (Pollard) Arslanian. Your personal input and story sharing played a big part in this work.

Through many in-person and phone interviews, I came to know Art Pollard as a friend, racer, and gentleman. Many thanks go out to local men such as Don Caskey, Jack Rodgers, Lee Holmes, Jack Timmings, Del McClure, Rolla Vollstedt, Mike Bell, Jack Corley, Harry Brown and Clyde Sullivan.

On a national basis, it was a privilege to gain insight about Art from others such as Bobby and Al Unser, Sr., Johnny Rutherford, Mel Kenyon, Dick Simon, Mario Andretti, Phil Casey, Dick Vermeil, Donald Davidson and Robin Miller. I thank you all for taking a break from your busy schedules to chat with me.

Many of the photos were sourced from the Pollard Family archives, but I would also like to thank others for their contributions. They include Ralph Hunt, the Rolla Vollstedt and Len Sutton families, the Indianapolis Motor Speedway, Dick Vermeil, Clyde Sullivan, various newspapers and other individuals who I befriended on Facebook.

In closing, I have been diligent in verifying the facts and circumstances surrounding the events recorded in this book. At the same time, though, I realize some may find slight errors here and there. If so, please contact me at bkehoe51@gmail.com and I will be happy to make those corrections. Judy Pollard Dippel can be contacted at judy@jldwrites.com.

Bob Kehoe
August, 2019

Please visit the Art Pollard website, created by David Owen: artpollardracedriver.info.

ABOUT THE AUTHOR

BOB KEHOE

A native of Portland, Oregon, Bob Kehoe is a freelance automotive journalist and photographer who wrote his first car column for his high school newspaper. Following a stint in the U.S. Coast Guard and a career in the high-tech industry, he turned to automotive writing on a full-time basis, beginning with the *Oregonian* newspaper in 1994. Additionally, he has written for other publications including *Speedvision Online, DRIVE! Magazine*, and *eBay Motors*. He has held positions as Media Coordinator for an SCCA Pro Racing Series, and Public Relations Coordinator for major hot rod shows.

Following the first publishing of this book about Art Pollard in 2016, Bob followed up with the biography of racer Billy Foster of Victoria, British Columbia. 'Billy Foster – The Victoria Flash', was released in 2019 and follows the career of Foster. The book includes a history of motorsports in the British Columbia area.

Bob and his wife Karen recently relocated from Oregon to Eloy, Arizona.

Now, Kehoe presents this expanded and updated version of "Art Pollard – The Gentleman Racer."

INDEX

A

Agabashian, Freddie · 137
Agajanian, J.C. · 93, 110, 112, 114, 118
American Racing Association · 51, 54
Amick, George · 21, 31, 34
Anderson, Bruce · 213
Andretti, Mario · 55, 78-79, 87, 90, 92-93, 97-99, 101-102, 107-108, 111-112, 116, 118-119, 132, 143-145, 147-150, 155-158, 160-164, 166-167, 169, 175, 178-183, 197, 201, 203, 206, 209, 217, 234-235, 248, 253, 258
Andrus, Mel · 65-66
Arnold, Chuck · 189
Arslanian, Dave · 188
Arslanian, Pat (Pollard) · 185-188, 211-214, 216, 218-222
Art Pollard Car Wash Systems · 173-174
Art Pollard Day · 256
Art Pollard Fund · 138
Atkins, Dick · 87, 93
Atlanta International Raceway · 90
Auto Racing Hall of Fame · 27, 34, 40, 102, 208
Autodromo Ingeniero Juan R. Bascolo · 192
Autotron Electronics · 78, 82

B

Banks, Henry · 208
Bay Cities Racing Association · 53
Bell, Mike · 244,
Bertrand, Norm · 237
Bettenhausen, Gary · 97, 112, 147, 149, 160, 166, 180, 189, 198, 204, 211
Bettenhausen, Merle · 216
Bettenhausen, Tony · 32-33, 77, 92, 144, 180, 197
Bignotti, George · 31, 33
Bliss, Mike · 241
Bobby Ball 150 · 184
Bobby Ball 200 · 167
Bobby Ball Memorial · 79, 93, 107, 149
Book, Bob · 15
Brabham, Jack · 164
Brabham/Offy · 183, 197

Brabham/Repco · 164
Brainerd International Raceway · 166
Branson, Don · 52, 79
Brawner, Clint · 160, 181, 187, 192, 221
Brawner/Ford · 97, 119, 144, 155, 160, 163-164, 166-167, 175
Brawner/Hawk · 167, 253
Breckenridge, Gavin · 62
Brown, Harry 'Fuzzy' · 248-250, 258
Bryan, Jimmy · 30, 97, 119, 175, 192, 200
Bryant Heating & Cooling · 78, 132, 138, 143-144
Bucknum, Ronnie · 144, 148
Burany, Frank · 78

C

California 200 · 109-112, 115, 155
California 500 · 181-182, 197, 205
California State Fairgrounds · 79, 147
Calistoga Speedway · 51
CAMRA · 68-69, 71-72, 202, 209
Cannon, Larry · 137
Capital Speedway · 43
Card, Dick · 65-66
Carnegie, Tom · 219, 252
Caruthers, Jimmy · 192, 196, 213
Casey, Phil · 94-97, 103, 105-106, 122, 145, 258
Caskey, Don · 7, 10, 13, 15, 24, 44, 57, 61, 220, 258
Caves, Myron · 110, 117
Champion Spark Plug Company · 135-136
Chapman, Colin · 90, 120-121, 123, 126, 130, 132
Christie, Bob · 21, 29, 32-33, 82
Clark, Jimmie · 93, 101, 114, 121
Cobre Firestone Special · 213, 217
Cochran, B.B. · 226
Cochran, Bob · 68, 72
Cole, Hal · 52
Collins, Don · 79, 93, 145, 242, 244
Collins, Sid · 190, 208
Colt/Ford · 175, 177-178, 196-198
Compton, Richard (Dick) · 80-81, 90-91
Continental Divide Raceway · 144, 163, 179
Cook, Duke · 137
Cooper, Gordon · 90, 136

Copper Cup · 62, 64-66, 70
Corley, Jack · 245, 248, 258

D

Daffodil Cup · 66
Dallenbach, Wally · 97, 111, 119, 137, 144, 165, 189, 203, 205
Davidson, Donald · 160, 207, 258
Daytona · 11, 23, 27, 29-31, 34
DelRoy, Frank · 189
Demler, Norm · 30
DePaolo, Pete · 51-52
Dickson, Larry · 87
Dioguardi, Nick · 175
Dippel, Mark · 256
Donohue, Mark · 167, 177, 196-197, 204, 214
Douglas County Fairgrounds · 15, 57
Drake, Albert · 246-247
Duman, Ronnie · 86-87, 94, 143, 169, 181
DuQuoin State Fairgrounds · 145

E

Eagle/Ford · 93, 97, 99, 108, 118, 143-144, 149, 163-164, 166-167
Eagle/Offy · 113, 148, 164, 193, 197, 205, 211, 213-214
Eaton, Jay · 18
Economaki, Chris · 54
Edmonton Gold Cup · 60-61, 63
Edson, Marc · 72
Ellefson, Norm · 61-62, 72
Etchison, Bobby · 43
Eugene Fairgrounds · 248
Eugene Speedway · 59, 237
Evergreen Motor Speedway · 67

F

Fairchild, Cy · 189, 215
Falk, Ron · 213, 226
Fanger, Jerry · 59
Fengler, Harlan · 83
Ferguson, Ranald · 26
Feuz, John · 237
Firestone · 105, 149, 213
Flaherty, Jack · 53
Flaherty, Pat · 32, 114
Fletcher, Bob · 213
Fosback, Ollie · 15

Foster, Billy · 61, 66-69, 71, 78, 80, 82, 85, 92, 209, 259
Foyt, A.J. · 31, 55, 78, 97-99, 108-109, 111, 116, 138, 144-145, 147, 157, 160-161, 164, 177, 183, 192, 194, 197-198, 200
Fuji International Speedway · 93

G

Garlits, Don · 199
Gerhardt, Don · 110, 114-115, 122
Gerhardt, Fred · 94, 96-97, 100-101, 104, 109-110, 121-122, 125, 143, 156, 180, 219
Gerhardt/Ford · 99, 105-106
Gerhardt/Offy · 78, 90-91, 93, 105, 119, 129, 143-144, 149, 155, 157, 160, 163-166, 175-177, 180
Gilman, Al · 60
Gilmore Broadcasting · 105-106
Gilmore Stadium ·114
Gilmore, Jim · 192
Glass, Ken · 19, 41, 56-57, 59-60, 68, 237
Gold Cup · 61-62, 64-65
Goldstein, Mel · 226
Goodyear · 149-150, 188
Granatelli, Andy · 98-99, 120-123, 125, 128-131, 143-144, 149, 152-156, 160, 163-168, 172, 175, 178, 182, 185-187, 200-201, 203, 205-206, 211, 228, 242-243, 253
Grant, Jerry · 101, 132, 204-205, 223
Green, Bob · 57, 226
Greenhut, Darolyn (Cooke) · 63
Gregg, Bob · 66, 68-69, 72
Grissom, Gus · 90, 136
Guerrero, Roberto · 97
Gurney, Chuck · 137
Gurney, Dan · 99, 108, 118, 123, 128, 132, 143, 149, 158, 163, 166-167, 169, 175, 182
Guthrie, Janet · 23, 97

H

Halibrand, Ted · 180
Hanford Motor Speedway · 105, 110, 155
Hanks, Sam · 55
Harris, Kurt · 42
Harvey, Ed · 226
Hawk/Ford · 99, 157
Hayhoe Racing Enterprises · 181
Hayhoe, Jim · 181
Hayhoe/Offy · 181
Hill, Graham · 93, 101, 121, 123-124, 128-129
Hiss, Mike · 205
Hulse, Chuck · 83, 110-111, 117
Hunt, Ralph · 258
Hurt, Bob · 112, 190
Hurtubise, Jim · 52, 94-95, 97, 127, 137, 182

Hutchinson, Pete · 165
Hyde, Bill · 237

I

Illinois State Fairgrounds · 92, 164
Indiana State Fairgrounds · 145, 166, 189
Indianapolis Fairgrounds · 170
Indianapolis Raceway Park · 91, 144, 164
Indy Racing League · 97
Irvan, Gary · 137

J

Jack, Rajo · 52-53
Janett, Frank · 62
Jantzen Beach Arena · 44
Johncock, Gordon · 78, 93-94, 99, 105-106, 109, 111, 115, 144, 163, 165-166, 175, 192, 209, 214, 224
Jones, Levy · 68
Jones, Parnelli · 97-99, 102, 120-123, 126, 129, 143-144, 149, 155, 161, 164

K

Kearney Bowl · 60
Ken's Martinizing Special · 20, 57, 59-60, 68, 81
Kenyon, Don · 95
Kenyon, Mel · 27, 94-95, 97, 100, 102, 105-106, 109-110, 113, 115, 119, 129, 158, 169, 187, 258
King, Grant · 155-156, 163, 173-174, 248
Kingfish/Offy · 175-178
Knepper, Arnie · 111, 132
Knoxville Nationals · 175
Koch, Ernie · 20, 56, 62
Koch, George 'Pop' · 21
Krisiloff, Steve · 137, 189
Kuzma/Offy · 166

L

Langhorne · 27, 33, 90, 92, 95, 143-144, 163, 253
Larson, Neil · 186, 226
Larue D. Carter Memorial Hospital · 136, 138, 209, 215
Laycock/Offy · 176, 182
Leonard, Joe · 78, 90, 93, 98, 102, 106, 110-111, 116, 121, 123-124, 128-129, 131, 133, 143-144, 148-149, 164, 178, 182, 196-198, 203, 206
Lewis, Vic · 226
Liguori, Ralph · 95, 189

Livingston, Gordy · 246
Lola/Ford · 93, 143-144, 148, 155, 164, 167, 205
Lola/Foyt · 203, 206, 211
Loquasto, Al · 189
Lotus/Ford · 79, 156
Lotus/Offy · 157-158
Lotus/Plymouth · 167

M

Mahler, John · 137, 215
Mallard/Offy · 127
Malloy, Jim · 61, 69, 71, 132, 143-144, 160-161, 164, 167, 178, 202, 248
Marlboro 300 · 198
Marshman, Bobby · 82
Mason-Dixon 300 · 164
Matan, 'Tiger' · 62
McClure, Del · 145, 241, 244, 258
McCluskey, Roger · 79, 90, 97-98, 101, 103, 108, 111-112, 114-116, 128, 143, 161, 164, 166, 177, 181-184, 189, 205, 206
McDonald, Larry · 62
McElreath, Jim · 79, 92-93, 97, 112, 183-184, 197
McGee, Jim · 160, 181
McGowan, Frankie · 21
McGrath, Jack · 26, 29
McGreevy, Mike · 53
McLaren/Offy · 196-197
McNabb, Richard C. · 138
McNamara/Ford · 178
McRae, Graham · 224
Mears, Rick · 97
Michigan 200 · 197, 209
Michigan 500 · 97
Michigan International Raceway · 148, 180
Millen, Armund · 246
Miller, Al · 101
Miller, Jimmy · 55
Miller, Robin · 31, 189, 209, 215-217, 221, 227, 254, 258
Milton, Tommy · 51
Milwaukee 200 · 171
Milwaukee Mile · 77, 90, 92, 143-144, 160, 164, 197
Mongoose/Ford · 106, 143, 150
Mongoose/Offy · 97, 145
Moore, Darmon · 237
Morris/Ford · 180, 184
Mosley, Mike · 161, 166, 193, 202, 204, 211
Murphy, Jimmy · 51
Muther, Rick · 166

N

NASCAR · 34, 55, 92, 153, 164, 180, 183
Nelson, Cliff · 237-238
Newcomer, John · 173-174

O

O'Connor, Pat · 52, 114
Olivero, Bobby · 137
Ongais, Danny · 97, 112, 116
Ontario Motor Speedway · 181-182, 197
Osborn, Howard · 68
Owl Garage · 52, 53

P

Pace, Dick · 42
Pacheteau, Jack · 51, 52, 54
Pacific Raceways · 92
Pacific Racing Association · 17-18, 251
Parsons, Johnny · 53, 189, 215-216
Peets, Ray · 62
Phoenix Intl. Raceway · 79, 107, 155, 192
Pikes Peak Hillclimb · 163
Plymouth · 153-156, 163-167, 169-170
Pollard, Art Sr. · 2, 3, 5, 7, 10, 226
Pollard, Bob · 2-4, 7, 9, 12, 15, 45, 77
Pollard, Bobbie · 1-2, 219
Pollard, Brad · 46, 139, 182, 220, 231-234
Pollard, Diane · 45, 219
Pollard, Harvel · 2, 46, 152, 182, 213, 219, 231
Pollard, Judy (Dippel) · 2, 9, 11, 13-14, 19, 77, 79-80, 90, 98, 104, 134, 170, 219, 222, 251-252, 256, 258
Pollard, Laurie · 46, 231
Pollard, Mark · 46, 182, 231-232
Pollard, Mary Lou · 46, 231
Pollard, Mike · 14, 19, 73, 139, 219, 229-231, 239, 219, 230
Portland Meadows · 35, 237-238
Portland Speedway · 20, 21, 35, 41, 68, 71, 237, 241, 242, 245, 250
Posey, Sam · 166-167
Puterbaugh, Bill · 189

R

Rager, Roger · 137
Randol, Keith · 86
Ranger Special · 237-239
Rasmussen, Eldon · 61-62, 65-66, 69
Rathmann, Dick · 32

Rathmann, Jim · 29, 32-33, 82, 90-91
Retzloff, Al · 148
Revson, Peter · 158, 164, 194, 197, 202, 204
Rex Mays 200 · 230
Rex Mays Classic · 90, 143, 160, 178
Riley, Mike · 51-52
Rindt, Jochen · 97, 101
Riverside International Raceway · 92, 108, 149, 167
Robbins, Jim · 78-79, 132, 143
Roberts, Jim · 42, 71-72, 247, 250
Robertson, George · 62, 65, 69, 72
Rodgers, Jack · 7, 10, 14, 45, 258
Rose, Bud · 55
Rose, Dude · 57, 59
Ruby, Lloyd · 92, 97, 107, 111, 119, 128, 143-145, 150, 158, 160, 161, 164-165, 175-176, 182, 192
Rupp, Mickey · 94
Rutherford, Betty · 186, 221
Rutherford, Johnny · 52, 78, 82, 93, 111, 116, 138, 144, 161, 166, 177, 182, 189, 197, 201, 211, 214, 218, 220, 234-235, 253, 258

S

Sachs, Eddie · 33
Salem Speedway · 42, 44
Salemi, Pete · 143
Salih, George · 30
Sauer, Sam · 65
Savage, Swede · 179, 184, 197, 214, 223-224, 253
Scorpion/Ford · 181, 192-194, 196-198
Seattle International Raceway · 167
Selley, Don · 72
Shelby, Carroll · 121, 123
Simon, Dick · 69, 137, 145, 167, 183, 217, 235, 258
Sirois, Leon 'Jigger' · 157
Smith, Al · 67
Smyth, Bill · 227
Sneva, Blaine · 72, 137
Sneva, Jan · 72
Sneva, Kay · 137
Sneva, Tom · 61, 137
Snider, George · 110-111, 137, 143, 198
Sorenson, Fred · 65
Spence, Mike · 121, 123
Squires, Larry · 62
Stainton, James 'Red' · 156
Stardust 150 · 118
Stewart, Jackie · 84, 93, 101, 121
Stewart, Tony · 55
STP Corp. · 131
Strickland, Dave · 192

Sullivan, Clyde · 250, 258
Sutton, Len · 21-22, 26, 33, 78, 82, 155, 209, 238-239, 258
Sweikert, Bob · 52-53

T

Taylor, Frank · 62
Teague, Marshall · 31-32
Ted Horn Memorial · 145
Templeton, Shorty · 82
Texas World Speedway · 211
Thermo King · 95, 97-98, 100-101, 104-105, 108-110, 118-119, 121, 125-126, 149, 180
Timmings, Jack · 42, 236, 258
Titus, Jerry · 149
Tony Bettenhausen 200 · 77, 92, 144, 180, 197
Trenton 150 · 97, 119
Trenton 200 · 78, 146, 175, 193
Trenton 300 · 166
Trenton Speedway · 198
Trentonian Split 300 · 211
Turkey Night Grand Prix · 30
Turner, Jack · 82

U

Umpqua Regional Timing Association · 57
United States Auto Club · 112, 114
United States Auto Club 500 All-Stars · 189
Unser, Al Sr. · 78, 92-93, 97, 102, 108, 111-112, 115, 117, 132, 137, 143-145, 148-149, 155, 161, 164, 166-167, 175-178, 180, 183-184, 192, 194, 196, 198, 204, 211, 224, 235, 258
Unser, Bobby · 93, 104, 108, 111, 113, 115-116, 118-119, 123-124, 128, 144-145, 148-150, 157-158, 162-164, 167, 175, 193, 197-198, 201, 203-206, 211, 223, 235
USAC Championship Car Series · 29, 168
USAC National Midget Championship · 95

V

Van Camp, Eric · 62
Van Osten, Bud · 59, 226
Vasser, Jimmy · 181
Veith, Bob · 52, 100, 102
Vermeil, Alice · 51-52
Vermeil, Dick · 46, 50, 258
Vermeil, Louie · 51-52, 55
Vidan, Pat · 21, 35-40, 101-102 190
Vollstedt, Rolla · 20-21, 23, 25-26, 56, 77-78, 80-81, 97, 102, 114, 143, 155, 235, 237-238, 258
Vollstedt/Ford · 78, 92, 143, 144, 179, 183
Vollstedt/Offy · 78, 93
Vukovich, Billy · 53, 109-110, 112, 117, 137, 197-198, 202, 205-206, 215-216

Vukovich, Joyce · 186

W

Walker, Don · 67
Walker, Ray · 71-72
Walkup, Bruce · 112, 181, 189
Walsh, Clay · 52
Walther, David 'Salt' · 180
Walther, George · 180
Ward, Rodger · 27, 29, 32, 82, 189, 230
Watson/Ford · 193
Watson/Offy · 79, 93
Webb, Spider · 55
Weld, Greg · 90, 160-161, 166, 175-178, 197
West Coast Vintage Racers · 244
Western States Race of Champions · 60
White, Marty · 72
Wilcox, Dean · 42, 61
Wilke, Bob · 113, 144
Williams, Carl · 128, 157, 182
Wilson, Dempsey · 33, 111
World of Speed Museum · 237, 256

Y

Yarborough, Cale · 102, 110
Yarbrough, Lee Roy · 90, 96-97, 105, 183, 195
Yarbrough, Sparky · 42

Made in the USA
Middletown, DE
07 October 2020